DECENTRALIZATION

DECENTRALIZATION
The Territorial Dimension of the State

B. C. Smith
Reader in Public Administration
University of Bath

London
GEORGE ALLEN & UNWIN
Boston   Sydney

George Allen & Unwin (Publishers) Ltd,
40 Museum Street, London WC1A 1LU, UK

George Allen & Unwin (Publishers) Ltd,
Park Lane, Hemel Hempstead, Herts HP2 4TE, UK

Allen & Unwin, Inc.,
Fifty Cross Street, Winchester, Mass. 01890, USA

George Allen & Unwin Australia Pty Ltd,
8 Napier Street, North Sydney, NSW 2060, Australia

First published in 1985.

British Library Cataloguing in Publication Data

Smith, Brian C.
  Decentralization: the territorial dimension of the state.
1. Decentralization in government
I. Title
351.09′3   JF1507
ISBN 0 – 04 – 352113 – 4
ISBN 0 – 04 – 352114 – 2 Pbk

Library of Congress Cataloging in Publication Data

Smith, Brian C.
  Decentralization.
Bibliography: p. 207
Includes index.
1. Decentralization in government. I. Title.
JS113.S59 1985   350.007′3   84 – 20419
ISBN 0 – 04 – 352113 – 4 (alk. paper)
ISBN 0 – 04 – 352114 – 2 (pbk.: alk. paper)

Set in 11 on 12 point Times by Grove Graphics, Tring, Herts, and
printed in Great Britain by Mackays of Chatham

Contents

Preface

There are, as far as I am aware, no states in the world that do not have governmental institutions of some kind operating at the subnational level. There are no totally centralized states in which all governmental authority is concentrated in the headquarters of national government agencies. The choice of regional or local institutions is one that all governments have to make. It is a choice that in some states is made with remarkable frequency as the structure of the state at the subnational level is reformed and reorganized in successive attempts to secure desired political and administrative objectives. The choice of subnational or decentralized institutions is, above all, a political one. The objectives which states pursue in forming or reconstituting a federation, or reorganizing a system of regional or local government, are political objectives. Such changes may be presented and debated in the technical language of administrative efficiency or constitutional principles, but they reflect the outcome of conflicts of interest between groups in society which feel they have something significant to gain or lose in the restructuring of local institutions, in the delegation of power to them, or in the redefinition of areas.

This book is about the political choices which are made when decentralization occurs. It examines the various options which are open to political leaders who believe that decentralization is one way of securing their political objectives. It presents a conceptual structure which helps us to understand the fairly wide range of possibilities for decentralized governments. These possibilities are illustrated by examples drawn from a number of different states in different regions of the world and with different types of regime and ideology. It also considers the political arguments for different kinds and levels of decentralization in different ideological and developmental contexts, and the controversies surrounding the practical operation of decentralized government – the delimitation of areas, the financing of subnational institutions, relations with higher levels of government and the choice of institutions at lower levels.

A recurring theme throughout is the delegation of power from one geographical level of government to another. Hence *Decentralization* as the title. How far a system of government is decentralized, however, cannot be prejudged from the mere existence of subnational institutions. The focus on decentralization, rather than on what would have to be a wider-ranging study of all aspects of regional and local politics and administration, concentrates attention on the political choices being made when political leaders at the centre decide to create or change a territorial structure of government.

The purpose of the book is thus not to formulate some universal theory of decentralization, though a relationship, real or supposed, between cause and effect will sometimes be found as part of the arguments which are examined in what follows. The aim is far more modest than this. The illustrative material that is included is not used to support causal generalizations of my own about decentralization. They are employed to illustrate an institution or to concretize a concept (such as a prefectoral system of field administration), or to aid comprehension of an argument (such as a perceived relationship between fiscal dependence and political autonomy). It is in this sense only that the book is comparative and not in the sense of arguing for one particular theoretical framework for understanding decentralization. There are many normative theories about the value of decentralization as well as about the operation of its different features. These constitute the object of study but no synthesis is attempted.

An academic's field of specialization will always owe much to the wisdom of others. My intellectual debts will be obvious from what follows. But I owe a particular debt of gratitude to my friend and former colleague at Exeter University, Jeffrey Stanyer, who has taught me more about decentralization than anyone else. Thinking recently about decentralization was made easier by a Personal Research Award from the Social Science Research Council for the 1979–80 academic year. This also enabled some fieldwork to be done in Nigeria. I am also grateful to colleagues at the University of Bath for helpful comments on parts of the manuscript: David Collard, John Cullis, Graham Room, Elizabeth Meehan and Brian Neve. The job of preparing the manuscript was made that much easier by the typing and word-processing skills of Maria Bez and Margaret Arnold to whom I am grateful for their patient assistance. All the defects of the book are mine.

1
Introduction to a Concept

Lexicographically, decentralization means both reversing the concentration of administration at a single centre and conferring powers of local government. The dictionary thus captures the idea of decentralization as a political phenomenon involving both administration and government. Decentralization involves the delegation of power to lower levels in a territorial hierarchy, whether the hierarchy is one of governments within a state or offices within a large-scale organization. Decentralization may be clearly distinguished from the dispersal of the headquarters' branches from the capital city, as when part of a national ministry is moved to a provincial city to provide employment there. It may also be distinguished from delegation, when a superior entrusts a subordinate with some of the former's responsibilities, though decentralization will involve delegation when the subordinate, whether it be an individual bureaucrat or an elected assembly, takes part responsibility for a designated area within the territorial jurisdiction of the organization or state concerned.

In the study of politics decentralization refers to the territorial distribution of power. It is concerned with the extent to which power and authority are dispersed through the geographical hierarchy of the state, and the institutions and processes through which such dispersal occurs. Decentralization entails the subdivision of the state's territory into smaller areas and the creation of political and administrative institutions in those areas. Some of the institutions so created may themselves find it necessary to practise further decentralization.

One focus of attention is therefore on the major subdivisions of the unitary state: the counties and districts of England and Wales, or the *départements* and communes of France, for example. Another is federalism, which presents evidence of two of the major constitutional forms which decentralization can take. Federalism divides political power territorially in a specific constitutional way. But, in addition, each of the constituent parts of a federation, such as the fifty states of the USA or the nineteen states of Nigeria, may be regarded as unitary states each with its own internal system of local government. Local governments themselves may employ various kinds of administrative decentralization within the internal organizations of their administrative departments.

Yet another aspect of decentralization is found within national administrative agencies such as government ministries or public corporations which find it expedient to delegate authority to officials responsible for the work of the organization in designated areas. Selected regions may have special agencies created within them, such as the Sudan's Gazira Board or the Scottish Highlands and Islands Development Board, and these agencies may find it necessary to split the region into smaller units for administrative purposes.

It follows that decentralization involves different kinds of hierarchy combining different institutions and functions. Each level of government within a federal or unitary state may be able to delegate powers to lower-level governments. And the administrative agencies of government at all levels may practise decentralization within their organizations. It also follows that the study of decentralization, unlike some influential but constricting traditions in political science and public administration, should beg no questions about the concepts 'local' and 'government' when discussing local government. Geographical areas and the state institutions within them are both highly variable.

The Demand for Decentralization

The need for some form of decentralization appears to be universal. Even the smallest states have some kind of local government with some degree of autonomy (P. King, 1982, p. 125; see also Duchacek, 1970, pp. 3 ff.). States with small populations may geographically and ethnically require decentralization, such as the Solomon Islands' population of some 180,000 spread over a scattered archipelago of 29,000 sq. km of land and 803,000 sq. km of ocean and speaking seventy-four different languages (Premdas, 1982).

All contemporary states must somehow meet this need. It may arise simply for reasons of practical administration. The functions of the modern state require it to operate at the local level. Taxes must be collected and laws enforced. In the welfare state, claims must be assessed and benefits paid. In developing countries the peasantry must be serviced with loans, seed and fertilizers. Decentralization is widely regarded as a necessary condition for social, economic and political development. Whatever its ideological foundation or level of intervention, the contemporary state must localize its governmental apparatus.

More dramatically, many states have to devise a response to localized political demands for greater autonomy. Few states can ignore public hostility to centralization and uniformity. In different regions of the world national governments are using decentralization as a strategy for coping with the political instability which is threatened by secessionist movements and demands for regional autonomy. The irony of this situation is that it is often brought about by minority groups that would dearly love to be 'integrated' if that meant enjoying equal rights with the majority population. However, it is a sense of discrimination within the larger community that so often forces minority cultural and ethnic groups to seek autonomy. Unfortunately the state which itself discriminates against them, or allows others to, is hardly likely to concede a right to self-determination. Whether *decentralization* constitutes an adequate response to demands for autonomy will depend on how extreme those demands have become, which, in turn will depend on the level of repression experienced in the past. It is nevertheless remarkable how universal the political significance of decentralization appears to be. In Chapter 3 an attempt is made to categorize the political and administrative forces leading to the adoption of decentralized methods of government in contemporary states. The countervailing forces supporting trends towards centralization are identified in Chapter 5 when relationships between different geographical levels of government are considered. Chapter 10 examines the role of decentralization in developing countries where so much faith has been placed in it as a foundation for progress.

The Value of Decentralization

The values of decentralization seem to have a wide appeal, regardless of ideology or political theory (Furniss, 1974). It is fashionable to deplore the over-centralization of contemporary government. In Britain, for example, we are told that there is extensive public dissatisfaction with over-centralization. It was claimed that the UK is the most centralized of the major industrial countries of the world, and that there is too little regional influence on public expenditure, inter-ministerial co-ordination and bureaucratic decision-making. The political life of the regions wastes away while uniformity is imposed by an increasingly congested Westminster and Whitehall. The government is accused of being both psychologically and physically remote.

As the pressures for larger organizational units, national minimum standards and central planning capabilities mount so the concern for local autonomy grows (Kuroda, 1975). One of the most disturbing characteristics of contemporary society is said to be the concentration of power in fewer and fewer organizations, whether public or private. This is seen as the inevitable result of technological, organizational and political development (D. K. Hart, 1972). Few governmental functions are now the exclusive responsibility of local institutions. Local needs outstretch local resources in both developed and developing societies. The threat, and in some cases the reality, is of a large, remote, impersonal administrative machine dominating the life of the individual (van Putten, 1971). A major theme underlying discussions of local government in the UK for the last thirty to forty years has been the assumed trend towards centralization, with the steady removal of services from local political control and the extension of central control mechanisms (Boaden, 1970). As we shall see in Chapter 10, in developing countries the over-centralization of authority and responsibility in ministerial headquarters and capital cities is generally regarded as a formidable obstacle to development (Heaphey, 1971).

The attraction of decentralization is not merely that it is the opposite of centralization and therefore can be assumed to be capable of remedying the latter's defects. Decentralization has a positive side. It is commonly associated with a wide range of economic, social and political objectives in both developed and less-developed societies. Economically, decentralization is said to improve the efficiency with which demands for locally provided services are expressed and public goods provided (Shepard, 1975). Market models of local decision-making see decentralization as a means of expanding the scope of consumer choice between public goods. Residential locational choice contributes to the realization of individual values and collective welfare. Decentralization is said to reduce costs, improve outputs and more effectively utilize human resources (D. K. Hart, 1972).

Politically, decentralization is said to strengthen accountability, political skills and national integration. It brings government closer to people. It provides better services to client groups. It promotes liberty, equality and welfare (Maas, 1959; D. M. Hill, 1974). It provides a training ground for citizen participation and political leadership, both local and national. It has even been elevated to the role of guardian of basic human values (van Putten, 1971). In Chapter 2 the roles ascribed to decentralization in different theories of government are analysed.

Yet decentralization is not without its critics. In the context of some theories of the state, decentralization appears parochial and separatist. It threatens the unity of the general will. It reinforces narrow, sectional interests. It is anti-egalitarian through its support for regional variation in the provision of public goods.

From a socialist perspective decentralization is likely to be discussed in relation to the nature of the state and economy in which it operates. Above all, decentralization will be judged by reference to the interests which benefit from and control subnational political institutions. A romantic, idealistic perception of decentralization, as some kind of absolute good to be valued in its own right, will be rejected. Local institutions will be seen to be just as susceptible to manipulation by dominant classes as national governments. A different view of power will be adopted to that which sees local democracy as egalitarian in political terms because of universal suffrage in local elections. Power will be seen as residing beyond the institutions of decentralized government and as unequally distributed among classes according to their material position in society. Far from guaranteeing political equality, local institutions may be accused of perpetuating the maldistribution of rewards and influence that characterises capitalist society generally. There may also be a feeling that the political education to be obtained from local democracy teaches the importance of recognizing the social and economic disadvantages which restrict the political power of certain classes and the lack of opportunity provided by local government to change the structural constraints on economic and social advancement. In the Third World, where decentralization is given the official objective of mobilizing the poor in development efforts, it may be recognized that local institutions have simply provided yet more resources and power to be commandeered by already powerful elites and propertied interests.

Critics have also observed how decentralization's major role in capitalist societies has been as part of liberal reformism. It incorporates what might otherwise be forces antagonistic to the regime into the state apparatus by extending the apparatus downwards (Katznelson, 1972). Decentralization thus creates the form of dispersed power without creating its substance. Chapter 9 examines the association between decentralization and participation and looks at some of the attempts made to bring power to the people by creating institutions at grass-root levels.

Even outside the ranks of radical critics of the capitalist state there has been no shortage of adverse comment on decentralized government. The moralizing which goes on about the quality of local elected representatives and the vested interests benefiting from the housing and planning functions of English local authorities may be pious but it exists. The manifest lack of improvement in efficiency and democracy following the last reorganization of British local government has not gone unnoticed (Sharpe, 1978). There have been warnings against assuming that more centralization in British local government is inevitably bad (Boaden, 1970). Not everyone approves of the extent to which the British state in its operational aspects is a male bourgeois gerontocracy (Smith and Stanyer, 1976, p. 110). Public confidence in their honesty as well as their competence declines as the number of councillors and officers convicted for corruption increases. Evidence from both public opinion polls and sociological investigation suggests that decentralization does not strengthen trust in the fairness of government (Yin and Lucas, 1973). The case of Northern Ireland where devolution was marred by gerrymandering, and by discrimination in the administration of law and order and municipal housing hardly inspires an automatic faith in decentralization, wherever the blame for all the trouble should lie (Birch, 1977).

In the USA, too, critics of decentralization have reacted strongly against what they see as the inefficiencies and diseconomies of political fragmentation leading to urban sprawl, inadequate open spaces, congested schools, mediocre administration, smog, traffic jams and the break-down of mass transportation systems (R. C. Wood, 1959). The disparities in the quality of life and public services between the central and suburban areas of the fragmented metropolis have attracted a good deal of criticism from American students of decentralization. Decentralization within urban governments to neighbourhood institutions has been opposed not only as 'a betrayal of integration' but also, in view of its anti-professional stance, as a denial of the merit system in urban government (Yates, 1973).

Students of underdevelopment have also warned that the proliferation of administrative arrangements at the local level can bring about a deterioration in the quality of administration as larger numbers of officials with less education, narrower outlooks and hardly any experience are employed (Mukerji, 1961). It is also possible for the goals of decentralization to conflict, as the experience of Yugoslavia, regarded as one of the most decentralized socialist states, has shown. Heterogeneous policy demands have produced the disparate and conflicting goals of regional economic equality, efficient investment within regions and the devolution of planning power to communal organizations and enterprise managements (Lang, 1975).

In view of such conflicting attitudes towards decentralization is it possible that it can mean the same thing to different people? It is clear that while the opponents and proponents of decentralization may agree on the institutions and processes involved, they begin from fundamentally different premises about the nature of power or the meaning of democracy. It is easy to confuse institutions and process. Or they visualize decentralization operating within very different kinds of political and economic system. Decentralization under capitalism and liberal political institutions will be judged differently by proponents and opponents of the capitalist state. And they often fail to specify the kind of political or administrative hierarchy they have in mind when recommending or condemning decentralization. It is often politically expedient to be imprecise. Ambiguities in politics sometimes flow from ambiguities in language. As Rondinelli has pointed out, in Kenya, Tanzania and the Sudan

> the early decentralization laws were quite vague about the extent and forms of decentralization to be established, the procedures for participation and the roles of and relationships among officials at various levels of administration. Public pronouncements in Tanzania and the Sudan implied that local governments would be created; the language of the decentralization laws – and even their titles – used the term 'local government', whereas in reality, leaders in both countries initially intended only to establish local units of administration that would act as agents of the central government. (Rondinelli, 1981a, p. 140)

It is not unusual to find institutions for maximum participation with minimum delegation (as when elected bodies have no powers) and institutions for maximum delegation and minimum participation (as when a field agent of the centre is given extensive powers) both parading under the label of decentralization. This is just one of the reasons for gaining some conceptual clarity, which is one of the purposes of this book.

The Elements of Decentralization

Elements of the state apparatus which are common to all systems of decentralization are implicit in what has already been said here. First, it is clear from the discussion above that decentralization involves one or more divisions of the state's territory. Decentralization requires the delimitation of areas. This is not an arbitrary process. It entails the application of principles which themselves embody particular administrative and political values. If the purpose of decentralization is to reflect the needs or wishes of local communities then the delimitation of areas will have to reflect settlement patterns and the spatial distribution of those communities. The spatial patterns of social and economic life thus may be thought an appropriate basis for demarcating communities for political and administrative purposes. When power is devolved to area governments that are intended to reflect the unique political forces within a territory it is obvious that some attempt will have to be made to distinguish boundaries on the political map which separate one political community from another. A sense of political identity may, however, be associated with many other factors than settlement patterns. Language, history, culture, location (for example, offshore islands) and tradition may preserve administrative and political boundaries which have a political significance and force of their own. Such areas are deemed by the political system to merit special treatment in constitutional and administrative terms. They are accepted as facts of political life.

An alternative principle which may be applied to the areal division of powers is that of efficiency. The state may be divided geographically by one of its administrative agencies into areas which contain characteristics (such as population size or density, watersheds, or topography) that are believed to be related to the efficiency with which a public service may be administered. The delimitation of areas then implies the notion of a technically defined optimum size and shape. The frequent lack of coincidence between areas defined technically and those defined by reference to settlement patterns or their 'special status' (Smith and Stanyer, 1976, pp. 91–4) is one of the lasting problems for the state when organizing a system of decentralization. Chapter 4 compares the different principles upon which territorial divisions are made in contemporary states and examines some additional ways in which areas can be defined according to criteria which are relevant to the functions of government.

Decentralization involves the delegation of authority. Such

delegated authority may be broadly classified as either political or bureaucratic. Political authority is delegated when power is devolved through legislative enactment to an area government (as in a unitary state) or allocated between national and area governments by the constitution (as in a federal state). Such delegation creates political institutions (usually formed by the application of democratic principles, though with varying structures) with the right to make policies for their areas over which they have jurisdiction. Area governments or authorities thereby acquire a measure of autonomy. They exercise powers which fall within their jurisdiction. They gain legitimacy from the unique local political system over which each government exercises some jurisdiction. They normally have some independent revenues. However, even in federal states and always in unitary states this autonomy is never complete. The discretion which area governments can exercise is limited by the influence and sometimes the control which the national government can exercise over its subordinates (in unitary states) or partners (in federations). The relationships between territorial levels of government are thus of prime importance to the student of decentralization. How intergovernmental relations may be approached is the subject of Chapter 5. Since finance is crucial to autonomy, and increasingly has become the medium through which intergovernmental power is exercised, the financial problems of area governments are the subject of Chapter 6.

Bureaucratic authority derives from the delegation of responsibilities from the headquarters of an organization to the field. The discretion which the field representative of the organization may be able to exercise depends on what decisions superiors in the organizational hierarchy are prepared to delegate. The exercise of decentralized bureaucratic authority is subject to organizational controls and influence. The legitimacy of the authority so exercised is based on appointment (that is, bureaucratic methods of recruitment rather than the democratic methods of recruitment normal in area systems of government). The authority delegated to field staff is managerial or administrative, though its political significance at the area level may be considerable. Bureaucratic decentralization, or deconcentration, is frequently employed to reduce the forces of localism and enforce uniformity in decision-making across the country, unlike political decentralization which is designed to reflect the unique characteristics, problems and needs of different regions and localities.

The decentralization of power entails the establishment of

institutions and the recruitment of office holders. The institutions of area governments normally require the recruitment of what have been referred to as lay personnel as distinct from the professionals and administrators in government bureaucracies (Smith and Stanyer, 1976). Lay office holders have a local political base, including connections with and membership of other organizations in the area, especially political parties. They are recruited from their area and generally only hold office within that area, at least as far as their participation in area government is concerned. They are recruited into political office by means of election (councillors, governors, representatives, mayors, deputies, assemblymen, and so on), or appointment by higher authority (the members of governing boards for health, water and parks, for example). Lay authority is generally exercised collectively (through a municipal council or area management board). Such corporate bodies usually employ their own professional staffs of administrators and professional specialists (engineers, doctors, teachers, planners and lawyers). The variety of institutions through which area government is carried on is great and an attempt at categorization is made in Chapter 7.

Decentralized institutions will be found at all geographical levels. In recent years attempts have been made to encourage participation in government by decentralizing different kinds of authority to the lowest levels consistent with some kind of effective action. Decentralization to 'neighbourhood' level has been an integral part of state-initiated programmes for urban rejuvenation in a number of countries. Chapter 9 looks at these experiments to see what kinds of institutions were involved and whether participation meant the real decentralization of power to neighbourhood governments and grass-root organizations.

Field personnel in the area offices of central departments, by contrast, are part of an administrative organization of which they are employees. Field officers are posted to their areas, districts, provinces, or regions and may be expected to move from area to area and between headquarters and the provinces. The field officer is thus part of a hierarchy. Typically, the field officer is a full-time career official, appointed, promoted, renumerated, controlled, deployed and retired by the bureaucratic procedures applicable to all members of the organization. So just as lay authority and institutions create a miniature political system (with elections, policy-making, pressure-group activity and policy implementation: Stanyer, 1976) so field authority and personnel may produce a miniature administrative system with its own hierarchy, levels of discretion, generalist and technical personnel and internal methods of co-ordination and control. Chapter 8 examines the political and administrative roles of field personnel and the different organizational structures in which they are employed.

If area government is exercised through political authority and lay institutions within areas defined by community characteristics a system of devolution (in unitary states) or federalism may be said to exist. Service-defined areas, bureaucratic authority and field personnel produce field administration or deconcentration. Any given political system will reveal a complex pattern of devolution and deconcentration combined, sometimes overlaid by federalism. The constituent parts of a federation will decentralize to lay bureaucratic institutions. Federal government agencies frequently operate field services. Field administration may be encountered within a system of municipal government as well as within the states or provinces of a federation, and alongside local government in a unitary state. Authority is delegated in different ways and to different degrees. Field administration and municipal government may be more or less integrated under a prefectoral system or function without one (see Chapter 8).

Political decentralization is usually assumed to entail democracy. Decision-makers are elected representatives accountable to voters who participate in other ways in the political life of local communities or regions. However, it should be noted that political decentralization does not logically imply democracy, even in the limited sense of accountable government by majoritarian elected assemblies. Decentralized governments may vary in the extent to which they satisfy democratic criteria just as they vary in the autonomy they enjoy from higher levels of government. Local-level government might be highly decentralized but based on traditional élites, as in some forms of indirect rule within colonial territories.

The different forms that decentralization can take also suggest that this part of the state apparatus may be viewed very differently depending on whether the viewer identifies with the centre or with a locality or region. A high degree of decentralization to an appointed state official exercising broad powers within a locality will look highly centralized from the perspective of the community. Administrative decentralization may coexist with political centralization, and it is wrong to infer, as P. King (1982, p. 125) does that administrative decentralization implies '*some* degree of political self-control among subsidiary units' (italics in original). Administrative decentralization in which subsidiary units have no *self* government, being governed by officials appointed by the centre, is both a logical and practical possibility.

Federalism

It is sometimes thought useful to arrange the different forms which decentralization in the state can take along a continuum which represents the varying levels of decentralization associated with different organizational and constitutional arrangements. The level of autonomy is said to range from complete independence to complete integration, as when, in theory, all administration outside the nation's capital is in the hands of field agents of central ministries. Federalism is usually regarded as a more decentralized arrangement than devolution to rural, urban, metropolitan, or regional governments (Kelsen, 1961; Ridley, 1973; Riker, 1975; Smith and Stanyer, 1976, p. 92). However, recent studies of federalism suggest that it may be mistaken to conclude that levels of decentralization can be inferred from the constitutional difference between devolution and federalism.

Federalism is sometimes thought to be a highly decentralized form of government because, unlike devolution, the main area governments receive their powers not from the national government but from the constitution upon which the central or federal government is equally dependent for its sphere of jurisdiction. The two levels are thus co-ordinate and independent (Wheare, 1963, p. 10). For example, the British North America Act of 1867 assigns 'classes of subjects' exclusively to the legislatures of the Canadian provinces and enumerates the exclusive legislative authority of the Parliament of Canada as well as giving the residue to the national government. The Act lists twenty-nine powers of the national government, including the regulation of trade and commerce, the raising of taxation, public borrowing and defence. The powers assigned to the provinces also include the levying of *direct* taxation in order to raise revenues for provincial purposes. Municipal government is listed as another exclusive power of the provinces. In so far as a federation is distinguished by a constitution which is superior to the individual governments of the states as far as the territorial division of powers is concerned, it follows that there must be a written constitution. It also follows that there should be a special (and difficult) amending procedure in which both levels of government participate. For example, in the USA a proposal for amendment requires a two-thirds majority in both Houses of Congress (one of which represents the states) or a convention called by Congress on the application of two-thirds of the states; ratification then requires agreement by legislatures or conventions in three-quarters of the states. It further follows that conflicts about rightful areas of jurisdiction have to be settled by a body which is 'independent' of both levels of government − a supreme court.

However, the comparative analysis of federations and unitary states reveals three things which make the distinction between federal and unitary states much less clear than it is sometimes believed to be, and the issue of whether federalism is more decentralized than a unitary constitution a matter for empirical investigation rather than definition.

First, it is not unusual for federal constitutions to contradict the principle of federalism by assigning some power to the federal government over the regional governments. In Switzerland the courts must find federal laws valid. In Canada the federal government may disallow provincial law and instruct the lieutenant-governor of a province to withold assent from provincial legislation. The national government also appoints lieutenant-governors and important provincial judicial officers. In the USSR constitutional amendment is the prerogative of the central government. Financial control is in the hands of the centre and the powers 'reserved' for the central government are so extensive that little is left exclusively to the republics. There are 'basic principles' governing the exercise of powers by the republics which are determined by the Union government. India is another federation in which such extensive powers are conferred on the national government that little of importance is left to the constituent parts. A study of American federalism concluded that 'the only aspect of state government that is beyond the reach of Washington is the very existence of the states with their present boundaries' (Reagan and Sanzone, 1981, p. 11).

Secondly, the way in which federations have evolved makes formal, legalistic definitions in terms of divisions of powers relatively useless. The two main levels of government have become increasingly interdependent. There has been a significant expansion in the concurrent powers of federal systems (Birch, 1955). Among other things this means that federations have a tendency to become more or less centralized than the founding politicians intended. It certainly means that different federations will reveal very different levels of decentralization. In the USA, for example, the growth in levels of federal spending has meant that many federal grant-aided programmes have been initiated.

These lay down policies which state and local governments are required to implement under close federal supervision. While some commentators speak of the USA as having a 'unitary-federal' political system, others see the new-style federalism as pragmatic, involving the sharing of functions between federal and state governments. Federalism changes in response to social and economic forces. The 'marble cake' metaphor, indicating an intermixing of federal and state decision-making, is now preferred in the USA to the 'layer cake' metaphor, implying autonomous spheres of decision-making (Grodzins, 1960; Reagan and Sanzone, 1981). Federalism has come to be characterized by the bargaining which goes on over concurrent powers. The federal government has also intervened to impose national standards.

In Canada, by contrast, judicial review has strengthened provincial powers despite the original determination to make the Canadian constitution highly centralized. Other political factors have also served to make Canada more decentralized than was originally intended. The Canadian political process emphasizes the mutual interdependence of federal and provincial levels, giving rise to what is sometimes referred to as a 'diplomatic' relationship between the two. Regional autonomy has been given higher priority than national political egalitarianism which elsewhere has led to centralization.

Thirdly, it is possible for a unitary state to devolve substantial powers to provincial governments so that a quasi-federal arrangement exists. Northern Ireland from 1920 to 1973 was a case in point as, more recently, is Papua New Guinea.

Such developments and comparisons have driven observers to redefine federalism in such a way as to make it indistinguishable from a unitary state. W. Livingstone, for example, abandoned the idea of federalism as a form of government in favour of federalism as a form of society in which differences of language, ethnicity, religion, class and race differentiate society on a territorial basis (1956). Friedrich also fails to distinguish federalism from other kinds of decentralized government when he defined it as a 'union of groups, united by one or more common objectives, rooted in common values, interests or beliefs, but retaining their distinctive group character for other purposes' (1968). Duchacek also feels obliged to define federalism in social and political terms which could equally be applied to some unitary states. 'A federal constitution may therefore be seen as a political compact that explicitly admits of the existence of conflicting interests among the component territorial communities and commits them all to seek accommodation without outvoting the minority and without the use of force' (1970, p. 192). Riker (1975) has even argued that so difficult is it to distinguish federations from other systems of government that it is a myth.

As Vile (1977) has clearly shown, such definitions of federalism fail to distinguish between a system of government and a socio-political system. Society may be perceived as diversified and its polity pluralistic, without anything being said about its formal structure of government. We are often told that formal structures are less important than socio-economic environment, but in comparisons of territorial government this is less true than it might be elsewhere. The crucial question that needs to be asked about federalism is whether there is anything about a federal constitution which is important for the way in which intergovernmental relations are conducted and which *in this respect* distinguishes federalism from a unitary state.

All that can be said in reply to this is that the crucial, and *politically* significant characteristic of a federation is that it is more difficult than in a unitary state for the centre to encroach upon the powers and status of regional governments. Federalism rules out the total elimination of provincial autonomy, a theoretical possibility in a unitary state (Duchacek, 1970, p. 194), to which one must add: a theoretical possibility within the normal procedures of government. The critical dimension of federalism lies in the procedures required to amend the structure of relations between governments. Hence the importance of independent adjudication and the representation of the constituent units at the central level of government. Federalism involves special techniques for managing a changing equilibrium between national and regional levels of government (Vile, 1973, pp. 2–3; Vile, 1977). Preston King, after a detailed analysis of the concepts of federalism and federation identifies one particular 'technique' as critical in distinguishing a federation from non-federal states. That is the constitutional incorporation of the regions into the centre's decision-making procedure (P. King, 1982, p. 146).

Thus the purpose of distinguishing federalism is not to produce abstract definitions or beg important questions about the distribution of territorial power. It is to see how far a special procedure for initiating and adjudicating upon changes in the distribution of power affect the final outcome along with all the other aspects of the political process, such as party system, political culture, judicial system and political interests. Federations cannot by means of definition be located on a continuum (P. King, 1982, p. 126). Furthermore, the representation of regional interests in the second chamber of the legislature may be differentially affected by internal political forces within federations. For example, Canadian and Australian experience, when compared with the USA, suggests that, by weakening the second chamber, a parliamentary regime may be incompatible with decentralized federalism (W. Livingstone, 1968, p. 111).

Federations are thus systems of government where it has been deliberately made difficult for the national government to alter the powers of the constituent units, their boundaries and their forms of government. Looked at in this way the contrast with unitary states is clear. Even when special provision is made for one part of the country, as was the case with devolution to Northern Ireland, there is never any doubt as to the unitary nature of the arrangements. Northern Ireland enjoyed more autonomy than England and Wales, but its constitutional status was clearly a case of devolution since political authority had been delegated by the United Kingdom Parliament to a legislative assembly which sat in Belfast. The Government of Ireland Act, 1920, was the province's 'constitution' and it clearly stated that 'the supreme authority of the Parliament of the United Kingdom shall remain unaffected and undiminished over all persons, matters and things in Ireland and every part thereof'. The UK Parliament could pass laws on any subject in the province. The two governments were not co-ordinate. The UK Parliament could change the powers devolved to Stormont and could disallow its laws. The government at Stormont was a dependent government (Wheare, 1963, pp. 31–2). The province was represented in Westminster, but by constituency members sitting in the Lower House, not through legislative entrenchment of the province. The powers exercised by the Northern Ireland government were residuary, which made it a strong form of devolution, but the *excluded* and *reserved* powers of the national government included defence, foreign relations, external trade, communications and taxation. Northern Ireland received transferred revenues and grants, especially for social services and agriculture. Much effort went into negotiating equality of service standards between the province and the rest of the UK. It was difficult for the province to act independently (Lawrence, 1956, p. 15). There was little deviation from British norms in policy formulation. Provincial legislation rarely differed from British law (Birch, 1956, p. 311).

Further evidence of the crucial constitutional difference between unitary and federal states is found in the reform of local government in Britain and the issue of devolution to Scottish and Welsh assemblies. The Local Government Acts of 1972 completely altered the system of local government in England, Scotland and

Wales. This fundamental and far-reaching change required no special legislative procedure. A simple majority in Parliament, as with all other legislation, was all that was required to effect this constitutional change (Brand, 1976). The powers of subordinate governments and their relations with the centre are similarly established by ordinary Acts of Parliament or, in some cases, executive discretion. The devolution proposals similarly required nothing more than ordinary legislation. The proposals were eventually defeated in exceptional referenda which did add an unusual stage to the process of constitutional change, though again only because Parliament decided to make approval in a referendum a necessary condition of implementation. This suggests that it is possible for a unitary state to move in and out of a condition of what Richard Rose called 'political federalism' when more than one level of power must accept constitutional proposals (Rose, 1977, p. 36).

The concept of decentralization used here, then, does not exclude federalism. It is not restricted to the unitary state, as it is for Duchacek, for whom it 'presupposes the existence of a central authority whose leaders deem it useful − or inevitable − to delegate a portion of their centrally held power to sub-national centres, for the sake of administrative expediency or in response to sub-national pressures' (1970, p. 112). Quite apart from the fact that this definition does not exclude federations which are created or reorganized by the centre, as in Nigeria in 1979, the range of levels of decentralization which federalism itself is capable of producing makes it necessary to include federations in our investigations into decentralized government. Federations as much as unitary states are confronted with the same classes of problem, whether it be in the delimitation of subnational areas, the allocation of powers including those to tax and the consequent intergovernmental relationships, the creation of democratic and bureaucratic institutions, and the need to legitimize the state.

2
Decentralization in Theory

Introduction

Decentralization now has almost universal appeal and is accommodated within very different views of the state. When considered in the context of political theory it is usually assumed that decentralization will be of the political variety. Decentralized government for those concerned with the normative evaluation of forms of political authority is taken to imply two fundamental conditions. The first is that the territorial subdivisions of the state will have a measure of autonomy. They will, to some extent, be self-governing through political institutions which have their roots within the territory for which they have jurisdiction. They will not be administered by the agents of a superior government but will be governed by institutions that are founded on the politics of the area. The second is that those institutions will be democratically recruited. They will take their decisions according to democratic procedures.

The first condition (self-government) does not entail the second (democracy), since a community might well be self-governing through hereditary kingship, feudal institutions or other forms of government. This was in fact the case with the forms of indirect rule practised by imperial powers such as Britain within their colonies. Furthermore, in the past some notable proponents of local self-government have specifically rejected democracy as an appropriate way of governing local affairs. For example, Von Gneist, the nineteenth-century Prussian idealist, though believing that local government was a necessary condition of the ideal state, rejected representative institutions and political equality in favour of appointed members of the propertied classes. Local government was in fact defined in such a way as to make it incompatible with democratic practices (Whalen, 1960). In England Toulmin-Smith, writing in the mid-nineteenth century, also rejected democracy in preference for an earlier tradition of parochial government by selected officials and nominated justices of the peace (D. M. Hill, 1974, p. 26).

But today the assumption is generally that self-governing territories within the nation-state will be democratically organized, though there is clearly room for differences of opinion as to how far a given set of institutions and procedures fulfil one's democratic requirements. Free and fair elections with universal suffrage may satisfy one view of democracy, whereas another view will regard them as a sham if large sections of the population are too uninformed, poorly organized, or repressed to articulate their political demands effectively.

There are also differences of opinion as to how necessary democratic, local self-government is to the political health of the modern democratic state. As will be noted below, territorial interests may be classed among those sectional interests which are seen as incompatible with society's 'general will' represented by the nation's legislature. Sovereignty may be regarded as unified, not dispersed. Democracy therefore implies centralization rather than decentralization. However, arguments about the desirability of localized democracy are usually in agreement as to its nature.

This chapter examines decentralization from a normative standpoint and consider the role which social theorists have ascribed to it in the modern state. It starts by looking at some of the more conventional views which writers in a broadly liberal political tradition have presented on behalf of democratic decentralization (or local government as it is more commonly known, though no particular significance should be attached at this stage to the geographical connotations of 'local'). It moves on to the support which economists have given to the case for a decentralized state, and concludes with an outline of how Marxist views of the 'state at the local level' are currently developing. This issue will be returned to in the chapter on area, as the problem of democracy is related to the problem of deciding on the optimal area for decentralized government.

Local Government and Liberal Democracy

Liberal arguments in favour of democratic local government as the best method of arranging for the local administration of public services fall mainly into two categories. There are those that claim local government is good for *national* democracy; and there are those where the major concern is with the benefits to the *locality* of local democracy. Each can be further subdivided into three sets of interrelated values. At the national level these values relate to political education, training in leadership and political stability. At the local level the relevant values are equality, liberty and responsiveness.

As far as national democracy is concerned it is not self-evident, as C. H. Wilson noted in his *Essays on Local Government*, that national democracy *entails* local democracy as a means of administration (Wilson, 1948, p. 13). And indeed there is a continental European view of the state which sees locality as just one more special interest at odds with the sovereign general will. Professor Langrod, a Frenchman, argued some years ago, in an exchange of views published in the journal *Public Administration*, that a political system without local self-government was not necessarily undemocratic; that local government is but a technical administrative mechanism; and that democratic values are not necessarily preserved by local democratic institutions which are inegalitarian, divisive and contrary to the public will (Langrod, 1953, p. 28). Leo Moulin, a Belgian, contributed to this debate and also argued that local government was a training ground in the defence of 'narrow' local and individual interests, which overlook the 'higher' interests of the nation (Moulin, 1954).

Contrary to this, most liberal theories of the state argue that local democracy (and it is to be noted that the Continental contributors to the debate often seem to be objecting to the *undemocratic* aspects of local government) makes a positive contribution to the health of the nation's democracy generally by offering opportunities for 'greater personal participation in the actual business of governing' and by creating 'a democractic climate of opinion' (Panter-Brick, 1953). Local democracy thus becomes a necessary condition of national democracy. It is clear that those who advocate democratic decentralization see it as having beneficial effects on the state as a whole, even though there have been few attempts this century to produce a general theory from which the form of decentralized government can be deduced (Mackenzie, 1961).

Political Education
The first function which democratic decentralization is said to perform for the democratic state is political education. De Tocqueville wrote that 'town meetings are to liberty what primary schools are to science: they bring it within the people's reach, they teach men how to use and how to enjoy it' (de Tocqueville, 1835, p. 63). Another classic formulation of this view is found

in John Stuart Mill's *Representative Government*. Mill re-commended local government on the ground that it provides extra opportunities for political participation, both in electing and being elected to local offices, for people who otherwise would have few chances to act politically between national elections. (Mill added that local government extends such opportunities to the 'lower grades' of society, local positions rarely being sought by the 'higher ranks'.) One of the underlying themes of *Representative Government* is the educative effect of free institutions, and Mill's belief was that 'of this operation the local administrative institutions are the chief instruments' (Mill, 1861).

This, writes C. H. Wilson in the *Essays* cited earlier, is the strongest case that can be made for local government. It teaches the possible, the expedient, and the uses and risks of power, ingenuity and versatility. This has also been a recurring theme in discussions of political development. For Maddick, a principal objective of local government is that it should foster 'healthy political understanding'. The citizen learns to recognize the 'specious demagogue', to avoid electing the incompetent or corrupt representative, to debate issues effectively, to relate expenditure to income, to 'think for tomorrow' (Maddick, 1963, pp. 59 and 106).

The extent to which the educative claim on behalf of local democracy is justified is open to debate. Sharpe has criticized the claim as being paternalistic, seeing the function of teaching ordinary people how to manage scarce resources as linked to the problem of 'councillor calibre' (Sharpe, 1981d, p. 34). But even if we accept a need for political education, does local democracy actually provide it?

Local elections and the continuing process of local politics between elections undoubtedly generate political information. A small minority of activists will learn from their experiences, and others may find the act of choosing between leaders and pro-grammes educative. But there is no shortage of information, in Britain at least, that turnouts are low, that choices are made more under the influence of perceptions of national policies rather than local, and that there is a large degree of ignorance of, and lack of interest in, local politics on the part of most citizens. If we place much emphasis on the educative act of voting, as indeed Mill himself did, then the majority would appear to learn little from local government. However, this probably overestimates the significance of voting.

Mill was no doubt correct in stating that increased opportunities for political participation would be created by local representative government, but we should guard against the assumption that the mere existence of these bodies will lead to 'the nourishment of public spirit and the development of intelligence' (Mill, 1861). More recent evidence suggests that it is unwise to expect too much in the way of educative benefits from local democracy. There are many factors which affect levels of interest, knowledge and understanding of local affairs. It would be a mistake to conclude that local government had failed in this respect. To look to the operation of local political institutions for political education is to place an unreasonable burden on them. More importantly, it may overlook the extent to which political education is the function of wider social processes and institutions, such as class and education generally. A failure to recognize this constitutes part of the failure to place democratic decentralization within its broader social environment, and contributes to the mystification of government.

Training in Political Leadership

Similar caution should be employed in handling the related claim that local government provides a valuable training ground for national legislators. Professor Mackenzie traced this idea back to Bentham's vision of a 'sub-legislative' constituting 'a nursery for the supreme legislative: a school of appropriate aptitude, in all its branches for the business of legislature' (1961). Harold Laski similarly claimed that 'if members were, before their candidature was legal, required to serve three years on a local body, they would gain the "feel" of institutions so necessary to success' (1931).

There is certainly evidence that some national legislators have prior experience as local councillors, though it is rare for local councillors in Britain to see their service in local government as a training in parliamentarianism and political leadership. In some countries, such as France, elected representatives often occupy seats in both national and local legislatives. It is one thing to identify common membership, or even local experience, as part of the legislator's political career. It is another thing altogether to identify whether the legislators with local government experience are 'better' than those without it. Obviously the paramount problem is deciding what constitutes 'better' in this context. There is also the problem of separating out the effect of local government experience from all other experiences which contribute to a politician's training. No doubt local government provides valuable political experience to the activist. But other organizations, such as trade unions, also provide experience of resolving conflicts, operating decision-making procedures and allocating scarce resources (Money, 1973). In addition, it may be that local government provides experience of a political institution that is in many ways unique and which therefore can hardly be said to provide training for a higher-level legislature or executive. Local government may provide experience of party systems, legislative roles, methods of policy formulation, legislative – executive – administrative relationships and executive accountability that are vastly different from what obtain at the national level. The councillor entering a national legislature may find himself in a very different political environment. The value of political experience on local councils for national politicians should not be exaggerated (B. C. Smith, 1972b).

Political Stability

Finally, democratic decentralization is said to contribute to 'the breeding of better societies' (Sharpe, 1981d, p. 34) and the establishment of social harmony, community spirit and political stability. This value is related to the vision of local government as political educator in that experience of local politics enables people to choose leaders they can trust. And trust in government is a necessary condition for stable democracy.

There are many objectives and reservations that can be made to this way of thinking. First, it has been pointed out that stable democracy at the national level has, in many instances, preceded the establishment of local democracy (Sharpe, 1981d). Secondly, many countries can be identified that have experienced political instability after a period of active local government. Against this it may be argued that their systems of local democracy were not functioning properly. Had they done so, instability would have been less likely to occur. The problem with this is that we do not know what constitutes 'proper' local government. In what sense can India's system of local government be said to be better than, say, Pakistan's? Finally, it is probably impossible to single out the effect on national political stability of local government from the multitude of other pertinent factors. The relationship between local democracy and national stability can be only a matter of faith. And even that entirely begs the question of whether 'stability' is a desirable state of affairs.

Turning now to the local political system, three values can again be distinguished as attaching to local democracy in the writings of political theorists that have contributed to a 'framework of values within which the areal division of powers is said to be structured and judged' (Ylvisaker, 1959, p. 31).

Political Equality

First, local democracy is said to contribute to political equality. By providing extra opportunities for citizens to participate in public policy-making it strengthens the political equality implicit in civil rights. Local government gives additional occasions for voting, forming political associations and exercising freedom of speech. It sets up a further barrier to the concentration of power. It contributes to the political development of the individual (Ylvisaker, 1959).

More participation, then, means greater political equality. And participation at the local level secures a greater measure of political equality than politics at the national level. Local government is said to reflect and be a continuation of a prior and more natural form of democracy than national democracy.

The history of the idea that local government in some sense precedes the nation-state has been traced by Wickwar. According to this view of political development, local government is the descendant of 'historic communities' and as such reflects 'more of the natural history of men than any other part of modern civilization'. Therefore, municipalities are no mere subdivisions of the state for administrative convenience or even civic education (as in utilitarianism) but rather they represent 'deeper instincts'. Local government is thus that part of a nation's government which has not been 'surrendered' by localities to the state, but which has been retained by the communities in which it originated (Wickwar, 1970, p. 53).

Robert Dahl, in linking the ideals of modern municipal government to the ancient city-states, argues that larger communities make the realization of democracy more difficult. As size increases, the proportion of citizens that can participate directly in government decreases (Dahl, 1981, p. 47). For Dahl the great virtue of municipal democracy is that it encourages rational participation in 'shaping and forming vital aspects of their lives in common' and fosters 'the sense of unity, wholeness, belonging, of membership of an inclusive and solidary community which we sometimes seem to want with such a desperate yearning' (Dahl, 1981, p. 49). Only the city will be small enough in the condition of the twenty-first century to enable everyone to believe 'that his claims ordinarily receive a fair hearing, and decisions, even when adverse to his claims, have been arrived at with understanding and sympathy' (Dahl, 1981, p. 60).

The question of size and democracy will be taken up again in the chapter on areas. Here the concern is restricted to contrasts between national and local levels of government, rather than between subnational territories of different geographical and demographic scales. The 'purer democracy' thesis is open to the objection that it presents a romanticized view of the local polity, a consideration of relevance to the goals set for decentralization in developing countries (see Chapter 10). As Fesler argues, the local polity often shows evidence of the maldistribution of power, and of domination by those who wield economic power (Fesler, 1965, p. 543). Dahl himself acknowledges that the village or small town is characterized by 'the oppressive weight of repressed deviation and dissent' (Dahl, 1981, p. 50), but gives no convincing reason for believing the city to be less repressive.

In fact it is futile to compare national and local government in these terms. Both levels are equally vulnerable to the realities of politics in stratified societies where power at all levels is, like wealth, maldistributed. Marxist theorists of the local-level state, to be considered below, understand this well and have shown how class-based power operates within the locality as well as between it and the national level of government, without denying that municipal politics have afforded working-class interests with opportunities to obtain power locally.

Studies of local government as a means of decentralization thus too often stress its virtues as a training ground in democracy and representative government, and too rarely indicate how privilege and exploitation can be maintained and strengthened through local politics. Decentralization is too readily 'transformed into a value in its own right' by romantic idealization. It is made an absolute good (Fesler, 1965). In other words when liberal political theory is applied to the local political system it defines away the conflicts inherent in the structure of local society and replaces them with the idea of power residing in electoral accountability. Power is thought to be equally distributed by the right to vote. The only problem is to obtain a majority decision in conditions which appear to be remarkably lacking in vested interests, structural conflicts between classes and sources of power lying outside the constitutional framework of representative political institutions. The possibility that the holders of economic power at the local level will dominate local political institutions to perpetuate privilege, hierarchy and conservatism tends to be ignored. Power is conceived in narrowly constitutional terms as if this adequately specifies the whole power structure within the locality. Decentralization should instead be seen as part of the process by which dominant classes, including those at the local level, articulate their interests through state policies and institutions.

Accountability

The second value of democratic decentralization to the individual and the local community is that it facilitates accountability and, thereby, liberty. Mill's idea of liberty as an absence of restraint on self-regarding actions can be extended to local communities. Most actions of government are self-regarding from the locality's point of view (Mill, 1861, p. 346). Just as the individual has the right to liberty in those matters which alone concern him, so there is 'a corresponding liberty in any number of individuals to regulate by mutual agreement such things as regard them jointly, and regard no persons but themselves' (Mill, 1859, p. 157). Such a number may well be the inhabitants of a local community: 'The very object of having a local representation is in order that those who have any interest in common, which they do not share with the general body of their countrymen, may manage that joint interest by themselves' (Mill, 1861, p. 350).

Mill establishes the accountability of local governments by asserting the right of individuals grouped in local communities to self-regulation. Others have drawn attention to local democracy as a defence against arbitrary power. Indeed, a traditional argument for the areal division of power under federal constitutions is that federalism discourages tyranny and strengthens liberty by preventing the concentration of power. Thomas Jefferson defended states' rights in the USA as 'the surest bulwarks against anti-republican tendencies' and 'the true barriers of our liberty'. A federation of 'single and independent' states could 'never be so fascinated by the arts of one man, as to submit voluntarily to his usurption' (quoted in Padover, 1954, pp. 32 and 53; see also de Tocqueville, 1835, Vol. 1, ch. 5). Ylvisaker recommends the areal division of powers as providing the individual with more readily available points of access, pressure and control than centralized government. Minorities more readily obtain governmental office and positions of influence. Governmental power is kept 'close to its origins, and governmental officials within reach of their masters' (Ylvisaker, 1959, p. 32). The creation of extra tiers of government assures friction and debate, both necessary for the protection of liberty. Dupré sees this as a reason for making the whole local government system complex. Freedom from arbitrary decisions is more likely when decision-making is difficult (Dupré, 1969). Professor Finer takes up the theme of liberty and accountability in more prosaic terms, emphasizing the accessibility of local councillors and their officials (Finer, 1957, p. 91).

There is some truth in the proposition that local democracy provides for greater accountability and control than field administration, public corporations or appointed agencies. The processes involved in local government make accountability more meaningful because of the elective element linking bureaucrat and citizen. The *political* activities inherent in local government – elections, rule making, political pressure, publicity and public debate – close the gap between the citizen and the administration and provide opportunities for grievances to be aired and wrongs remedied. It must be remembered, however, that serious doubts have been cast on the effectiveness of the ballot box when it comes to grievances arising from discretionary decisions and maladministration in local government.

There is danger, too, in this line of argument that the liberty of the individual will be confused with the liberty of communities (Sharpe, 1981d). Local self-government will, by definition, preserve the liberty of the local community against centralizing power. Whether it *also* protects the liberty of the individual is another matter. Local government is just as capable as central government of restraining the freedom of the individual in pursuit of some collective end. It may be equally reluctant or unable to liberate the individual from restraints and oppression originating elsewhere in society. Local government may make it easier for individual grievances to be redressed when individual rights are threatened by collective action. But collective action often threatens those with power and property. Local government may provide members of such classes with effective checks on public action designed to ameliorate the condition of the underprivileged. The redress of grievances is also more concerned with how policies are implemented than with what policies are chosen.

The relationship between the areal division of power and liberty gives grounds for scepticism, as Riker has pointed out in relation to the 'wise saw' about federalism. There are societies which preserve liberty without federalism, and dictatorships which operate federations. The territorial separation of power may actually promote tyranny by constantly frustrating majorities. The freedom of the national majority may be infringed by local majorities (such as the reversal of decisions on civil rights for negroes in the southern and border states of the USA in the mid-nineteenth century). 'To one who believes in the majoritarian notion of freedom, it is impossible to interpret federalism as other than a device for minority tyranny' (Riker, 1964, p. 142). When considering a possible relationship between decentralization and liberty it is important to ask, as with all discussions of liberty, 'freedom for whom?'

Responsiveness

The final value of local government to the community is its responsiveness and therefore ability to provide what people demand. In this sense it is an efficient way of managing local affairs and providing local services. This is sometimes referred to as the *welfare* value of local government (Ylvisaker, 1959).

Local government, it is argued, is responsive to the needs of the community. Needs are identified by decision-makers with intimate knowledge of the locality and answerable to local interests. Despite his conviction that local representative bodies and their officers were inferior to the national legislature and executive, Mill believed the locality had a compensating advantage: 'a far more direct interest in the result'. Local opinion acts 'more forcibly' on local administrators. Their authority depends on the will of the local public. Mill, however, did draw a distinction between principles and details (Mill, 1861, p. 357). C. H. Wilson emphasizes the importance of local knowledge and information to services where local diversity is required (Wilson, 1948, p. 20). Maddick makes a similar point for Third World states (Maddick, 1963, p. 106).

L. J. Sharpe draws attention to a hitherto overlooked contrast between central and local government that is highly relevant to the aim of meeting the individual needs of localities. Central government is based on functional specialization and departmentalism. The mixture of services and functions required locally varies from community to community. There must therefore be a co-ordinating body to determine the appropriate mixture of services for each community (Sharpe, 1981d, p. 36).

Local knowledge is thus seen as a prerequisite of responsiveness and flexibility in the determination of local priorities. Elected bodies are more able than other forms of local administration to acquire and utilize this information and intelligence. The political dimension in democratic forms of decentralization means that local government enjoys the advantage of the two-way flow of information between government and governed which is an important feature of democracy. The apparatus of representation in the localities may thus increase the local policy-maker's capacity to reflect local demands and opinions.

There are, of course, important factors which militate against local flexibility and responsiveness. Many of the important services administered by local authorities have national implications (Sharpe, 1965). There are political pressures to maintain such services at an equal standard regardless of area. Local flexibility and responsiveness are correspondingly reduced in many areas of local policy. However, although local authorities have to meet certain demands in standard of performance, there is wide room for discretion in local administration. A local authority satisfies purely local needs in the provision of many services. In fact local authorities effect a difficult compromise between the demands of their electorates and the controls of the central government.

The problem with this formulation of the local political process is that it adopts a holistic view of needs. It comes too close to presenting the identification of needs, and the right 'mix' of services to meet them, as a technical exercise in which a correct answer to the problem is found by tapping local knowledge and experience. The local people whose wisdom is accumulated for this purpose are presented as a unified mass with a common interest in getting things right. Clearly this is an unsatisfactory way of describing politics at any territorial level. The 'co-ordination' required to meet local needs is a highly political process involving conflicts of interest which have to be resolved by all the means available to the apparatus of the state. The members of some classes are better placed than others in protecting their needs and articulating their demands. Achieving a way of resolving conflicts may be much more to the advantage of some classes in society than others. What constitutes the right 'mix' of services provided by decentralized governments depends very much on what one's needs are, how they are best met from the individual's point of view and how one's interests are affected by the demands which collective action make on private resources.

That said and bearing in mind the factors which make for effective political demand, it may be argued that decentralization provides what is to some extent a unique opportunity for the measurement of 'consumer satisfaction'. The elective process allows for demonstrations of discontent or satisfaction at the general way in which the affairs of the locality are administered and managed in those spheres where local authorities can be parochial. When a large group in the community (for example, council house tenants) feel aggrieved, they probably stand a better chance of bringing about reform through representative institutions than through other forms of local administration (other things being equal, which they are not). The power which lies with the local electorate may thus ensure that local policies reflect local demand.

Sharpe has argued that local governments can be a valuable defence of consumer interests which are so often placed second to producer interests by central governments (Sharpe, 1984). Local government is better able than central government to respond to changes in demand, to experiment and to anticipate future changes. It provides a form of government in which people from non-producer groups can more easily participate (Sharpe, 1984).

The politics of local government create one of the essential elements of representative government − the two-way flow of information between local leaders and the public. Elections not only select leaders but also allow views to be aired. The activities of political groups provide for the further expression of opinion. Elected representatives hear grievances and explain policy. Because of its frequent contacts with the public the local administration becomes aware of popular feelings towards local policies and can bring them to the attention of the relevant policy-makers. All such channels of communication are important characteristics of representative government at the national level (Birch, 1964, ch. 15), but are equally valid as descriptions of the interrelationship between government and the public in the localities.

Presenting local government as a system which responds to demand, thus endowing it with the quality of 'economic efficiency' in a context in which the price mechanism is absent (Sharpe, 1981d, p. 38), has attracted the attention of economists. Their interpretations of the nature of local, decentralized governments have had interesting and important implications for issues which are often debated and decided upon without reference to such economic formulations. To these we now turn.

Economic Interpretations of Local Government

If approached from the perspective of theories of public choice and collective goods, decentralization becomes an important medium for increasing personal welfare. According to this approach individuals are assumed to choose their place of residence by comparing packages of services and taxes on offer by different municipalities. The rational individual will locate himself where the best combination is found according to his own preference schedule and will choose so as to gain the greatest net advantage. A system of local government offering the widest range of choices is therefore to be preferred as it will increase the chance of any given individual being better off than if faced with less variation. The citizen should be able to 'vote with his feet' if he is dissatisfied with the benefits received from the local authority, and move to a locality where the level and mix of services relative to taxes comes closer to meeting his preferences (Tiebout, 1972; Oates, 1972, pp. 11–12). These assumptions have important implications for the design of local government systems, for it follows that a fragmented pattern of areas and jurisdictions is preferable to a system of large, all-purpose authorities (Bish and Ostrom, 1973).

Public Responsiveness to Individual Preferences
The public-choice approach proceeds from the assumption that a diversity of individual preferences needs to be matched by a diversity of goods and services. It is assumed that the citizen is informed of the alternative packages available. The goods and services on offer from local governments are, unlike private goods, enjoyed by all members of the relevant community, so that one's consumption does not detract from another's. The significance of government in this model is that it ensures contributions are made towards the costs of providing 'local' public goods and services when voluntary effort is ineffective. It also provides, through elections and other political procedures, a means by which preferences are communicated.

The structure of the municipal system thus has an effect on the responsiveness of public officials to individual preferences. It becomes necessary to visualize different 'communities of users' which participate in decisions which affect their interests. These communities are not conterminous (Ostrom, Tiebout and Warren, 1961). For example, a community of interest for neighbourhood streets is smaller than a community of interest for urban thoroughfares or national highways (Dupré, 1969, p. 152). For efficiency to be maximized the number of jurisdictions should thus be equal to the number of areas needed to internalize the public goods to be provided, assuming that such goods are unlikely to be internalized within any single area. In this way the 'externalities' of public goods are internalized to the public served, that is, when the scale of operations internalizes the benefits from governmental intervention. The annexation of surrounding areas and the consolidation of local jurisdictions enables the coincidence of taxation and consumption to be established at least for services where 'free riding' reduces the benefits to the local population (Walker, 1981, pp. 172–3). In this way the number of opportunities for people to affect decisions which are not of interest to them is minimized. Obviously such an approach implies a tiered system of local authorities, especially in metropolitan areas. If the number of levels has to be restricted for other reasons, a system of conditional grants should be able to take into account the marginal social benefits and marginal social costs of the resulting spillover effects and equalize them out (Dupré, 1969, p. 153).

Decentralization organized according to public-choice principles is said to overcome many of the problems which public provision of goods and services creates for efficiency and responsiveness. The problem of *responsiveness* is here seen as one of determining community-wide demand in the absence of competitive pricing. The test of *efficiency* is whether governments actually supply the goods and services citizens prefer in the absence of measures of consumer satisfaction (Bish and Ostrom, 1973).

The Demand for Public Goods

On the *demand* side, whereas in private markets consumer preference is indicated by willingness to pay, in political systems it has to be expressed through voting and other political activities — lobbying, petitions, public inquiries, opinion polls, demonstrations, and so on. 'Demand' is difficult to identify in politics because: goods are disassociated from their 'prices' (taxes); these 'prices' may be met disproportionately by others (through progressive taxes); and votes have to express in a single choice a multitude of preferences or at least an 'all-or-nothing' choice as in a single-issue referendum. Different citizens have different opportunities for access to the means of expressing political preferences. The benefits need to outweigh the costs of participation. The costs of attaining positions of leadership vary from one individual to another, a factor which also distorts demand.

The public-choice approach to decentralization claims to reduce these problems by increasing the number of governmental units and their degree of specialization of function. This eases the voting problem, though it is usually acknowledged that the physical characteristics of service supply will have an unavoidable effect on size of area (as in the case of a water supply or pollution control agency). Smaller jurisdictions are also said to create proportionately larger benefits to individuals in return for their participation than larger units of government, another argument for the proliferation of small and specialized jurisdictions. The costs of becoming candidates with a chance of success are also lower in small communities. Larger units of government generate the need for costly political organizations and the spoils of office.

This, in turn, increases the risk of domination by a single political organization, the rise of political 'bosses', corruption and coercion. However, it is again recognized that there are high costs involved to the citizen who has to articulate preferences to many different special-purpose agencies (education boards, health authorities, water councils, police services, highways authorities, and so on). Multi-purpose decentralized governments are recognized as having benefits too.

Decentralization is also said to tie expenditure decisions to resource costs, so overcoming to some extent the problems which citizens have in judging the benefits of expenditure in relation to its cost (Oates, 1972, p. 13).

The Supply of Public Goods

On the *supply* side, there are many problems of allocative efficiency with collective goods − of determining whether the costs of production exceed the value of services to the community. There is also in public organizations less incentive to economize than in private ones − the problem of X-efficiency. The larger the organization, with its bigger management cadres and greater access to fiscal resources, the greater the tendency to exacerbate this weakness of public organizations. Also, the more monopolistic the government, the less the incentive to innovate (Oates, 1972, p. 12). Nor can it be assumed that a monopolistic public organization will produce a range of public services equally well. The theory that fragmented jurisdictions, rather than consolidated local authority, maximizes consumer satisfaction is in part based on the theory that public goods and services have different production characteristics − the optimal scale of production for one is not the same as for another (Magnusson, 1981).

A diverse range of jurisdictions is therefore preferable, encouraging rivalry and competition between fragmented and overlapping authorities. Consolidation reduces consumer satisfaction by creating huge monopolies inefficiently consuming large quantities of taxes and producing unwanted services (Ostrom, Tiebout and Warren, 1961). When, on the other hand, an area is divided and local government functions are 'split between special-purpose bodies which use differing territories and are separately accountable to the electorate' (Magnusson, 1981, p. 577), consumer satisfaction will be maximized.

Theoretical and Practical Problems

The public choice approach to the value of local government

provides a fresh insight into democratic accountability at the local level. It also challenges some of the more conventional wisdom about the scale of production problem and the areas required for different goods and services. It draws attention to the costs involved in the exercise of choice and the expression of preferences in politics and implicitly to the question of whether these costs are equally distributed. However, the approach encounters problems of both a theoretical and practical kind.

First, the theory prescribes small jurisdictions, though the concept of externalities points to jurisdictions of greatly varying scales. In fact it may be impossible to contain externalities within an area smaller than the state itself, such is the extent to which local decisions have implications extending beyond the boundaries of the locality. For most of the major functions of government assigned to subnational units the principle of externalities would lead to a high level of centralization if applied rigorously (Sharpe, 1984). Most 'local' services would have to be disaggregated to reveal the purely local goods. The greater the number of separate municipal jurisdictions, especially in metropolitan areas, the more collective decisions there are which need to be made by a wider jurisdiction, such as land use, environmental and transportation decisions. The spillover effects of decisions by smaller municipalities demand metropolitan action (Jackson, 1975, pp. 22–3). In so far as public-choice theory assumes that pure local goods exist for which there are no spillovers into adjacent jurisdictions, it is deficient (Bennett, 1980, p. 31).

This leaves the choice of scale still to be made. There is a similar ambiguity about the need for single-purpose and multi-purpose authorities. Here the political traditions of a country are likely to be more influential than economic considerations, especially in the case of *ad hoc* bodies which, if appointed, conflict with the principle of participation but, if elected, may run counter to political tradition (Dupré, 1969).

Second, political demands have, like other demands, to be backed up by resources. These are as unevenly distributed among citizens as among consumers. Freedom to choose in politics, as in private consumption, is only valuable if it can be exercised. To move from one locality to another in response to a preferred level and cost of public service requires 'demand' to be made effective. To many groups for whom public services are especially important (because they cannot afford the private provision of, say, education and health care, or no private provision exists) the 'right' to move to a preferred 'bundle' of services and taxes is empty. To the aged, the unskilled worker, the one-parent family, the unemployed and the ethnic minority, the recommendation to move to Long Island or Gerrards Cross is either cruel or stupid (Stanyer, 1979). Alternatively, who is going to 'prefer' Toxteth or Harlem, even though the costs might be lower? And the chances of them being lower are slight since areas with the highest needs require the highest levels of expenditure. If all those who can afford to have moved out into more salubrious jurisdictions, isolating themselves in separate municipalities 'where a high level of services can be provided at a low rate of tax, and planning regulations can be used to enhance and protect the desired environment' (Magnusson, 1981, p. 578), the costs of services will fall on those unable to pay for the package of public goods for which they have expressed a preference. Land-use zoning is often used by richer communities to restrict the access of poorer migrants, and so further undermines the assumptions of the theory. Income differences also limit the validity of the theory in that wealthier communities with large tax bases can provide a range of public goods with lower rates of tax than a poorer community. Inequalities and polarization thus result as different areas provide the same goods but tax people differently (Bennett, 1980, p. 37). Any application of public-choice theory needs to be aware of the problem of income distribution.

Any theory of public choice which ignores the effect on consumer demand and existing levels of service provision of past and present patterns of deprivation is unsatisfactory. The natural growth of local government systems reflect the past interests of dominant classes who have a continuing interest in the kind of fragmentation recommended by the public-choice theorists. Responding to the needs of the privileged members of society, municipal government is likely to produce uniformity rather than diversity.

Residential choices are affected by factors other than local government services and taxes, such as social environment, physical appearance, work opportunities and costs of mobility. 'Demand' in politics generally is affected by many different factors, such as ideology, socialization, false consciousness and educational levels. Powerful interests will gain additional advantages from the increased complexity of government which makes the system more difficult to comprehend and paralyses decision-making (Dupré, 1969, p. 157). Information and organization are more easily obtained by some groups than others:

'preference intensities are imperfectly articulated' (Walker, 1981, p. 185). Public-choice theory offers no correctives to these distortions. The kind of local government environment experienced by a citizen will be far from having been chosen. The exigencies of employment and other factors may make it necessary for certain classes to tolerate a very unattractive combination of services and taxes.

Thirdly, the use of conditional grants to internalize spillover effects is likely to concentrate power at higher levels of government. This negates the expression of preferences by inhabitants of the locality. Economic efficiency may be served at the expense of participation and autonomy if fiscal considerations locate power outside the community (Dupré, 1969).

Fourthly, a theory of locational choice based on individual preferences is undermined when the unit of residence is the family. The costs and benefits of location are 'consumed' by its members. The assumption that every individual is the best judge of his or her own interests conflicts with the fact that family decisions have to compromise between the different utilities of different members of a household standing in different relations to the system of taxation and consuming different public services. Any decision to relocate a family will not necessarily maximize the utilities of all its members (Stanyer, 1980).

Fifthly, the existence of a multitude of suppliers is no guarantee of an unrestricted range of provision. A market may be intensely competitive with a large number of separate suppliers but their small scale, high costs and inability to employ the latest technology can mean the buyer is better off with a monopoly than a host of small entrepreneurs. The public sector is presumably open to the same considerations. In a comparable system of public service provision the citizen may merely have the freedom to choose between different degrees of inefficiency (Stanyer, 1980), unless the 'supply' of services is separated from production.

The 'locational-choice' model of decentralization has another disadvantage. Since the characteristics of communities affecting locational decisions by individuals and families are extremely varied there has to be a great multiplicity of communities before people can trade different benefits off against each other. The greater the multiplicity of communities the fewer compromises people have to make among the community attributes which they value. But even with a large variety of communities 'people will still be left with demands to satisfy through other means once a location is chosen' (Jackson, 1975, pp. 22–3).

The public-choice approach seems unable to offer a satisfactory solution to the problem of contradiction between the need for a fragmented jurisdiction to maximize consumer welfare within a small-scale community of interest and the need for an organization to reflect consumer values for public goods that extend over a number of contiguous communities. Competition between local authorities may widen consumer choice of public goods that can be internalized within the boundaries of neighbouring jurisdictions. But in urban areas competition may take a very different form. A fragmented system may permit competition in the sense of conflict between municipalities seeking to avoid the cost of public goods whose beneficiaries include citizens from neighbouring areas. Competition here may mean one jurisdiction effectively blocking administrative intervention that would disproportionately benefit people in a neighbouring jurisdiction (Ostrom, Tiebout and Warren, 1961, p. 840). Avoiding control by an 'external' agency (that is, a higher tier of government) may mean not having the public good provided at all.

Marxist Interpretations of the State at the Local Level

Until relatively recently Marxists have tended to see the state as a unity that did not need to be differentiated as between geographical levels. The Althusserian position of placing institutions in the realm of appearances and concentrating on underlying social relations 'can lead to an undifferentiated assimilation of all governmental agencies into an apparently monolithic "state apparatus" ' (Dunleavy, 1980a, p. 127).

In recent years, however, Marxist writers have offered increasingly more complete explanations of the state at the subnational level, particularly in the context of contemporary capitalism. In part the aim has been to identify the interests which are expressed through subnational institutions whether based on class or consumption patterns. But the main theoretical advances have resulted from attempts to identify the specific roles of the local state and to integrate these into a dialectic of intergovernmental relations.

The Local State and Capitalist Reproduction
Recognition is thus at last being given to the role of local institutions in the state's reproduction of conditions in which capitalist accumulation can take place. Local and regional

governments, in federal and unitary states alike, are seen as having a crucial role in the reproduction of both the forces and relations of production, as well as having a contribution to make to production itself, particularly in the provision of a necessary infrastructure of communications and energy. It is in capitalist reproduction that localized governments are seen as most heavily involved. The reproduction of capitalism entails renewing the conditions and means of production. Many such activities involve other levels of government and substantial central funding, but local government retains considerable autonomy (Saunders, 1980, p. 148).

The renewal of capitalism's *productive forces* requires not only the continuing provision of capital, raw materials and manufactured goods but also labour power. The process of reproducing labour power involves the state which has to plan for and provide an educated, trained and healthy labour force to meet the current needs of industry. This labour force also requires the provision of a social wage. Local authorities have had an historic role in state provision in many areas of state intervention relevant to the reproduction of labour. Collective consumption organized locally has come to play an increasingly significant part in the reproduction of labour power providing many of the material and cultural conditions of existence, such as low-rent housing and recreational facilities, as well as educating the economy's human capital.

Class conflict between labour and capital thus takes on a new dimension in which the local state is heavily involved. This conflict now extends beyond employment, wage-labour and the workplace to encompass struggles over 'indirect wages' made available by local governments in the form of housing, education and social welfare. According to this line of investigation local government, particularly in the industrial city, not only helps to ensure the national existence of labour power but its existence in a form needed by capital. It is through the provision of 'means of consumption' that the extended reproduction of labour is achieved. In advanced capitalist societies the means of consumption are increasingly socialized, that is, provided collectively rather than through the market (Saunders, 1980, p. 106). This interpretation of state intervention in capitalist society has led to the 'dual-state' thesis. According to this, social investment expenditure by the state on such things as an economic infrastructure is centralized within bureaucratic and corporalist institutions, while social consumption, designed to reduce the cost to capital of labour, is assigned to tightly controlled local authorities (O'Connor, 1973; Offe, 1975; Cawson and Saunders, 1983). In practice, however, the distinction is much less clear-cut than this (see below).

Collective Consumption and Local Government

Local government, particularly in urban areas, has become an arena within which a major contradiction of capitalism is experienced, that between the allocation of resources to profitable production or unprofitable consumption in housing, education, health and public transport. 'The intervention of the state becomes necessary to take charge of the sectors and services that are non-competitive (from the point of view of capital) but necessary for the functioning of economic activity and/or the appeasement of social conflicts' (Saunders, 1980, p. 108 quoting Castells).

Hence collective consumption becomes politicized. It affects the interests of all classes. It produces new inequalities in educational opportunity and health care. It creates occasions for new alliances between the working class and other classes against the state: 'collective consumption, defined as those facilities provided by the state on account of their unprofitability, has qualitatively different political effects from individual consumption via the market' (Saunders, 1980, p. 123). Hence the argument that class cannot be applied to the local state and should be replaced by social cleavages based on the individual's position in collective consumption (Dunleavy, 1979; Saunders, 1982).

Renewal of the *relations of production* must also be carried out if capitalism is to persist. The appropriate relations of labour to capital must be maintained, involving a system of wage, property and authority relations. A system of ownership and a supporting ideology must be sustained. The economic and the political must be kept separate in the public's political consciousness. These objectives are partly achieved through the state's repressive and coercive apparatus but mainly through ideological means to induce consent and sustain the mystification of bourgeois society.

In this, local government is involved through the provision of services such as education and through the institutional procedures of representative democracy. The maintenance of order and social cohesion requires state intervention at the local level for the purposes of coercion (through local police forces), support for the 'surplus population' (through social services) and legitimation (through schools, social work and programmes of public participation).

Local Government and Working-Class Interests

The legitimating role of local government brings to the surface another contradiction within the capitalist state. Democratic ideology requires majoritarian government at the local level. This, in theory, should place local power in the hands of the numerically predominant working class. There are many ways to ensure this solidarity does not emerge and produce a threat to the overall dominance of the propertied classes, but there are occasions when the contradiction between the logic of democracy and the logic of capitalism is starkly visible. Representative institutions at the local level are an important symbol of liberal democracy. Yet they logically and sometimes actually imply the capture of the local state apparatus by classes or fractions hostile to the interests dominant at the centre. Local authorities may become controlled by political parties representing working-class interests, or the interests of small business. However, while it may be politically impossible to dispense with local democracy, the independence of local government can be reduced by fiscal controls and the allocation of local functions to appointed regional agencies (Dunleavy, 1980a, p. 128). ·

This line of analysis leads to yet another contradiction, that between the ideological presumption in favour of local self-government, and the growing propensity of the central apparatus of the state to increase its hold over all levels in the structure. But before moving on to see how Marxists have interpreted intergovernmental relations it is necessary to consider briefly the role of the local state in production itself. The state's contribution to capitalist production includes direct investment in industry, tariff protection and infrastructure. The provision of necessary urban infrastructure, and the management of the urban environment to accommodate a restructured industrial economy, again involves the local state acting on behalf of capital as its political agent in the provision of roads, water supplies, energy, communications, physical planning and urban redevelopment thus blurring the 'dual-state' distinction.

Intergovernmental Relations

This perspective on the state at the local level requires a new interpretation of intergovernmental relations, one that offers an explanation of centralization in terms of class interests and conflicts and moves away from seeing different levels of government as cohesive forms of authority in conflict with each other independently of the interests represented and in conflict at each level.

Centralization has been interpreted as a reflection within the state apparatus of the needs of monopoly capitalism. It is argued that the interests of monopoly capital are increasingly represented by central institutions and policies. When the interests of monopoly capital are dominant within the state, local government as a 'residual element' of earlier stages in the development of capitalism will be controlled (Dunleavy, 1980a, p. 129).

In the USA, too, the needs of monopoly capital account for shifts in power to higher-level jurisdictions. Monopoly capital has large fixed investment in precisely those central cities where tax bases are declining as the middle classes leave for the suburbs, a movement originating in the interest of competitive capitalism. In order to protect the profitability of urban investments monopoly capital needs massive expenditure by the state on services and infrastructure. It must 'rationalize the metropolis'. To do this it needs access to the resources of the suburbs. That, in turn, requires the political autonomy of the suburbs to be destroyed. 'Capital must destroy the political fragmentation which it helped to create and which it has exploited so profitably' (Ashton, 1978, p. 83).

The management of large national and multinational corporations also sees advantage in more centralized administration when planning expansion. Municipalities can impede corporate decision-making with zoning regulations. Corporate interests look increasingly to urban planning on a metropolitan scale. 'Thus a struggle may ensue between suburban subclasses militant in their desire to preserve their local public-sector autonomy and large capitalist interests pushing for planned, rationalised, metropolis-wide government' (Markusen, 1978, p. 107). A possible solution is the creation of larger *ad hoc* jurisdictions for land use and infrastructural planning in the interest of monopoly capital, with public consumption and class reproduction left to existing fragmented authorities. In the USA there have also been federal programmes for slum clearance and urban renewal in order to protect central business districts.

Monopoly capitalism has a more general significance for the local-level state. O'Connor has shown how the state's role in economy and society has grown in support of monopoly capitalism. In addition, a heavy burden of cost, especially of social capital expenditure, generally falls on local government which is less able, because of its weak fiscal position, to bear it than higher levels of government. Hence the fiscal imbalance observed in the USA, for example. Such imbalance can often only be resolved by assigning a larger role in budgeting and technocratic planning to levels of government with the greater tax-raising capabilities (R. C. Hill, 1978, p. 231). Cities in the USA, especially those established in the early phases of industrialization, present a classic instance of the contradiction within capitalist societies between the historical residues of an earlier social formation (fragmented local administration, suburbanized manufacturing, fiscal imbalance and class segregation) and the municipal requirements of monopoly capitalism (social capital outlays and social expenses in O'Connor's terms). Shifting the cost of such social expenditure to higher levels of government meets resistance from powerful coalitions of suburban and rural interests which dominate most state-level governments (R. C. Hill, 1978, p. 232).

Castells (1978) has argued that the evolution of monopoly capitalism requires a transformation in the realization of profit. Individual commodity consumption must be stimulated by, among other things, collective consumption. Thus, in France the state apparatus was mobilized for monopoly accumulation in the period from 1958 to 1969, during which time it exercised a relative autonomy before being brought under closer control by the dominant class. The state became more centralized throughout the period, even though it moved from a pre-occupation with political and ideological legitimation to the dominant function of aid to monopoly capital. The main determinant in this centralization was the reproduction of labour power in areas of accelerated and spatially concentrated industrialization. Centralization was reflected in housing policy, infrastructural planning, transport, new towns and 'growth poles' for large-scale industry (Castells, 1978, p. 52). Often the central state apparatus bypassed the municipal authorities in favouring private capital, particularly in housing developments. The failure of these policies, and the economic crises and class struggles they provoked, led to a fundamental change in French urban and regional policy to one which supported the ideological functions of integration and preserving social relations. This reminds us again that the relationships between the territorial levels of the state will be determined by the priority given by the state to accumulation or legitimation. Political struggles will be one determinant in how the state as a whole manages collective consumption in general and the urban system in particular (Castells, 1978, p. 170).

The fiscal crisis of the local state illustrates this. In more than one country the structural limitations imposed by capitalist relations have changed the relative positions of central and local apparatuses, though often substituting one kind of central control for another. The increasing socialization of the forces and relations of production by state intervention has led to an increasing public debt at the local level. Political forces prevent taxation being used to finance these increasingly costly public services, and question the socialization of production, exchange and consumption, especially by large metropolitan authorities. Hence the imposition of central controls over municipal budgets and cuts in social programmes (Castells, 1978, p. 176). In Britain, too, the need for physical renewal and social support for a growing dependent population see revenues with a declining tax base relative to inflation failing to keep pace with the demand for increased expenditure (Cockburn, 1977). Marxists have drawn attention to the way class conflicts cut across intergovernmental conflicts. Working-class aims may require centralization, but in pursuit of egalitarian and redistributive objectives. The response of local interests in prosperous middle-class districts is to demand local autonomy in order to preserve their advantageous fiscal and social position. The ideology of local 'community' is brought into play in order to de-radicalize and even de-politicize issues. More important, the structural fragmentation characteristic of local government systems in some capitalist societies, such as the USA, enables the bourgeoisie to withdraw from responsibility for urban problems in depressed areas, inner cities and minority ghettos and frustrate redistributive policies (Dunleavy, 1980a, pp. 129–30).

Constraints on Local Governments

Finally, Marxists have drawn attention to the wider economic and political setting in which local government is situated. This leads them to present a very different picture of the constraints on local government action from that which is commonly acknowledged. For example, Cockburn has shown from a study of Lambeth that we cannot assume that the local state can be separated from the national and indeed international political economy and 'captured' by working-class representatives on behalf of working-class interests. Local authorities, especially in urban areas, are constrained by class interests outside the territory of the council, such as the shareholders and directors of firms employing local residents, the finance companies from which the council borrows and which determine much capital movement in the locality, the property dealers and speculators, the shareholders of building firms engaged for municipal housing programmes, and the professionals in the big firms of estate agents, solicitors and quantity surveyors. Local government 'is part of a structure which *as a whole and in the long term* has other interests to serve' than those of the majority, a structure which protects the interests of the bourgeoisie by culturally and politically dominating the working class (Cockburn, 1977, pp. 41–5, italics in original).

Saunders identifies three sets of limiting conditions with which local democracy operates: ecological, political and economic. Ecologically, towns and cities encapsulate inequalities in the urban environment which impose different living conditions on different categories of people (Saunders, 1980, p. 190). The urban system also corresponds to market forces rather than managerial direction by elected councils and public bureaucracies. Redistribution in pursuit of social justice inevitably fails as the market diverts funds away from areas of greatest social need into areas of greatest economic return (Saunders, 1980, p. 191).

Politically, elected representatives become increasingly dependent on bureaucrats and professionals as corporate management practices spread. Central government imposes further limitations on local political autonomy. Economically, local authorities are constrained by the need to maintain conditions consistent with private ownership and production and to spend in support of them. Dependence for revenues on the private sector also means that areas of highest need experience a shrinking revenue base. The only alternative is to be dependent on the central government or finance capital.

Conclusion

What has been presented above should be seen more as a series of controversies within different intellectual traditions than as coherent and self-contained theories. There is, for example, no single Marxist theory of the localized state. Nor can there be any aggregation or synthesis of the arguments examined in this chapter into some monolithic theory of decentralization. What counts as reality varies from perspective to perspective. There is, however, a good deal to be gained, when making prescriptive statements about decentralization, from an awareness of different orthodoxies and approaches, explicit or implicit, to politics and the state provided that it is remembered that the purposes of these theoretical traditions are different. Liberalism argues a normative case for political democracy at the local level on the basis of a political model of man. Neo-classical economics predicts behaviour under specified conditions on the basis of an economic model of man, though providing some analytical confirmation of some of the positivist elements in liberal theory. Neo-Marxists are concerned with social movements and collective interests within specific historical circumstances.

3
Administrative Needs
and Political Demands

Introduction

The need to decentralize is felt in all systems of government, though the responses made by different states to that need differ greatly. The varying political significance of geography, economy, ethnicity, history and ideology explains why what one state administers through democratic decentralization is in another thoroughly bureaucratized: or why a public service is regionalized in one country, localized in another, and centralized in a third: or why one federation displays centralist tendencies while another disintegrates.

Sometimes a particular need for decentralization will indicate the kind of institution required. Controls over municipal authorities are likely to be the responsibility of field officers of the central ministries, though even here the type of field administration used varies considerably. Other kinds of administrative decentralization will tell us little about the institutions required. Public highways, for example, can in principle be planned, built and maintained by central or local governments. Public utilities or hospitals might be managed locally by municipalities or appointed boards. The practical need for decentralization has to be placed in a particular setting before it can be decided how the state at the subnational level will be organized.

It is in fact easier to see why the state apparatus needs to be geographically dispersed, with decision-makers in different areas reflecting in their decisions the particular needs of their localities, than it is to understand why different forms of decentralization are utilized in different states. In Chapter 7 on institutions an attempt is made to distinguish basic types of decentralized state systems and account for those differences in broadly ideological terms. Beyond that it requires an intimate knowledge of political and historical forces in the individual states to know why the state apparatus is organized as it is in the provinces. In this chapter a distinction is drawn between the pressures on states to decentralize and the pressures leading to a particular kind of decentralization being used. It will be shown that these pressures are felt at all levels in the territorial hierarchy — at neighbourhood level, in urban and rural localities, in metropolitan areas and in regions. How the state responds to the need to decentralize and the demand for particular institutional forms will, of course, reflect the balance of political forces in each individual case.

Pressures to Decentralize

One of the most distinctive features of modern state administration is the need for close contact between the individual citizen and officialdom. The day-to-day management of many public functions requires members of the public to have direct access to state agencies and for state agencies to be able to reach individuals, families, firms and private associations. Administration has to be geographically dispersed for the purpose of revenue collection, the maintenance of law and order, land registration, the provision of cash benefits to people in need, and a host of other activities that simply cannot be conducted from the nation's capital (Paddison, 1983, p. 53).

The need to disperse the management of state functions throughout a network of local and regional offices tells us little about the level of decentralization involved, the discretion given to field officers of central ministries, or what role, if any, is assigned to localized governments. Functions may be managed locally to provide access points for claimants and clients, but local officials may be limited in their discretionary powers in order to ensure an equal standard of service or level of benefit to people whose circumstances are the same wherever they happen to live. If policy implementation varies from area to area it may be because the centre decrees that it should, rather than because officials have exercised discretion or institutions have exercised autonomy. The centre may formulate different agricultural policies for different agricultural regions, or different levels and patterns of expenditure for areas with different historical legacies in, say, health care facilities. However, it is unusual for local agencies and officials to have no discretion. Police authorities have to decide on what priorities to deploy scarce resources. Tax inspectors have to judge whether a tax-payer's expenses can be allowed against tax. Social security officials have to decide on eligibility for benefit; and so on.

Managerial pressures for decentralization operate at all levels in the geographical hierarchy. Effective community development work may require a neighbourhood-level organization. Tax collection requires an organization in the main urban centres. Urban transportation will need to be planned and managed by an organization with a metropolitan-wide jurisdiction. Regional development defines its own sphere of operations according to the economic criteria chosen to delimit regions, whether it be levels of unemployment, growth zones, or industrial structure.

The forces of geography may demand a decentralized structure. Modern systems of communication obviously reduce the extent to which size of territory, such as the USA, Canada, India, China, or the USSR, or other natural topographical features inhibit political and administrative centralization. But in less-developed countries decentralization is still associated with the inaccessibility of remote regions. Mountains, jungles and vast archipelagos 'demand a decentralised system if the programme for development is to reach outside the capital to the people for whom the programme was designed' (Maddick, 1963, p. 38).

Cultural variation, uneven economic development, ethnic diversity and persistent primordial loyalties often produce irresistible pressures for decentralization, though the political pressure may emanate from movements demanding complete separation from the state, that is, secession. Many states have had to devise a response to nationalistic demands for special treatment and regional autonomy for ethnic minorities. The United Kingdom Parliament felt in the mid-1970s that Scottish and Welsh nationalism had become a sufficiently powerful political force to warrant the establishment of devolved governments in each country. Spain's new constitution contains 'statutes of autonomy' in order to contain the secessionist pressures of the Basques and other communities. Belgium has experimented with regionalism in an attempt to manage the country's cultural, linguistic and economic diversity. Decentralization enabled the new government of Papua New Guinea to meet the challenge to unity posed by the country's several regionalist movements. Regional autonomy and the rights of nationalities to self-determination have been officially recognized in Ethiopia as part of its attempt to deal with the Eritrean problem. Canada devised the concept of 'sovereignty association' in an attempt to curb Quebec separatism.

There is, of course, a limit to the extent to which decentralization can constitute an adequate response to demands for total independence. National governments may attempt to contain secessionist movements by offering 'home rule' concessions which fall short of separatism. Alternatively, separation may be resisted with repression. Responses to nationalism and separatism have included genocide, expulsion, assimilation, language policies, quotas in political and bureaucratic élites, revenue-allocation formulae, positive discrimination, cultural autonomy and varying degrees of political autonomy. It is unusual for national governments to acquiesce in the breaking away from the nation state of a distinctive region, especially if part of that distinctiveness is an endowment with valuable natural or other economic resources. Demands for full autonomy are revolutionary from the perspective of the centre (Connor, 1973). History teaches us that 'attempts at secession are generally seen by governmental leaders as a threat to the authority of their regimes which is so intolerable that it is worth spilling blood to prevent it' (Birch, 1978, p. 340). However, national governments may be assisted in their negotiation of a compromise, involving political decentralization in some form or other, by factions within the nationalist movement which are prepared to accept less than complete political autonomy and independence.

Decentralization to culturally distinctive subgroups is regarded by many as necessary for the survival of socially heterogeneous states. Decentralization is seen as a countervailing force to the centrifugal forces that threaten political stability, especially in the relatively new states of the Third World (Paddison, 1983, p. 51). Such reasoning is supported by the claims made by some psychologists and social geographers. Territoriality is said to reduce the potential for conflict between subgroups by segregating them. A 'sense of place' is natural and therefore important to human-beings. If this can be recognized in the organization of government, tension can be eased (Sommer, 1969; Gold, 1976; Paddison, 1983, pp. 15–16). The significance of such constitutional or administrative design increases with greater ethnic diversity within the boundaries of a state.

However, the causal relationships involved here are clearly not one-way. The state itself is capable of creating territorial identities and loyalties. So the 'naturalness' of territorial identity is questionable (Paddison, 1983, p. 16). Intervening factors between stability and diversity may exist. Decentralization may lead to greater regional disparities of wealth which may, in turn, feed discontent and separatist tendencies. It has been suggested, for example, that in federations it is highly stabilizing for the characteristics, such as religion or language, which divide people to overlap so that within any one area there will be people separated by one factor (say, language), but united by another (say, religion). It can be hypothesized that the greater the diversities, the greater the chance of such overlapping occurring. Discrimination on the ground of area will be less feasible politically. Stability will be enhanced (Dikshit, 1975, pp. 234, 237).

Whether decentralization will accommodate linguistic, religious, or ethnic diversity will depend on a large number of factors — political, economic and social — as the discussion of federalism below shows. That is assuming that some form of decentralization is used as a means of political integration. Empirical studies have revealed only weak correlations between levels of decentralization and cultural diversity, though there is room for a good deal of argument about the significance of the measures employed in such analyses (Paddison, 1983, p. 44).

Another reason for decentralization is that different areas within the territory of the state have different needs. This does not just mean that national policy implementation may have to vary from area to area because of local circumstances (the managerial problem referred to earlier). It also means that local circumstances will require different responses from decision-makers in the priorities they attach to the multiple needs of a particular area. An appropriate mix of services, with resources allocated accordingly, has to be produced for each area. What that mix should be can only be determined by political decisions, since what are perceived to be 'needs' that require governmental intervention is a highly political matter dependent on values and ideology. There has to be some state apparatus which can give public policy some meaning by placing it in a specific spatial setting. Examples are land-use planning, urban redevelopment, resettlement projects, public health programmes, the management of natural resources and community development. Uniformity of service provision can also exacerbate inequalities by ignoring crucial factors affecting the level of need for services (Stewart, 1980b).

The localized nature of state functions are not, even in this case, a clear indication of the type of decentralized machinery that will be found. In principle, such an integration and co-ordination of localized service provision could be performed by a high-ranking officer of the state representing the central authorities, such as a prefectoral official or provincial governor. Alternatively, it could be the responsibility of an elected council or assembly with prescribed powers under statute or the constitution.

Such political demands for responsiveness to the needs of particular areas is felt at all levels in the territorial hierarchy. Municipalities may find it administratively necessary and politically expedient to create area institutions in acknowledgement of the special needs of particular neighbourhoods, especially ones with high levels of social and economic deprivation. This has been a motivating force for internal decentralization *within* local government in both Britain and the USA (see Chapter 9).

Over larger areas, urban municipalities and rural authorities provide multifunctional organs of decision-making designed to meet the needs of particular areas in a democratic way. Conflicts may arise between what are perceived as the territorial requirements of efficient administration in particular services, such as education, water supply, or urban planning, and the necessity to co-ordinate individual services within a single area in order to meet other objectives, such as democratic participation and easier access for the citizen to services or elected representatives. Hence compromises have to be worked out between the sometimes conflicting requirements of local government functions in order to provide governmental machinery that can respond to the needs of an area and its community rather than a single client group.

Finally, some kind of regional or intermediate tier of government or administration may be set up if this type of area is spatially significant in some field of public policy. Regional variations, particularly in industrial structure and other economic dimensions, may need to be reflected through appropriate institutions. Economic planning is the policy area which, in Western European states at least, has most commonly included the establishment of regional institutions to reflect the needs of distinct regions. In Britain, for example, the regional economic planning institutions set up in 1964 were intended to 'refine' the National Plan by analysing the needs of each region in the light of economic resources and trends. They were also to establish regional priorities in public expenditure (Lindley, 1982). In the 1960s a regional dimension was common to the national planning efforts of many developed and underdeveloped countries (Hackett and Hackett, 1963, p. 88). Once it has been decided that the state should intervene to redress regional imbalances by stimulating growth in some parts of the country and restraining it in others, regional institutions are required, if only with the minimal function of providing information on regional disparities. Even when national governments reserve for themselves the power to plan regional development it is common for regional institutions to be set up which are entitled to present national decision-makers with how different interests within each region perceive the needs of their part of the country.

We can see in the regional machinery which Britain, France and some other countries have employed in recent decades another cause of decentralization. That is the need for communication between national policy-makers and the wide range of diverse interests affected by public policy. An area organization enables the state to assess public reactions to government policy; to evaluate administrative performance; to collect data for policy reviews; and to inform various sections of the public of their rights and duties under the law. The national authorities not only seek contact and communication with private organizations, client groups, associations, corporate bodies, industrial firms and voluntary agencies. They also use an area organization to monitor and control other parts of the governmental apparatus, such as municipalities, public enterprises, courts of law, collectives, co-operatives and the institutions for which such subordinate parts of the machinery of government are responsible – schools, technical institutes, hospitals, welfare centres, prisons. Hence the need for a decentralized apparatus of inspectorates, auditors, controllers and advisers to oversee the decentralized machinery of government itself.

Institutional Responses

How the state responds to the pressures for subnational institutions will depend on a complex set of historical, ideological and political forces. Only the need for agencies to supervise decentralized institutions suggests a particular form of decentralization. The state's control agencies will, almost by definition, have to form part of the central bureaucracy and be organized as field services. In almost all other respects a political choice has to be made between the multiple options available. The few functions which are inevitably national will, in so far as they need to be decentralized, require field administration. Beyond that it is essentially a political decision whether the maintenance of law and order or the provision of welfare services are devolved to area governments, administered through field hierarchies, delegated to *ad hoc* regulatory or executive agencies, or even left to voluntary effort. The state apparatus can be adjusted to the physical features of the state's territory by either political or bureaucratic means. Cultural and community heterogeneity may or may not be accommodated by the devolution of power to the homelands of minorities. The unique needs of neighbourhoods, towns, rural districts and regions can be met by co-ordinating bodies of different types which may or may not be directly accountable through political processes to the inhabitants of the area. Bureaucratic or representative institutions, both elected and appointed, may serve as channels of communication between the centre and territorial or functional communities.

Given the need for a decentralized state apparatus, it is necessary to ask what values and pressures lead to the politicization of that apparatus, a politicization which generally involves the setting up of representative assemblies and the political processes which inevitably flow from their existence.

Democratic forms of decentralization may reflect a long political tradition of representative local government that has become an established part of the political culture which is hard for even the most centralist of national governments completely to overlook. Institutions in which people can participate may be conceded by the central authorities in response to demands for territorial self-determination, whether the territory be neighbourhood, city, region, or aspirant nation (Sharpe, 1979). All states appear to recognize an obligation to devolve at least minimal powers to a level of municipal government.

The consolidation of municipalities into larger units of government and a transfer of functions from local government to appointed *ad hoc* boards under the influence of managerialist ideology has generated two countervailing pressures. One has been for community participation through institutions of different kinds at village or urban neighbourhood level. The other has been for the democratization of an intermediate tier of government so that functions deemed in need of a regional scale of operations can be made directly accountable to the people of the region.

Regionalism

Demands for decentralization to regions and for the creation of intermediate levels of government thus extend beyond nationalist movements and demands for autonomy to national territories (Kolinsky, 1981, p. 85). Regionalism has origins which are quite distinct from the aspirations of nationalist movements, and constitutes a political demand for devolved powers to governments at the intermediate level, that is, with jurisdictions larger than those of existing municipal authorities.

Such demands may be a response to the use of the region by central governments for their own political and administrative objectives, such as economic planning. In France, for example, regionalism has been less a response to social cohesion and national identity and more a development from the use of centrally controlled co-ordinating and consultative machinery for regional planning (Kolinsky, 1981). Even then, there were contradictory goals set for the regional tier of the state: to strengthen national unity or weaken centralism; to increase economic growth or territorial equality; to increase participation or administrative efficiency (V. Wright, 1979).

Here, then, we have 'functional' regionalism with institutions set up at the regional level to serve the administrative needs of the centre. Those needs may include the participation of representatives from local interests in consultative machinery. Such interests may also have nationalistic overtones when they are associated with the claims of a district cultural-linguistic group (such as the Bretons). But this is not a necessary condition of regionalism. Any political benefits which may flow from participation in regional administration to the constituent communities of the regions is incidental to the centre's need for information and collaboration at the regional level. Regional decentralization is thus a particular geographical expression of the centre's more general need to organize its activities at the subnational level. Similarly, any response it may be forced to make to demands for the democratization of such activities, making regional institutions accountable to the region rather than to the centre, is an extension of the political culture which requires certain parts of the localized administrative apparatus of the state to be placed under the control, albeit incomplete, of a locally recruited political leadership.

In France, for example, functional regionalism has been transformed into political regionalism largely as the result of the Socialists coming to power with a programme of reforms that included the creation of directly elected regional councils with their own fiscal powers. In Britain, by contrast, functional regionalism in the shape of regional economic planning boards and councils did not give way to political regionalism, though the Scottish and Welsh Nationalists pushed the government to the point of passing legislation for devolution to Scotland and Wales, the implementation of which was defeated in referenda. Within England there are periodic calls for regional government in order to democratize the bureaucratic institutions which exist in the regions. Some of these are field offices of the central ministries and some are *ad hoc* agencies created to administer functions for which local authorities are judged too small. So far there has been no attempt made in Parliament to democratize the regional level of administration.

Regionalism may also be prompted by important geographical and historical factors which cannot be ignored by the political system. For example, the historical regions of the Italian mainland were incorporated into the postwar constitution not because of cultural or linguistic diversity (though these factors are significant to varying degrees in Sardinia, the Aosta valley, Trento-Alto Adige and Friuli-Venezia Giulia) but because of a persistent sense of regional diversity stretching back to the *Risorgimento* and of a reaction to the extreme centralization of Fascist dictatorship.

Federalism

Federalism may constitute a further development of regionalism when it is thought necessary to limit the power of central government by constitutional means. This is what Preston King (1982) refers to as a 'decentralist federalism' since it represents a move from a unitary state to one in which constituent territories are given constitutional safeguards. Germany in 1949 is a case in point. The need to secure the continuation of a precarious nationhood, which as has been noted is often a force behind decentralization in multi-ethnic states, has been experienced by many post-colonial states which originated as the artificial creations of competing European powers. Federalism may thus preserve a nation against disunity and disintegration. The timely constitutional recognition of communal and ethnic diversity may preserve the state. Examples are the creation of linguistic and communal states in India and the transition from a unitary to a federal state in Czechoslovakia (Duchacek, 1970, p. 206).

Federations in the Third World have often proved fragile arrangements leading eventually to a more centralized federation in an attempt to contain fissiparous tendencies. In Nigeria, for example, the number of constituent units has been increased, first from four to twelve and then to nineteen in an attempt to remove the destabilizing effect of overpowerful regions. The constituent states have become increasingly dependent on federal funding and their revenues from federal allocations are increasingly tied to specific, federally approved activities. The federal government has become more insistent on the implementation of nation-wide policies, especially in education and agricultural development. Centralization has gained ideological approval because of the close association in people's minds of regional autonomy with political instability. Nigeria has moved from a 'peripheral' to a centralized federalism (B. C. Smith, 1981a). Though successful in reducing the political significance of tribal divisions, this reorganization could not prevent a second displacement of civilian government by a self-appointed military junta.

Most of the attention paid to the origins of federalism has been concerned with 'centralist federalism'. This occurs when a stronger central authority is sought by regions loosely allied in a confederation; when a 'more enduring union' is sought; or when sovereign states seek political union, foregoing a measure of their sovereignty in pursuit of some other political objective (P. King, 1982, p. 24). What circumstances lead to a number of more or less independent areas wanting to go beyond alliance, league, or confederation to subordinate themselves to a federal agreement and constitution?

First, there is the fear of a common enemy, either actual or potential, against which the pooling of military resources will give protection. Fear of the USA among colonies to the north was a factor leading to Canadian federalism in the nineteenth century. The threat posed by the capitalist states of Europe to the Bolshevik Revolution in Russia prompted a union of socialist republics. Malaya, Singapore, Sabah and Sarawak formed Malaysia in 1963 in the face of Chinese communism and Indonesian aggression. The Founding Fathers of the American Constitution argued in *The Federalist* (1788) that union would secure a better defence against aggressors, including internal insurrection.

One authority on federalism, William Riker, has even argued that a necessary condition for the creation of federations is some internal or external threat which federal union serves to overcome (Riker, 1964 and 1975). Before striking a federal bargain, political leaders will desire to extend territorial control either to meet a military or diplomatic threat or to prepare for military or diplomatic expansion. If such conditions do not exist, Riker argues, federations are likely to fail. The necessary conditions for federalism are political rather than social. Dikshit has argued that a sense of insecurity is not only important in the establishment of federations (especially when the sense of separation is stronger than the sense of union): it is also a 'favourable factor in the maintenance of federalism' (Dikshit, 1975, pp. 237–8).

The USA provides an example of the second factor in the creation of federations which may be discerned, that is the provision of a better foundation for trade and prosperity. Federation provides an enlarged market and trading area. Beard (1965), for example, argues that merchant capital in the USA sought federation because a strong federal government would further their economic interests, as well as repressing agrarian radicalism. Economic unity may also be an attractive proposition in the Third World if it attracts foreign investment. The Federation of Rhodesia and Nyasaland may be cited as an example of such an attempt. Clearly such arguments recur in movements for European integration and African unity (P. King, 1982, p. 30).

However, some other impetus is probably needed if a 'common market' is to become a federation. Riker would argue that an external threat is necessary. Others, such as Duchacek, claim that a political or ideological commitment to the principle of federation is required (Duchacek, 1970, p. 201). The absence of a positive commitment to federation, seeing it merely as a means to mutual economic advantage, defence against a common enemy, a stronger position in international power politics, or unity in diversity, is unlikely to produce a federal union. These factors may be necessary, but not sufficient, conditions for federalism. Studies of federations that failed (the West Indies, Central and East Africa and Malaysia, in so far as Singapore broke away) suggests that a lack of ideological commitment to the value of federation caused the rupture despite economic advantage and even a common institutional heritage. Hence to the political leaders involved, federalism was used for contradictory ends, by promoting rather than reducing the independence of constituent units.

Clearly, federalism constitutes a delicate balance between the autonomy of constituent territories and complete integration under a sovereign national government. Since factors generally associated with the creation of federations may prove strong enough to produce a unitary system, as in the formation of the United Kingdom in 1707 by the Union of Scotland and England, in federations there must be factors contributing to the determination of the constituent units to retain a measure of autonomy. There is a large number of possibilities here. One is the existence of a federal model to be followed. So Canada, despite having similarities in legal system, religious beliefs, and literary and cultural traditions to Scotland and England, opted for federation rather than unity because of the model to the south. Other possibilities include the individuality of social groupings making up the population, prior experience of at least a measure of self-government if not complete sovereignty, geographical features such as vast territory and other natural barriers between communities, and the importance of political leadership, or the lack of it, at crucial moments in history (Wheare, 1963, pp. 40–4). The nature of the federation formed will depend on a particular combination of factors pulling diverse units together with those pulling towards regional autonomy (Dikshit, 1975, pp. 223–32).

A recent move in West Africa towards federation illustrates most of the political forces that historically have been associated with this type of political union – economic needs, fear of external powers, internal insurrection, the artificiality of colonial political boundaries, and so on. The Confederation of Senegambia came into being on 1 February 1982 when the two neighbouring West African states of Senegal and The Gambia ratified an agreement to integrate their armed forces and security services 'to defend the sovereignty, the territorial integrity and the independence of the Confederation'. An economic and monetary union has been formed, foreign policy will be co-ordinated and agreements will eventually be extended to communications and other areas of policy.

The Gambia, or at least its ruling élite, appears to have more to gain than Senegal from confederation. A left-wing coup, allegedly supported by Libya, was attempted in July 1981 and put down with the assistance of Senegalese troops who have remained in the country to maintain order under a mutual defence agreement made in April 1970. Senegalese troops constitute an essential bulwark of the Gambian regime. Discontents in The Gambia have been fuelled by a declining economy dependent on groundnuts which provide over 70 per cent of its export earnings. Production has fallen and there has been a downturn in the tourist industry. The balance of trade has steadily worsened since the mid-1970s. Per capita income fell by 16 per cent in 1979–80. The drought of 1980 produced an emergency necessitating relief under the World Food Programme.

Senegal has an interest in improved communications across the River Gambia and the establishment of a custom's union to eliminate cross-border smuggling. The fact that The Gambia forms an enclave within the territory of Senegal is illustrative of the division of West Africa between the European imperial powers. Integration was recommended by the United Nations in

1964. The two countries have similar economic, cultural, religious and ethnic characteristics, though The Gambia is Anglophone and Senegal Francophone, having been colonialized by Britain and France respectively.

Perhaps the most interesting aspect of the case of Senegambia is that it reminds us of the significance in the creation of federations of internal political conflicts and the benefits sought through closer union with a neighbouring territory by the ruling factions within a state whose dominance is threatened by internal dissidence. Even when internal insurrection does not form a significant threat it is important to recognize that federalism, like any other political arrangement, will not benefit all sections of society to the same degree and will be sought vigorously by those who believe it favourable to their own interests, such as the growing class of industrial capitalists, mercantile bourgeoisie and land-owning classes of Canada in the nineteenth century, for example.

Conclusion

Reference has been made to the political choices inherent in decentralization, and this point may be underlined by way of conclusion. The 'need' in contemporary states for decentralization reflects no less than the power of different groups to promote and defend their political interests. Federations are brought into being by groups seeking to benefit from wider economic associations and territorial mobility. They develop as more or less centralized according to the interplay of political forces. They disappear or are fundamentally restricted when a part breaks away or the centre is captured by a unitarist group, such as the military. In unitary states the choice of institutions for decentralized administration, or the level of autonomy devolved to subnational governments will reflect the political interests represented at the centre.

The conflicts that occur when such political choices have to be made are rarely expressed exclusively in territorial terms. That is, it is rare for all sections of society within a subnational territory to be united in their opposition to the centre. Whether the central authorities in federal or unitary states move to centralize or decentralize decision-making, the political response at the periphery is likely to be mixed. The authorities at the centre themselves reflect political and economic interests which are locally based. It is rare for the central authorities – legislature, judiciary, bureaucracy — to be structured in such a way as to exclude totally people representing any of the interests from a particular region.

It follows that if the centre, controlled by middle-class interests, centralizes in the interest of the middle classes it will be opposed locally by groups representing the working class, but supported by organizations and parties representing the middle class. Conversely, if a central government centralizes on behalf of working-class interests, the reaction from the periphery will be reversed. This is likely to hold true even when different classes at the periphery share a common ethnic origin, though cultural factors, especially language, may exclude all classes from the economic benefits of the larger union. Greater decentralization will similarly be differentially received, according to which interests control the peripheral governments and therefore the way in which they utilize, if at all, their new-found powers. Such alignments along other than territorial divisions cut across relationships between geographical levels of government. Dominant alignments will determine the 'need' for decentralization according to their own interests. Conflicts at the centre will be replicated at the periphery in choices about forms and levels of decentralization.

4

Area, Community
and Efficiency

Introduction

Decentralization of whatever form, requires the division of the
state's territory into areas. With federalism, the constituent parts
may be predetermined and remain the same after a number of
political units come together to form a federation. Elsewhere,
federations require the constituent areas to be delimited, especially
when there is a major political reorganization and the number
of constituent parts is changed, as in Nigeria after the return to
civilian from military government in 1979. Each region of a
federation will need to subdivide its territory further for the
purposes of decentralization below the regional level, and in this
respect the problems facing the constituent governments of a
federation correspond to those facing unitary states.

Within unitary states decisions have to be made about the appropriate territorial jurisdictions for urban and rural governments: the
counties and districts of England and Wales; the regions and districts of Scotland; the *départements* and communes of France; the
provinces and districts of Zambia; the provinces, autonomous
regions, counties, people's communes and production brigades of
China, and so on. Field areas have to be delimited for government
departments, both central and municipal, that cannot operate from
headquarters. A municipal social services department, for example,
may decentralize some operations to community development officers responsible for designated neighbourhoods, as well as create
a field organization for its professional social workers.

Areas have also to be delimited for special-purpose government
agencies – health boards, planning committees, water authorities,
development agencies, and so on. Some statutory bodies, such as
public corporations, are national in scope and may require a field

organization comparable to that of a central government department. A public utility, such as water or electricity, may be provided throughout the national territory, but by quasi-autonomous regional bodies which are co-ordinated centrally. Elsewhere a particular region may have a special agency for a special purpose and in this respect be different from all other regions — the Scottish Highlands and Islands Development Board, or the Sudan's Gazira Development Board, for example. Special governmental areas (Fesler, 1949) may also be needed for functions coming under local political control rather than bureaucratic administration — school districts in the USA, for example.

At first glance, the problem of delimiting subnational areas for government and administration appears to be quite straightforward. It is simply a case of matching area to function and creating a governmental jurisdiction encompassing the natural boundaries of a problem (Fesler, 1973, p. 8). However, the matter is far more complex than this. Everywhere there seems to be conflict between area and function.

The reasons why the area problem is so intractable are numerous. In government it is simply not possible to restrict a problem area (say, public housing provision) to a geographical area in some objective fashion. The 'natural' boundaries of a problem which governments may have to face are created politically, so that it becomes a matter of changing political judgement as to what the 'right' jurisdiction is for a particular function. Furthermore, many of the criteria for delimiting subnational areas are incompatible with each other. Jackson and Bergman (1973), for example, give four criteria of territorial organization. The first — that each 'activity area' needs its own territory — runs into the problem already mentioned. The others are that areas should be large enough to attract sufficient resources, have boundaries that avoid 'superabundant overlapping jurisdictions', and guarantee effective popular control (see also Bennett, 1980). All three may be in conflict, depending on what political decisions are made about 'sufficient' resources, a permissible level of 'overlapping', and 'effective' popular control.

One of the most persistent problems in systems of municipal government has been the reconciliation of the resources and political accountability requirements. Lipman, whose study of administrative areas published in 1949 has not been surpassed, identifies a fundamental conflict within municipal government that remains to be resolved in many countries not least the UK. The two main purposes of local government — civic education and the provision of beneficial public services − need areas that reflect both community and efficiency (Lipman, 1949, p. 1).

It should not be thought that the area problem in decentralized government is simply one of conflict between objective principles. Different criteria for delimiting governmental and administrative areas also have their own political proponents whose interests and values conflict, a point returned to later in this chapter.

The choice of areas is also conditional upon choice of institutions. Area does not, in practice, follow logically from function. The territorial scope of a particular subnational service will depend on the arrangements made for its administration regionally or locally. If, for example, water supply and related services are devolved to subnational governments some compromise with the territorial requirements of other local services is inevitable. The administration of water services will also be affected by beliefs about the optimum size of political jurisdictions. If such services are separated out from other functions of government and decentralized to single-purpose authorities, there will be much greater scope for defining areas according to the technical requirements of that particular service. If, in addition, the form of local administration chosen is bureaucratic rather than political, with decision-making for each area delegated to a board of appointed managers rather than a council of elected representatives, the public accountability factor can effectively be ignored in defining areas.

The choice of criteria for delimiting governmental areas will depend upon both the form of decentralization chosen (political or bureaucratic) and the functions to be performed by subnational institutions. At the level of local government, prominence may be given to the definition of *communities*. Social geography rather than government function then creates political boundaries, though it may be necessary to define a hierarchy of communities corresponding to the different scale of operations demanded by different devolved functions. Hence, the *efficiency* principle by means of which areas are defined according to assumptions about the scale of operations necessary for optimum performance. A third principle is *managerial*, when areas are defined according to the management structure of the decentralized organization. A fourth principle of delimitation is *technical*, where the optimum area for a government function is determined by the landscape or economy: watersheds, climate, soil conditions, topography, and the location of natural resources and the distribution of industry. Finally, there is the *social* principle, when areas define themselves regardless of administrative rationality. The following discussion is based on this classification.

Community

It would seem self-evident that an area defined for the purpose of government should correspond to a territory recognized by its inhabitants as forming a natural socio-economic unit, one to which they feel some sense of attachment and identity. Only then will such government have the necessary legitimacy. Such an area would already be defined by the behaviour and attitudes of the people who live and work in it (Paddison, 1983, p. 234). In Europe, local self-government has been based historically on the cohesion derived from close contact between inhabitants of towns and villages, the religious and cultural aspects of community life, and the social, commercial and economic characteristics of towns. Where ties of common values and interests are still strong it is argued that public affairs should be conducted by a council whose jurisdiction is limited to the urban or rural community (Leemans, 1970, p. 40). A belief that government areas no longer correspond to settlement patterns and the spatial behaviour of communities has often prompted the reform of local government systems (Schnur, 1969). In Britain, for example, the reorganization of local government in 1972 had the 'socio-geographic objective' of bringing government boundaries into line with settlement patterns which had changed dramatically since the existing system had been created at the end of the nineteenth century.

Drawing administrative and political boundaries around communities is far from easy, and requires a good deal of knowledge not only about the spatial distribution of settlements but also about the spatial patterns of socio-economic activity. The physical boundaries of settlements − villages, towns, cities and conurbations or metropolitan areas − are reasonably easy to identify since the social landscape is an objective reality. The spatial patterns of social life are much more difficult to ascertain and require systematic research into the behavioural relationships between spatially defined groups − economic transactions, personal mobility for commuting to work, shopping and recreation, and cultural linkages.

It has long been argued that local government areas should recognize the 'daily tide of people journeying to or from work', and correspond to the spheres of influence of towns as economic and social centres (Gilbert, 1948, p. 176; Cole, 1947; Smailes, 1947). In Britain, the Royal Commission which investigated the defects of the local government system prior to its reorganization in the early 1970s argued that a subjective community of interest derived from the objective relations between town and hinterland

and that administrative boundaries should reflect the interdependence of centre and hinterland to make efficient land-use planning, traffic management, highways development and public transport possible. Making government boundaries coincide with service centre hinterlands would also 'internalize' the service externalities generated by local government functions and therefore produce a more equitable distribution of goods and benefits (Sharpe, 1978, p. 90). Elsewhere in Europe the process of urbanization, strengthening the links between urban centres and their hinterlands and the dependence of rural areas on urban, has increased the popularity of the 'central town' concept, notably in Yugoslavia, Sweden, many West German *Länder*, Belgium and France. Urban and metropolitan centres have been favoured in many countries as the foundation for spatial planning (Leemans, 1970, pp. 116–17).

There is a long history of research into spatial behaviour, starting mainly with the work of American geographers in the early twentieth century who mapped the areas of influence of metropolitan centres by analysing economic and social activity, showing the economically dependent surrounds for which cities provided marketing and financial facilities. Rural areas were included in this kind of analysis when Wilson and Galpin studied the 'social anatomy' of rural communities by analysing the dependence of hinterlands on rural centres for education, trade and recreation. In Germany a theoretical basis was provided for the study of urban-rural relations by Walther Christaller's *Die Zentralen Orte in Suddeutschland* in 1933. Christaller developed the concept of a hierarchy of service centres, each level of which provides a higher grade of social, professional and commercial services for a more extensive population than the level below (see Dickinson, 1964). In Britain this kind of research has been associated with Professor R. E. Dickinson in the 1930s, the reconstruction planning of the postwar period and the work of Ebenezer Howard, Patrick Geddes (who coined the term 'city-region'), Smailes, Green and Bracy on urban hinterlands. Common to all these studies is the idea of different grades of urban centre forming the centre of 'functional' regions or areas with 'functional coherence' or interdependent parts (Lipman, 1952; Glasson, 1974; Dawson, 1981; Paddison, 1983, p. 24).

The methods by which the spheres of influence of service centres are defined involve identifying the urban status of centres by the services they provide (banks, shops, schools, hospitals, newspapers, and so on) and the number of inhabitants employed in service occupations. The area served by such services is then measured by the catchment areas of such institutions as schools, libraries, churches, professional firms and voluntary organizations, and by the hinterland served by communications, using traffic flows, passenger transport use, telephone calls and zones of newspaper circulation. The economic status of different centres may be established by identifying the area served by markets and retail or wholesale outlets. The coincidence of service areas determines the general area of influence on a given urban centre.

Social and economic geography should, in principle, be able to provide information on where administrative and political boundaries might be drawn so as to demarcate one locality from another according to the patterns of social and economic life which already separate one community from another. In practice, however, there are many difficulties to be overcome before such an analysis can form the basis of a decentralized system of government. Doubts have also been expressed as to the appropriateness of such concepts for the delimitation of governmental areas.

In the first place, different functional flows (journeys to work, recreation and shopping) are rarely spatially matched. There inevitably seems to be a lack of correlation between regions defined according to different criteria. As the prosperity of particular centres vary, and firms expand and contract, flows and spheres of influence change (Glasson, 1974, p. 30). Furthermore, settlements and urban centres become increasingly interdependent, making the demarcation referred to above increasingly difficult. Discontinuities in the spatial aspects of social and economic behaviour, the non-coincidence of behaviour patterns and the problem of knowing how to weigh the different hinterlands and areas of influence produced by different patterns of behaviour mean that service area patterns cannot automatically be applied to local administrative areas (Lipman, 1952, p. 214).

Even assuming that the relationships between urban centres and their dependent hinterlands can be mapped with confidence, the area of influence does not necessarily weld the inhabitants together into a natural community of interest (Paddison, 1983, p. 235). In so far as public services contribute to the sphere of urban influence another problem may be created by basing the city region on the scope of municipal institutions, such as hospitals, schools and libraries, which may not be operating according to the areas needed for maximum efficiency. Any proposed municipal reorganization based on the city-region may thus incorporate suboptimum spheres of operations built into the existing local government system.

Another reason why the city-region concept may not be appropriate for municipal reorganization is that it incorporates into a single governmental jurisdiction urban and rural areas. Urban areas have distinctive needs requiring more collective action and more integrated government than rural areas. This is an argument for keeping rural hinterlands under different governments from urban nuclei (Sharpe, 1978). Furthermore, public-choice theory would suggest that the greater the homogeneity of the community's socio-economic composition, the greater the likelihood that governmental outputs will be close to the collective preferences of citizens. It is thus more rational to create small jurisdictions than large, complex social entities as the area basis of decentralized government (Paddison, 1983).

Efficiency

The areas of decentralized government are often based on the belief that there is a systematic relationship between the quality of administrative performance in government services and the characteristics of local areas which can be varied by altering geographical boundaries. Hence the belief that local government efficiency will be increased by the creation of larger government areas. It is very widely accepted that local units of government need to be of a minimum size if they are to be financially viable, avoid central control and satisfy the local public and their representatives. Urban services, in particular, such as planning, housing, water, sewage and transportation, are thought to need large-scale organization. Also the more specialized the service the larger the population catchment area required to support the staff and institutions required (Newton, 1982). Small authorities are thought to be unable to attract staff of sufficient calibre because of the lack of career opportunities. Enlarged jurisdictions should permit a unit of government to provide a greater range of functions by crossing thresholds in population, tax base and workloads, or because of economies of scale. They should internalize externality spillovers and counteract 'migration of the tax base and fiscal imbalance' (an important consideration in the United States – Bennett, 1980, p. 306). In Europe, attempts to relate functions to the minimum population believed necessary to support efficient administration have produced increases in population size for the basic units of municipal government in Sweden, Finland, Norway, the Netherlands, Belgium, West Germany and the UK (Leemans, 1970, pp. 45–8; van Putten, 1971, p. 225). In Europe the trend since the war has unmistakably been towards fewer, larger units of municipal government, though there are considerable differences in prescribed minimum levels, levels which in some states have varied over time (Council of Europe, 1980, p. 18). Table 4.1 shows how the number of municipalities has been reduced by amalgamation in European states, sometimes dramatically as in Denmark, West Germany, Britain and Sweden. The odd ones out are Italy, where municipalities favour intermunicipal co-operation and where the regions, within whose sphere of competence local government falls, have not been politically moved to reform; and Greece where amalgamations are voluntary.

The service-efficiency argument has undoubtedly been extremely influential within processes of administrative reform in many countries. Yet it is an argument that carries with it so many qualifications and exceptions that it is almost totally useless as a guide to the delimitation of boundaries for devolved government.

Determining the relative level of efficiency in the provision of local goods and services by jurisdictions of different sizes requires a measurable output which can be 'costed' (Hansen, 1981). But the 'measurement' or evaluation of local government output involves both qualitative and quantitative judgements. It is extremely difficult to find objective criteria for measuring the 'output' of teachers, social workers, policemen and the other service providers found in systems of local government. Other services do have more quantifiable outputs, such as highways, sewage systems and water supplies, but any measurable economies of scale to be had in these cases require operating these services separately and not as part of a multifunctional system of government. Even if units of output are identifiable, these may show considerable variation across local governments whose services may differ in content and character. Since it is difficult to identify unit costs in local government, it is difficult to know whether an increase in size of population will automatically produce an increase in resources (Sharpe, 1978, p. 92).

The argument that there are economies of scale from which local authorities can benefit by operating over large areas with larger populations is thus difficult to prove. There is hardly any firm evidence of economies of scale in local government services (Bennett, 1980, p. 309). There is certainly no conclusive evidence that larger jurisdictions are more efficient than smaller ones. As Newton puts it, the only thing we can conclude with confidence is that, 'under certain not well understood circumstances, it may, or may not, be more, or less, economical to have larger, or

Table 4.1 *Changes in the Number of Western European Municipalities.*

	1940s	*1950s*		*1960s*		*1970s*		
Austria				3,183 (1966)		3,183 (1970)	2,414 (1972)	2,417 (1974)
Belgium	2,670 (1947)			2,663 (1961)		2,359 (1970)		
Denmark				1,387 (1961)		277 (1970)	275 (1974)	
France				37,708 (1968)		36,489 (1970)	36,413 (1980)	
Great Britain		1,347 (1950)		1,349 (1960)	1,288 (1965)	1,357 (1973)	410 (1974)	521 (1975)
Greece				5,993 (1962)		6,037 (1979)		
Italy		7,810 (1950)				8,056 (1972)		
Luxembourg		126		126		126		
Netherlands		1,015 (1950)		994 (1960)		913 (1970)	862 (1973)	811 (1979)
Norway						443 (1974)	445 (1975)	454 (1977)
Spain	9,265 (1940)	9,214 (1950)		9,202 (1960)		8,655 (1970)	8,049 (1978)	
Sweden		2,500 (1950)	1,037 (1952)	1,006 (1963)	848 (1969)	464 (1971)	278 (1974)	279 (1980)
Switzerland		3,097		3,095		3,072 (1970) 3,034 (1977)	3,050 (1975)	3,038 (1977)
West Germany		24,512 (1959		24,438 (1965)	24,282 (1968)	14,242 (1974)	8,514 (1978)	

Source: Council of Europe (1980).

smaller, local authorities' (Newton, 1982, p. 193). Only political judgements can establish the level of service required, or the importance to attach to these parts of a service for which scale economies can be identified when there is no conclusive evidence for the whole service (Hirsch, 1970). Changing technology can alter the scale economies applicable to a service, making the problem of finding an optimum area for a range of services even more complex. Changes in professional opinion about optimum areas and changes in function from time to time make the economies-of-scale argument a recipe for constant reorganization (Sharpe, 1978), despite the fact that what happens currently cannot be taken as an indication of what would happen under a reorganized system (Foster *et al.*, 1980, p. 569). Different population densities may affect operations, leading to diseconomies in some urban areas (Hansen, 1981). The relationship between population size and economies of scale is also likely to be affected by the geographical distribution of population as between, say, an urban area and an area containing an urban centre with a rural hinterland (Sharpe, 1978).

Another important factor affecting the economies-of-scale argument is that such economies need not be regarded as imperatives of system design. Their implications can be avoided by separating service provision from service production, as when local authorities enter into contracting arrangements with each other, an arrangement used extensively in the USA (Paddison, 1983, pp. 222–3). Indeed, joint arrangements between local authorities deserve far more attention than they usually get, especially as a means of preserving smaller authorities (Foster *et al.*, 1980, p. 571). The assumption that local efficiency is best served by the expansion and consolidation of jurisdictions needs to be seriously questioned, especially if there are political arguments for smaller rather than larger areas of local government.

Another pressure for larger areas comes from the notion that efficiency depends on the internalization of costs and benefits, so that area boundaries coincide with groupings of users. Yet the identification of such areas under conditions of population and resource mobility is virtually impossible. Such an exercise could lead to the creation of larger and larger units of government, or complete centralization since the central government is the only level of operations at which many local services, and some parts of others, can be completely internalized. Furthermore, the aggregation of services for the purpose of multifunctional government would again involve many compromises being made. Any level of general government is bound to generate some service externalities; and there is no guarantee that an area in which externalities have been internalized will coincide with a population having a sense of identity and civic consciousness (Sharpe, 1981c, pp. 96–7).

The main consideration which is in conflict with the economies-of-scale argument is the democratic quality of local government. Making democracy and efficiency compatible is arguably the greatest challenge confronting decentralized government (Dahl, 1981; Dahl and Tufte, 1974; Newton, 1982). If a democratic government is one that acts in accordance with the wishes of its citizens, and is not remote and inaccessible, 'then democracy is undeniably a diminishing function of scale' (Sharpe, 1978, p. 98). Smaller units of government, it is sometimes argued, produce more responsive political leaders, make participation easier and are more likely to be socially homogeneous, thus producing clearer majorities for decision-makers (Sharpe, 1978; Bennett, 1980, p. 309). There may be 'control-loss' diseconomies of scale which increase as the size of territory increases together with increased problems of co-ordinating expenditure decisions with revenue raising. Rather than assume falsely that policy planning needs better-qualified staff which only large authorities can afford, a local government system should be scaled down so that co-ordinated planning of taxing and spending is possible (Foster *et al.*, 1980, pp. 564, 569). In this respect, it is noticeable how much larger Britain's local authorities are compared with her European neighbours, despite the fact that there have been trends throughout Europe towards municipal consolidation (see Table 4.2).

Against this it might be argued that large units of decentralized government have no worse a record than small ones in some aspects of political participation. Newton, arguing in favour of large authorities, points out that there is no systematic relationship between size and social attachment to, or interest in, local affairs as measured by such indicators as rates of participation, knowledge of the system and the locality, and attitudes to local services, elected representatives and the system of representation. British evidence also suggests that larger authorities have councils which in social composition are more representative of the population and more strongly attached to the area than smaller ones. Larger areas also afford more opportunities to participate in and influence public affairs than smaller units, because of the proportionately greater number of voluntary organizations,

Table 4.2   *Size and Number of Local Government Units in Selected European States.*

Country	Total Population	No. of Units	Average Population of Units	Units over 100,000 Population
Belgium (Communes 1977)	9,788,248	596	16,255	—
Denmark (Kommuner 1972)	4,995,653	277	17,963	5
France (Communes 1968)	49,778, 500	37,708	1,320	37
Italy (Comune 1973)	54,136,547	8,059	6,717	47
Netherlands (Gemeentin 1972)	13,599, 092	841	16,170	16
Norway (Kommuner 1973)	3,947,775	444	8,891	11
West Germany (Gemeinde and Kreisfreie Städte, 1975)	60,650,600	22,510	2,694	69
Sweden (Kommuner 1976)	8,208,442	278	29,527	11
England and Wales (Districts 1972)	49,219,000	401	122,740	173

Source: Council of Europe (1980).

citizens' associations, community groups and organized political parties to assist the articulation of political demands (Newton, 1982; Sharpe, 1984).

Other political factors have to be built into the democracy/ efficiency equation; and the weight they are given will reflect personal political values. Small communities can be conservative and oligarchic, enforcing social conformity and suppressing political dissent, while larger units of government may provide opportunities for the achievement of egalitarian social objectives as well as a more politically egalitarian decision-making arena. Small units will reinforce territorial and therefore personal inequalities by seeking to minimize their levels of expenditure and taxation, while large units can help reduce territorial inequalities by combining rich and poor neighbourhoods in the same area (Newton, 1982). Large units of government may be more redistributive, if not more efficient, than small units.

Another value which may be in conflict with efficiency, if efficiency requires the consolidation of communities into large areas for decentralized government, is local autonomy. The benefits of autonomy in a system of fragmented jurisdictions has at least to be set against the costs of any diseconomies of scale, assuming they can be demonstrated (Bennett, 1980, p. 309). Furthermore, creating fewer, larger units of government may make central control easier by narrowing the centre's span of control. This would also have the effect of reducing autonomy. Against this, however, it might be supposed that larger units would be more powerful in their dealings with the centre by virtue of the political leadership and professional expertise that they could muster.

Finally, it has to be remembered that there are likely to be very powerful vested interests in large-scale organizations at the local or regional level, especially within the bureaucracy itself. These interests have been successful in promoting a technocratic view of decentralized government, through which the economies-of-scale argument has been very persuasive in political circles. Once changes have been implemented on the basis of such arguments, as they have in Britain and some other European states, it is difficult to reverse the trend, especially when cynicism sets in as to the expectations that can reasonably be had for socio-economic welfare from institutional and administrative reorganization.

Managerial Convenience

A division of the state's territory into areas may be made

according to the administrative needs of a national agency or department. Boundaries are then drawn which reflect the perceptions of the central decision-makers of how best to manage the flow of work. The number and location of field offices will then be determined by the span of control thought optimum by headquarters, or by the workload which it is thought appropriate for a field office to take in. Such a workload may be, in part, made up of political considerations, especially if the objects of administration are subordinate governments (Fesler, 1949, pp. 50–8).

Here, then, the aim will be to divide the territory into roughly equal, manageable parts. Aggregations of local communities will be delimited, but not to reflect local identities. Rather the object is to maximize the efficiency and effectiveness of administrative operations bearing on the recipients of government services, whether they be individuals, firms, institutions, industrial establishments, or other governments and government agencies. Such a principle of delimitation may be as important to the administrative departments of local or regional governments, which have to divide their areas further for administrative purposes, as to national governments. But the division is made by the 'centre' in each instance to meet its needs and values rather than by the identification of naturally coherent communities (Lipman, 1949, p. 310).

Technical Requirements

The natural properties of regions may have significance for administration and so provide a pattern of areas determined by physical features. Although the term 'region' is given different meanings in geography and public administration, administrative regions are often based on geographical regions, that is, areas with unifying characteristics or properties. For the geographer those properties may also be social or economic, as in the case of a coalfield or an agricultural region. By influencing patterns of settlement and communication, natural features shade into socio-economic and so may affect perceptions of community in the delimitation of governmental areas.

Physical geography is most obviously a basis for the drawing of administrative boundaries when governments attempt to manage natural resources for purposes such as water supply, land drainage, coastal-erosion control, irrigation, soil conservation, forest development, recreation, waste disposal or wild-life conservation. A geographical region, such as a river basin, may offer an appropriate area for economic and social planning if the lives of the inhabitants are tied closely to the exploitation of natural resources. The Tennessee Valley Authority is perhaps the most famous example of a multi-purpose development authority based on a watershed area (Selznick, 1949).

In Britain, the organization of the water industry provides another example of administrative structure based on geographical features. The ten water authorities in England and Wales are responsible for a range of functions connected with water usage − conservation, supply and distribution; sewerage and sewage disposal; land drainage; pollution control; and recreation. The regional boundaries of the water authorities are determined by catchment areas − areas of land draining to a particular river. Each authority deals with a self-contained water cycle: the natural system of water circulation between land, air and sea. The administrative structure is thus based on hydrological boundaries, unlike the earlier system in which different parts of the water cycle were divided into a fragmented structure of local authorities, river authorities and commercial undertakings. However, illustrating the point that administrative criteria can never be totally overlooked, each region is made up of a number of catchment areas, and local authority boundaries are taken into account in the subdivisions of some water regions. The size of each region thus reflects managerial perceptions about the amount of work that can be handled by a single organization (there is only loose co-ordination by the national level) (Gray, 1982).

Socially Distinct Regions

The territorial structure of government and administration may have to accommodate a division of society into socially distinct regions based on history, ethnicity, or language, or some combination of these. Areas which formed the major constituent parts of a country during the process of unification may continue to experience a sense of identity which cannot be overlooked by the constitutional and administrative system. In most European states, for example, there are provinces that are sanctified by history to the extent that it is difficult, if not impossible, to change boundaries in pursuit of administrative reform (Leemans, 1970, p. 41). A regional social identity may persist when territorial units can claim some degree of past political autonomy, as in West

Germany where minor attachments remain to regions that can be traced back to the German principalities of the nineteenth century (Urwin, 1982b).

The spatial units of federations are even more intractable, however inappropriate they might be for national purposes. It has been said that 'federation starts with a tacit recognition of the immutability of regional personalities' (Dikshit, 1975, p. 10). Artificially delineated territories can come to have an historic appeal based on vested interests and loyalties. In the USA, for example, some states were arbitrarily and geometrically defined as immigrants pushed the frontier westward. Yet these synthetic creations have been transformed into 'natural' areas which, while not constituting physical or economic regions, are occupied by people with a sense of loyalty and identity such that the states constitute, in part, social regions (Duchacek, 1970, p. 31). In federal states such regional identities, which may or may not have their origins in political or cultural associations predating unification, are usually protected by constitutional guarantees that make it doubly difficult to change the territorial structure of federations. Only where federal boundaries owe their origins to the artificial creations of an external power is it relatively easy to restructure a federation. This has happened in a number of post-colonial states, such as Nigeria, where regional boundaries originally reflected the administrative needs of British colonialism rather than cultural identity.

Ethnicity and culture usually form part of a socially distinct region's history though ethnicity and culture are made up of different elements which may vary in their significance from one region and ethnic group to another (Urwin, 1982a). The Basques, for example, are more a moral and political community than a descent or language group. Which factors are emphasized in defining the Basques and therefore their territory — ideas about provincial autonomy, language, and so on — depends on the particular political conflicts being engaged in. Historically, religion, language and folklore distinguish one section of Basque society from another in the competition for resources within the Basque country; but the *fueros* and ideas of original Basque sovereignty symbolize a nationalism that distinguishes Basques from the rest of Spain (Heiberg, 1982). Similarly in Belgium: though the linguistic border 'represents the most stable division that Belgium has ever known' regional attachments are not based exclusively on one factor. Economic, social and denominational conflicts make the definition of social regions more complex (Frognier, Quevit and Stenbock, 1982).

The Spatial Requirements of Administration

The delimitation of areas for decentralized government and administration is far from being merely a technical exercise. Crucial political choices have to be made about the objectives of decentralized institutions. Conflicts over these objectives will inevitably lead to conflicts over the appropriate criteria to be used in drawing administrative boundaries. Such conflicts become most apparent when reforms and reorganization have been initiated. Reconciliation of the different criteria which may be employed in the delimitation of areas is difficult. Final decisions will be determined by the pressure which vested interests can generate. A particularly effective form of pressure is ideological, when a set of beliefs about decentralization become common currency among key decision-makers in the reform process. An example was the widely accepted assumption at the time of local government reorganization in Britain that large units of local government were more efficient than small. This conventional wisdom, reflecting the wider technocratic and managerial approach to political problems fashionable at the time, held sway despite the absence of conclusive supporting evidence.

It is unlikely that any state will have a standard set of areas to which all decentralized administration is expected to conform. Special-purpose agencies will operate with specially designated areas. The flow of work within the field offices of central departments and between the field level and headquarters will differ from department to department. A standard pattern of field areas will be difficult to establish even when great weight is attached to interdepartmental co-ordination at field level. Even the regions of a federation will not necessarily constitute the optimum areas for federal field services.

It is only with the creation of multifunctional devolved governments that the problem of reconciling principles and territorial needs of different services becomes most pressing. The adoption of the efficiency principle will set up conflicting pressures as each service lays claim to its own optimum area. Only the creation of a multitude of special-purpose districts can overcome this problem. A multi-purpose government is almost bound to violate the spatial requirements of some services.

Settlement patterns and a sense of community may be resorted to. Even if the technical problems of defining 'communities', referred to above, are ignored it does not follow that the spatial requirements of particular administrative processes will coincide with boundaries based on community. And neither set of criteria will necessarily coincide with areas that have the strength of tradition, ethnicity, culture, or language behind them. The designers of decentralized systems are forced to compromise between the requirements of different sets of factors, each of which is certain to be supported by strong political pressures; the bureaucracy in the case of 'efficiency' factors; local political élites in the case of community factors; and primordial loyalties in the case of culturally distinct regions.

5
Intergovernmental Relations

In Chapter 3, pressures towards decentralization and the formation of area institutions were discussed. This chapter looks specifically at the relationships between levels of government and at the way these relationships have been investigated and interpreted by social scientists. It begins by examining the centralist tendencies of contemporary politics before analysing how intergovernmental relations have been, and might be, profitably explored.

Centralist Trends

Economic Development
Economic development seems inevitably to lead to industrial and demographic concentration. Modern economies are increasingly dominated by large corporations and conglomerates, with populations becoming more concentrated in major urban and industrial centres (Sharpe, 1979, p. 11). To the extent that governments are involved in regulating and promoting industrial institutions it is likely to be national governments that alone have the capacity to do this. Municipal authorities will have to cope with the problems of urbanization, but even here managing the metropolis seems everywhere to require large and remote jurisdictions that coincide with the growing metropolitan areas. In broader historical perspective, economic development leads to the erosion of territorial loyalties and groups, and to their replacement by the solidarity of occupational groups. As Durkheim recognized almost a century ago, political and social organization based on a territorial bond had lost its force and, though the 'material neighbourhood' persisted, it was to be superseded by the corporation or occupational group (Durkheim, 1893, pp. 28–9).

Economic Management

The involvement of the state in the economy is another factor that has strengthened the powers of central governments relative to local. This applies to both developing and developed countries. 'In the developing countries, where resources are scarce, it is inevitable that central government should keep a close watch to ensure that these are used to the best advantage' (van Putten, 1971, p. 227). In developed countries, national governments have attempted to manage the economy on behalf of oligopolistic corporations. They also provide the infrastructure on which industrial production is dependent (Sharpe, 1979). Again, central rather than local governments are responsible for such intervention. State action for planning and welfare, involving projects and services beyond the financial and technological means of territorial communities, 'results in a formidable increase in the number and power of national administrators' (Duchacek, 1970, pp. 311–12).

In federal systems the jurisdictions of federal governments have also tended to increase relative to the states. Government intervention in an integrated national economy inevitably falls to a jurisdiction that overlaps the boundaries of constituent parts. If the dominant forces in politics demand the regulation of trade, aid to agriculture, improved national communications, the control of commercial activity and protection against poor-quality goods only the central authorities are in a position to respond.

In the unitary state the legacies of earlier reliance on devolved power has serious implications for national economic management. In Britain, for example, local government expenditure has considerable economic significance. Local authorities compete for resources with both the rest of the public sector and the private. They account for over a fifth of total domestic investment and have been spending a growing proportion of the national income (Dunleavy, 1980b, p. 59). Government attempts to manage the economy and, in particular, control inflation have affected the expenditure levels of individual local governments as well as their negotiations with their employees over pay, the level of local taxes levied and the management of individual services.

Egalitarianism

Equality as a political principle has also produced centralizing pressures in the state. The realization of a degree of political equality releases demands for social and economic equality. The state is required to perform redistributive and welfare activities.

Only the central government can achieve such national equality. Territorial equity may be achieved without necessarily overcentralizing, but territorial equity that is consistent with local autonomy, and therefore decentralist, will almost certainly be inconsistent with interpersonal equity (Heald, 1983, p. 243).

Since area governments tend to be involved heavily in the provision of services relating to social and economic welfare their activities have spillover effects which extend beyond their boundaries, increasing the tendency to transfer functions to higher levels of government (Sharpe, 1979, pp. 14–15).

Federal systems are equally affected by the egalitarian pressures on contemporary state structures. 'The demand for equality, taken to its extreme, is the logical antithesis of federalism' (Vile, 1977, p. 5). When it is argued that the citizens of one state or region should receive equal benefits in welfare protection, housing, or education it becomes increasingly difficult to preserve a system in which different regional governments decide on priorities for their areas. The definition and enforcement of civil rights has also fallen increasingly to central governments (Riker, 1964, p. 66).

Equality not only enlarges the activities of the centre at the expense of the localities, it requires that the standards of administrative performance by area governments are territorially equal (van Putten, 1971, p. 226). Territorial justice relates not only to costs and benefits of public services, but also to the right to freedom from maladministration. The increased geographical mobility of the population and the influence of the mass media have increased awareness of disparities between areas and strengthened political opposition to such differences (Smith and Stanyer, 1976, p. 124). It is, however, still a matter of some debate and disagreement as to whether common standards for local services have emerged as a result of the imposition by the centre of national minimum standards or as a consequence of locally elected councils responding to social and political pressures for common standards (Greenwood, Jones and Stewart, 1982).

The Nationalization of Culture
What has been called 'cultural nationalization', brought about by developments in communications, is a powerful socially homogenizing force that undermines parochial sentiment and interest in the uniqueness of regional cultures. Modern politics reflect the tension between such forces and the attempts of cultural movements and organization to preserve local culture, especially language (see Chapter 3). The nationalization of attitudes and

culture has contributed to the decline in the significance of 'place' in politics and a growth in the significance of social and economic interest as the tie binding people together in pursuit of their political objectives (Sharpe, 1979, p. 11). The development of a specifically unitary political culture is encouraged by the growing relevance of national pressure groups to represent interests at central government level. Ultimately the level of centralization within a state will reflect the balance of forces within the dominant ideology which support the political identity and integrity of the nation or its constituent parts.

The Growth of Government

Many of the political forces mentioned have led to an overall growth in the level of government activity and this itself is said to breed centralization. After surveying all fields of government action in the USA, Riker concluded that, as government has grown, so the federal government has acquired more duties relative to the states (Riker, 1964, p. 81). Within government there are built-in pressures for further expansion and growth (Sharpe, 1979). Such growth is said to benefit the central institutions of government at the expense of the local. The external forces that lead to the growth in the scale of government can act as a centralizing influence. Wars, economic recessions, dependence on foreign aid and external economic, political and military threats seem everywhere to contribute to the centralization as well as the growth of the state. Only national governments have the capacity to mobilize and negotiate in times of crisis and dependence (Duchacek, 1970, pp. 324–9).

Governmental growth has been accompanied by the professionalization of the state and the growth of bureaucracies based on technical expertise. Such bureaucracies are themselves part of the capacity in government for self-sustaining growth. But more importantly in the present context is the centralizing effect of bureaucratization and professionalism. Professional knowledge cuts across territorial divisions and professional judgements take precedence over political ones, notably in public functions where area governments have traditionally been active, such as public health, public works and environmental planning (Tarrow *et al.*, eds, 1978). Professionalism means that the power of occupational communities reduces the autonomy of territorial communities.

Political Stability

Centralization is sometimes seen as the inevitable response to political instability and the crisis of the urban areas experienced in many industrial states. In the USA, for example, the deterioration of the urban environment and the accompanying periodic breakdowns of public order 'raises the prospect of pervasive federal dominance in the name of security'. National intervention in urban problems may be encouraged when the political interests represented at the intermediate level conflict with those represented by city governments (Duchacek, 1970, p. 322). However, the relationship between political stability and centralization appears from comparative studies to be far more complex than this. There is evidence to suggest that the authority of the state needs to be widely accepted before power can successfully be devolved, but that destabilizing forces can be contained by the careful manipulation of the centre's powers over local governments, whether they be black townships in South Africa or communist municipalities in France and Italy (Schulz, 1979, pp. 2–4).

Measuring Decentralization

It would certainly seem necessary to be able to make comparisons over time and between countries to see to what extent changes in the level of centralization had actually taken place in response to the forces mentioned earlier. There is, after all, sometimes disagreement about what is happening in a particular country. For example, it has been part of conventional wisdom in Britain since the 1930s that central control over local government has been increasing (Jones, 1980, p. 1). Yet, as Stanyer has pointed out, neither statistical nor longitudinal studies bear this out (Stanyer, 1976, p. 212). And repeated pressure for changes desired by the centre are successfully resisted by local governments. This still leaves the possibility that what the centre has done is take functions away, leaving local authorities to exercise their discretion over fewer matters, but even this is not an entirely uncontentious proposition. In any event, the facts of the British case are less important for the present exercise than devising a way of testing whether changes of this kind have occurred in Britain or elsewhere.

Certainly countries are often compared by reference to levels of decentralization. It would seem that decentralization is accepted as a variable, not an attribute. American local government is said to be more decentralized than English (Newton, 1974). West Germany is supposed to be more decentralized than Austria, and

Switzerland more than West Germany (Fried, 1974, p. 315). It is often argued that American federalism has become more centralized, while Canada has become less so. We are told that in Britain there is widespread public dissatisfaction with the over-centralization of British government and that the UK is the most centralized of the major industrial states.

There are, however, theoretical difficulties in the way of making systematic comparisons between states or within states over time. In a seminal paper on decentralization James Fesler (1965) identified three methodological problems facing political scientists who want to move the discussion of decentralization from generalities to a degree of precision. The first is linguistic – the way the terms 'centralization' and 'decentralization' tend to dichotomize our thinking. The second is a problem of measurement and the weaknesses of indices of decentralization. And the third is the problem of differentiating in terms of decentralization between the regions of a single country. All three problems might be subsumed under the heading of 'measurement' since replacing a dichotomy with a continuum, differentiating between areas, and constructing indices to measure the territorial distribution of power are all interrelated methodological issues. The same solution would serve all three. Fesler regretted the bluntness of available tools of analysis but directed his attention to other approaches to an understanding of the subject. Other scholars since then have found the problem insoluble. Yet it is necessary to be able to measure decentralization if we want to know whether changes have in fact occurred and what the consequences of these changes are. The greatest problem is that of holding the other determinants of local autonomy and policy formation constant so that the variable impact of decentralization may be assessed. Cross-national comparisons are particularly difficult because it appears impossible to compare the delegation of power when it occurs in such different contexts and takes such different forms. Comparisons over time, however, are not so difficult though they are undoubtedly complicated by the fact that changes in devolved powers are often accompanied by changes in area, so like is not being compared with like.

If it is to be tested whether the relationships between different levels of government have moved towards greater centralization, there are some changes which directly influence the balance of power and others which may make one side or the other politically stronger though the influence on intergovernmental relations is more hypothetical.

Functions

One obvious test of change in levels of decentralization relates to the functions and powers of subordinate governments. Legislation or constitutional interpretation to switch a governmental function from one level to another will change the level of decentralization in the state. Centralization can be reduced by expanding the jurisdiction of subordinate governments. This test is complicated by the fact that the provision of many public goods (such as education) is often shared between levels of government, but it is not unknown for the centre to take over responsibility for a service in its entirety, thereafter administering that service through its own field administration or a quasi-independent appointed board of management (see Chapter 7). When investigating the distribution of state services between devolved governments (or federal units) and field administration it is important to remember that some field services are responsible for a substantive executive activity (such as agricultural extension work) which could, in principle, be performed by subordinate governments, while others represent aspects of central control over the machinery of government (such as inspection, audit and policy control). Chapter 8 discusses the different roles of field administration.

Indicators of shifts in the territorial balance of power, augmenting information on changes in the allocation of government functions, may be obtained from data on spending and personnel. The volume of 'local' expenditure as a proportion of total public spending may be used as a measure by which to compare states or a single state at different time periods. Increased decentralization will be, in part, reflected in a growing proportion of public spending incurred by area governments. State and local expenditure in the USA has been used for this purpose. Most of the expenditure involved below the federal level could, in principle, be the responsibility of either the locality or the state (the 'central' government as far as municipal authorities are concerned). For the USA, Stephens defined a 'services index' to measure the distribution of services such as police, education, penal institutions and highways between state and local governments. This is based on the proportion of total public expenditure allocated to each level of government. Functions can then be classified as central, local, or 'joint'. Each state can be ranked and compared with others in terms of its level of decentralization (Stephens, 1974). To use this test in a unitary state would require adjustments to be made to take into account those items of expenditure which could never be devolved, such as foreign affairs and defence (B. C. Smith, 1980, p. 140). It is also important when carrying out comparative research, to ensure that the authorities to which expenditure is assigned are comparable entities (Sherwood, 1969).

The proportion of public servants working in a locality employed by central compared with local organizations has also been used to measure decentralization. Stephens (1974) measured the distribution of public service personnel between state and local levels of government in the USA to see what proportion of total public servants performing relevant government functions are employed by central agencies. Adjustments were made in the central-local personnel ratio to account for the fact that local services tend to be highly labour–intensive. Once again, 'relevant' functions need to be defined as those which, in principle, could be administered in the localities by either central or local personnel.

The sharing of functions by different levels of government is also significant in federal systems. This is because the practice of federalism rarely conforms to the strict allocation of powers contained in federal constitutions.

In the USA, for example, the idea that federalism involves the clear-cut delegation of powers to each tier of government (a 'layer cake' model of intergovernmental relations) has given way to the idea that each tier might, and often does, contribute to some aspect of policy-making and implementation in most spheres of state intervention. The relationships between the tiers vary over time and according to the policy concerned. This is the 'marble cake' image of intergovernmental relations in which federalism is characterized as involving co-operation, sharing, interdependence and even creativity between national, state and municipal authorities (Grodzins, 1960, p. 265).

Such imagery tells us more about how federalism does not work than about how it does. The nature of the relations between tiers of government, and whether any theory explaining those relations can be produced, as distinct from labels and concepts like 'creative', 'co-operative', or just 'new' which characterize federalism in a particular state at a particular time, remain to be seen. However, there is ample comparative evidence that all federations experience the interdependence rather than isolation of internal governments. One general pattern seems to be a growing dependence of regional governments on the centre for finance, and dependence of the centre on the regions for policy implementation. Such mutual dependence produces complex institutional and procedural devices for consultation and co-operation (Duchacek, 1970, pp. 318–19). It makes the evaluation of shifts in the territorial distribution of power all the more difficult.

Delegation

Changes in the type and extent of delegation to area governments affect the territorial distribution of power. Three factors are important here. The first is whether the area governments have, as in some Western European countries, a 'general competence' to do whatever is considered necessary to meet the needs of the area as perceived by area decision-makers, or need to find some statutory confirmation that they can act on a particular matter or provide a particular service (the *ultra vires* doctrine). The second is the form of central administrative control employed. It is possible (see below) to distinguish between control (backed by sanctions) and influence which area governments are free to resist. Comparative analysis, even within one state over time, is difficult here because of extensive variation in the forms of control used. The significance of such variation, for example between selective financial controls and general budgetary approvals, has to be evaluated (Kaufman, 1963; Hepworth, 1976). So, too, does a comparison of a wide range of decentralized functions and minimal delegation with a narrow range but greater delegation. A third variation between states is whether central control mainly takes the form of initiation or veto. This will depend on the attitudes of the central agencies to the local governments for which they bear some responsibility. In Britain, for example, central departments have been shown to exhibit very different sets of attitudes – some regulatory, some promotional and some *laissez-faire* (Griffith, 1966).

Revenue

A third test of decentralization is the revenue-raising power which is delegated to subordinate governments. The level of decentralization in a system of government will be changed if legal restrictions on the level of local rates of tax are imposed. It will also be dependent on whether the tax powers delegated permit area governments to expand their revenues in line with increases in the rate of inflation and the growth of the economy (Grumm and Murphy, 1974; Davey, 1971). Ashford has shown that for Britain, France, West Germany, Canada and the USA decentralization has been affected by the availability of 'elastic' taxes to local government (Ashford, 1979, p. 82). However, the proportion of local revenues raised locally as distinct from originating in central grants should be regarded as a factor whose relationship to decentralization is more problematic (see below). The subject of area government finance will be discussed in Chapter 6.

Creating Area Governments

Fourthly, the method adopted by the state to create area governments is an important variable in unitary constitutions. This will influence whether centre and area institutions operate as partners, or whether area governments are the agents of the centre. Local governments may receive their powers and duties through legislative enactment or executive delegation. Where the source of area authority is the legislature there will be more decentralization than where the source is the executive. Decentralization will be greater if area governments have a legal existence independent of the central executive.

Dependency

There are other features of area government which may be altered by the central legislative and executive authorities which may affect the territorial distribution of power, though the influence is less direct than those already mentioned. The first, and one of the most contentious, is the proportion of local revenue raised from local services compared with dependency on central grants. There is a widespread view that if central funding increases so will central control. However, empirical evidence does not always support this conclusion. Nor can it be assumed a priori that greater financial dependency means a loss of local independence of action. Grant dependency does not seem to be causally related to wide variations in local expenditure priorities in Britain, for example. However, variations in patterns of local expenditure do not *necessarily* mean there is extensive decentralization, any more than uniformity equals centralization (Foster, Jackman and Osborn, 1976; Brand, 1965). And, as Stanyer has pointed out, '*A priori*, the conjunction of central finance and central control and influence is as consistent with the hypothesis that grants are paid because control exists, as the opposite' (Stanyer, 1976, p. 233). Central control and influence are exercised independently and regardless of the way local services are funded. More important is whether the grant system has built into it a device by which the centre can set a ceiling on total local expenditure or (even more centralizing) establish local priorities. Methods of grant administration may be more important than the size of grants to intergovernmental relations (Grumm and Murphy, 1974).

Areas

The size of area governments, a factor which can be changed by local government reforms and reorganization, may also be important for decentralization. Larger local authorities should be better placed to resist central domination than smaller ones. They will have stronger revenue bases, larger professional organizations, greater ability to meet the needs of the area because of large catchment areas, and more experience at managing large-scale organizations and resources. Legislation creating fewer but larger governments in terms of population and territory might thus be a decentralizing measure. Against this, however, is that after such reorganization the centre is left with fewer subordinate governments to control and fewer chief officers, political leaders, departmental organizations, policies and spending programmes to manipulate. Also the hypothesis that the smaller the authority the greater the conformity to central wishes has not been verified. So the relationship between size and control is still very much open to debate (as was seen in the previous chapter).

Party Politics

The effect of political parties on decentralization is an important though under-researched issue. Politics in both federal and unitary states tends to be dominated by national political organizations with local branches seeking electoral office in national and subnational government. Riker has argued that centralization within federations may be measured by the degree to which one party controls both levels of government and how far central party leaders control party members holding office locally. He concluded from his analysis of federalism in the USA that the country's 'decentralized party system is the main protector of the integrity of states in our federalism' (Riker, 1964, p. 101). In Canada a centralized constitution is modified by a decentralized party system in which the dominant provincial parties are not part of national organizations and national leaders find it difficult to control their fellow partisans at provincial level. By contrast, the Soviet constitution is on paper extremely decentralized, but this is negated by the strictly hierarchical and centralized single political party (Riker, 1964, pp. 116–24; Duchacek, 1970, pp. 329–37). The nature of the party system as well as the internal organizations of parties are, in turn, influenced by the territorial structure of power in which they operate. For example, in the USA the powers of the constituent states are thought to explain the federal structure of American political parties (Duchacek, 1970, pp. 338–40).

John Gyford has drawn attention to the importance of distinguishing between the different roles of national parties in subnational political arenas. First, local election candidates might fight under national party labels but with locally decided programmes. Secondly, party headquarters might provide policy advice to partisan office holders. Thirdly, the 'nationalization' of party politics might move from advice to exhortation with party headquarters encouraging local councillors to adopt certain policies. Finally, headquarters might instruct and monitor local action. These roles can be thought of as points on a continuum of party decentralization. Location on this continuum will depend on the resources available for control, the party's philosophy of decentralization and the party constitution (Gyford, 1980).

In considering the effect of party politics it must not be assumed that there can only be a one-way flow of influence from headquarters to local party branch so that the effect of national parties in local politics is a centralizing one. This is not only because a national party may be national in name only. It is also because ideas, information, experience, opinion and demands will flow from the grass-roots upwards. National parties may be localized to some degree, just as local parties may be nationalized (Gyford, 1980).

The Structure of the System

Finally, the structure of area government itself may be significant to the level of decentralization. This is again open to manipulation, since it is up to the centre to decide whether the system should consist of a single- or multi-tiered structure with primary or secondary forms of local government and single-purpose or multifunctional institutions (see Chapter 7). The more levels in the territorial hierarchy of the state, the more opportunity for 'discretionary gaps' and 'leakages' of authority to occur. This should therefore increase the discretion available to lower levels in the system (Downs, 1967). However, if a unitary system has areas which correspond closely to areas of natural community and do not take in parts of neighbouring communities, then decisions and policies made locally will require fewer compromises to be made between community interests. It may then be hypothesized that a simple (or single-tier) system of unitary all-purpose authorities will be less decentralized than a complex (or multi-tiered) system of authorities with co-ordinate jurisdictions.

The discussion is beginning to turn towards the politics of local autonomy rather than decentralization. As Ashford has shown, states vary in the power of their local governments to bargain with the centre over the allocation of new functions, the size of revenue allocations and the form of taxation power delegated to them (Ashford, 1979). This distinction between autonomy and decentralization will be examined next in the context of dominant approaches to the study of intergovernmental relations.

Approaches to Intergovernmental Relations

This section is, of course, exclusively concerned with the territorial aspects of intergovernmental relations. It looks at the study of relations between different levels of government in the state hierarchy, though, as will be seen, this subject has recently benefited from applications of some of the concepts employed in interorganizational analysis. The dominant approaches to intergovernmental relations adopted by social scientists interested in the spatial distribution of power are outlined. An alternative approach is suggested which superimposes non-territorial divisions and conflicts within contemporary industrial societies upon the geographical divisions which are represented in the political and administrative structures of all modern states.

Law and Administration

The study of intergovernmental relations has been heavily influenced by the historical-legal tradition in political studies and public administration. It has focused on the different formal relationships of power and influence between central and subnational governments expressed through the main categories of central control – legislative, judicial and administrative. In Britain, for example, methods of central control and influence can be classified by distinguishing, first, between administrative control and influence, and legislative/judicial control. Two other methods of control stand midway between the strictly legislative and judicial controls exercised by Parliament and the courts, and the administrative controls, including powers of approval, appointment and default, available to ministers. These are the statutory power given to ministers to make regulations; and the machinery of district audit by which the legality of expenditure is tested. All these aspects of central–local relations 'exercise a general influence on the atmosphere of local authority decision making' without necessarily producing conflict (Stanyer, 1976, p. 221). Administrative controls include powers of approval, appointment and default.

By contrast, methods of influence are more common and seek

agreement before action rather than sanction and enforcement after it. Influence by the centre on the local decision-makers is exercised in Britain by means of circulars and other communications, specific grants and central inspection. Discussions of intergovernmental relations in terms of controls often centre on whether local authorities should be regarded as agents or partners of the centre, and whether financial dependence increases central control (Griffith, 1966; Davey, 1971; Ashford, 1974; Dearlove, 1979, pp. 242–5). However, the main conclusion drawn from the application of these categories of control is that intergovernmental relations are generally characterized more by negotiation, persuasion and dialogue than by the resolution of overt conflict by the use of ultimate sanctions. Local authorities are by no means the passive recipients of central directives. Such an approach to the legal and administrative relationships between levels of government permits the political context of such relationships to be explored. It requires the political analyst to examine the power resources which the institutions on each side of the relationship can deploy.

The importance of this approach is that it reminds us how far decentralization within the contemporary state *is* a matter of formal organizational arrangements between the different geographical levels of the state hierarchy. How far a state is decentralized can usefully be kept separate from the question of how much autonomy local areas enjoy. This enables decentralization to be considered as a necessary, though not sufficient, condition of local autonomy. Decentralization is essentially a question of central–local relations, to use the language of traditional British public administration. It is a function of the rules which delegate authority from one level to another either within an organization or within a state. It may be affected by other factors which support or undermine the autonomy of a particular subnational territory or community. Decentralization, then, is open to official manipulation. It is the consequence of political and administrative decisions. It is by the manipulation of central–local relations that a system of government is made more or less decentralized.

What this approach has not been able to do is evaluate the consequences for political power and public policy of greater or less decentralization. As far as the 'outputs' of the system are concerned, some policy studies have asked whether one system of central control produces uniformity in local policy-making or permits diversity of local political decisions which can then be explained by reference to the characteristics of the local political system. But this approach has not been concerned with the effects of different levels of decentralization on such outputs. Variations among the internal characteristics of local communities, such as population size and financial resources, have been analysed to see if they relate causally to variations in the level of local autonomy. But levels of decentralization have not been analysed to see what the implications of such variation here might be.

In addition, the approach has not been particularly concerned with the political forces behind changes in one direction or another, and the tendency towards centralization in some states. To do this requires intergovernmental relations to be placed in a wider context than is usually the case and an examination of political factors cutting across the central–local dimension of intra-state relationships.

Community Politics

An alternative approach to intergovernmental relations is found within the political science of community, and particularly urban, politics. To a large extent the concern here has been to locate political power within communities – in a plurality of interests, in an élite, among multiple élites, and so on; and to compare the relative importance of political and socio-economic variables on policy outputs. The outputs of community governments have been explained by reference to the internal characteristics or structural attributes of the area – its dominant community values, the degree to which power is concentrated, the level of community integration, or the formal structure of the local government system, for example. Again, the level of decentralization is assumed to be a constant factor, despite what Fesler has said about particular regions, provinces and local governments being differentially treated in practice (Fesler, 1965, p. 537).

When students of community power turned their attention to the 'interpenetration of levels of government' they were concerned primarily with local autonomy. Decentralization was seen as just one among many variables influencing local autonomy (Clark, 1973). The local community characteristics relevant to local political autonomy are the natural, social and economic resources of the area, its cultural distinctiveness and political structures.

Such an approach to intergovernmental relations is important and legitimate in that it distinguishes between central–local relations and local autonomy. Autonomy is a function of numerous aspects of national and local politics. It is to be accounted for, in part, by economic, social and political structures which lie outside the relationships between different institutional levels in the state hierarchy. Changing the pattern of these relationships, which administrative reformers are often tempted to do, may have less effect on autonomy (if that is the objective) than might be intended. In France, for example, the power of local notables strengthens the localities in their conflicts with the centre, while in the USA decentralist provisions in state constitution do not seem to have prevented centralization (B. C. Smith, 1980, p. 142).

The question of whether variations in decentralization, or the extent to which the management of local affairs is in the hands of representatives of the area rather than of the centre, make any difference to policy outcomes remains unanswered. The man-made constraints on local autonomy need to be separated out from the other relevant facets of the area's socio-economic structure before an answer to this question can be attempted.

Interorganizational Politics

A distinction has been made between decentralization and autonomy, and earlier it was pointed out that discussions of formal relationships between levels of government are incomplete without an examination of other aspects of politics which are relevant to the territorial allocation of power. Central governments are not always willing or able to use the controls available to them, and some area governments possess resources which enable them to resist pressures from the centre. There is great scope for bargaining, negotiation and initiative. Area governments vary in their willingness to use political, financial, legal and administrative resources to resist control. Interaction is probably a better term than control when describing central–local relations (B. C. Smith, 1980, p. 141; Scharpf *et al.*, 1978; Jones, 1974). Co-operation, collusion and competition characterize the relations between governments as much as coercion. Co-operation occurs because each political unit offers something of value to the other (especially in the case of fiscal transfers). Thus in all aspects of multi-organizational government we should not expect to find a single policy in each functional area being pursued by all units. Rather there will be different policies pursued by institutions with different capabilities, constituencies and preferences (Bish, 1978). The study of intergovernmental relations needs to abandon its preoccupation with formal hierarchies of authority and focus on networks of 'antagonistic but interdependent actors' engaged in permanent bargaining and the formation of alliances (Thoenig, 1978).

Such interaction and interdependence between levels of

government are affected by many different political and organization factors, such as inconsistent central policies and local influence over central projects and priorities (Harris, 1978; Rhodes, 1976). Technology is also relevant to control (B. C. Smith, 1980, p. 142). Physical distance may also be important. Discretion at area level may be strengthened, especially in less-developed countries, if physical distance reduces the frequency and effectiveness of central supervision. Hence decisions to vary the level of decentralization in the state might be offset by geographical, demographic, political and economic factors.

Awareness of this has led some students of intergovernmental relations to turn to organizational sociology and seek inspiration from the study of interorganizational networks. The fullest exposition of an approach based on such adaptation has been made available by Rhodes (1976, 1977, 1979 and 1981). Rhodes finds the popular models of central–local relations as 'partnership' or 'agency' descriptively inadequate. The relationships are too often described legalistically and are presented as uni-dimensional rather than multi-dimensional. The centre is presented as a monolithic entity when it consists of a large number of diverse institutions. The same is true of each local authority.

The alternative approach, based on interorganizational analysis, expresses the relationship between centre and area as 'a complex system of dependencies' (Rhodes, 1979). Organizations are seen as being dependent on others which make up one part of their environments. Strategies have to be employed to manage dependency (which all organizations experience to a greater or lesser degree) on others for necessary resources. A 'focal' organization, then, has to be studied both as part of an 'organization set' consisting of other organizations with which it interacts, and of a 'network' of wider and less direct influences, the boundary of which is very hard to demarcate empirically. Within its 'domain', or goals and objectives, an organization has to establish 'domain consensus' or legitimacy in the eyes of other members of its set.

Politics within and between organizations centres on the employment of strategies by the organization's 'dominant coalition' to secure needed resources. Power in interorganizational terms is thus reciprocal since all organizations experience dependency rather than domination. Power and dependence rest on access to five major types of resource: finance, political access and support, professional expertise, jurisdiction and administrative relationships. Information and expertise, in particular, have been widely acknowledged as political resources which may strengthen the power of lower-level governments despite their formal subordination. Conversely, a shortage of technical expertise and information may undermine the powers formally delegated to local authorities (Mayntz, 1978; Baestlein *et al.*, 1978; Garlichs and Hull, 1978; Thoenig, 1978). Variations in the pattern of dependence between organizations determine the structure of the set — its size, 'compactness' (or directness of relations between organizations), 'density' (or extent to which potential linkages are made actual) and diversity of interactions. They also determine its behavioural characteristics — the frequency, durability, intensity and form of interaction between organizations. The dominant coalition can employ either co-operative or conflictual strategies, the latter involving disruption, manipulation and authority (Rhodes, 1979).

When controls have to be employed as 'corrective interventions' by higher-level governments their effectiveness is likely to be highly dependent on the consent of the interests and institutions to be controlled. Many different strategies are available to reduce conflict and secure agreement, including persuasion, problem-solving, bargaining, coercion, reducing the complexity of the problem and limiting the scope and content of public policy. The likelihood of disagreement between levels of governments is affected by the number of participants, their previous experience of collaboration, the political context and characteristics of the issue itself — how complex it is, how much disagreement over substantive goals there is and whether the instruments of control employed are matched to the 'control requirements' of a particular policy problem (Scharpf *et al.*, 1978).

This framework for analysis should be very useful to future research in the area. It has one outstanding merit. It explicitly rejects the idea that the relations between levels of government in contemporary states operate along a single dimension, with both levels united in their opposition to the other over-centralizing or decentralizing tendencies. It draws attention to the fragmented nature of both central and area governments. It shows area government to be fragmented, whether it be the whole system or an individual local authority. It provides a systematic method for analysing the resources available to both levels in their conflicts with the other. It acknowledges the possibility of *co-operation* between organizations and therefore between levels of government.

This last point is particularly significant. Unlike the approach in traditional discussions of central–local government relations, the 'local' level is not treated as if it were a homogeneous entity, united in its resistance to central control. The interorganizational analysis approach implies that the response of area governments to central initiatives, and vice versa, will not necessarily be a co-ordinated and unified one. There may be vertical alignments cutting across the central–local divide and linking the 'dominant coalitions' of different levels of government in pursuit of a common interest.

While the interorganizational analysis approach classifies the resources available to dominant coalitions in their conflicts and strategic bargaining, such conflict is still, as in more traditional approaches, very much internalized. Interorganizational conflict is presented as having its origins in command over resources, leaving open the question of the uses to which such resources are to be put and the interests to be served by their use. The concept of 'network' would perhaps encompass such interests, though again networks are defined largely in organizational terms. A network can, however include 'the larger pattern of societal dominance'.

Conclusion

The spatial dimension of intergovernmental relations may be analysed using different methodologies. Each can be instructive. The historical-legal approach enables us to distinguish decentralization from autonomy. It focuses on institutional and procedural changes which may be made to alter the distribution of power between levels of government. The community-politics approach reminds us that officially instigated 'reforms' in intergovernmental relations may be neutralized by the political and economic context in which they are made. Factors supporting local autonomy may impede national government attempts to centralize power. Interorganizational studies inform us of the multi-dimensional nature of intergovernmental relations and the power resources which can be utilized when governments interact.

One problem with contemporary approaches to the study of intergovernmental relations is that they tend to isolate conflicts between levels of government from other political conflicts in society. Central government incursions into local autonomy are not related to other state interventions to manage such conflict. Changes in the status of local governments relative to the centre are usually analysed in managerialist terms. The problem is depoliticized. Explanations of centralization are sought in the technical deficiencies of local institutions. Local needs are said to outstretch local resources. Technological changes are said to demand larger units benefiting from economies of scale. Professional expertise needs to be freed from political 'interference' and organized in special-purpose bureaucratic agencies. Jurisdictional conflicts between local authorities, especially in metropolitan areas, have to be erased. Hence local government must expect greater central intervention and control. The centre must maintain national standards. The centre must produce territorial justice by equalization measures. The centre must provide the funds. He who pays the piper calls the tune. And so on.

Yet a Marxist analysis of local government (see Chapter 2) suggests that we ought not to regard each side of the central–local equation as self-contained and homogeneous in its dealings with the other. Conflicts within local communities will include different reactions to central interventions, depending on whose interests the centre is perceived as promoting by its attempts to restrict local autonomy. Changing patterns of central government policy and expenditure generate conflicts not only between the geographical levels of the state but also between classes and groups at the local level. At the local level class interests cut across the divisions between central and local government.

From such a perspective, intergovernmental relations reveal many contradictory political forces. State intervention, particularly of the corporatist kind, generates pressures for centralization which conflict with the need to legitimize the state through participation and decentralization. Changing forms of intervention encounter political forces and interests which are the product of earlier phases in the development of the capitalist state. The administrative apparatus of the state contains within it powerful forces which conflict with the institutional requirements of new directions in state policy. The support given by different classes to movements in the territorial location of power depends on the particular class interests represented at the centre.

Hence it may be important to locate a study of intergovernmental relations within a framework of conflicting interests that are reflected in changing patterns of state intervention and their institutional expressions. Conflicts between levels of government may be one response to attempts by the state to manage conflicts within society at large. Intergovernmental relations will then reflect alliances between national and local political interests which cause conflict within, as well as between, levels of government.

6
Financing Decentralized Government

Introduction

The decentralization of government, whether in federations or unitary states, raises some of the most intractable problems in the field of public finance. It is obvious that the exercise of governmental power at the subnational level entails expenditure by subnational governments. Those governments have to secure revenues to finance that expenditure. Beyond those two self-evidently obvious propositions there seems nothing but disagreement on all the issues and decisions that flow from them: what revenue sources are the best; why there is a widespread, almost universal, growing dependency on higher-level governments for the incomes of area governments; whether that dependency reduces the autonomy of area governments and undermines their accountability and responsiveness to their electorates and communities; what effect inflation has on local and regional spending; why some central governments resist the devolution of extensive revenue-raising powers; and so on. This chapter examines these issues, first, by examining the main sources of revenue available to area government; secondly, by looking at recent trends in subnational expenditure and the implications of these for revenues; thirdly, by examining the reasons for the growing dependency on higher-level governments and, fourthly, by trying to disentangle strands in the argument about the relationship between dependency and autonomy.

The overall focus of the chapter is thus on the question of autonomy. This is because it is a basic assumption in all systems of decentralized government that the political institutions created for the territorial subdivisions of the state must, if they are to have any political credibility, have some measure of independence in the level of revenue they raise and the choice of public goods on which to spend it. Unlike the field offices of national public organizations, area governments are assumed to need some power to decide at what rate to levy the taxes assigned to them by the constitution or the national government, and some freedom to allocate their spending among the functions similarly devolved to them, according to their own sense of priorities.

The financial problems of area governments are inevitably closely interrelated with most of the other decisions that have to be made about decentralization in contemporary states. Most notably there is a clear link between the financing of area governments and their relations with the centre. Intergovernmental relations and decentralized public finance can only be separated artificially. A central controversy for many years has been that concerning the effect on levels of central control of local government's dependency on central allocations for an adequate income. There is also the question of how far the central government's responsibility for managing the national economy limits the extent to which revenue powers can be devolved and area governments left free to decide on the overall scale of their budgets. Finance is also closely linked to the area problem and the question of whether a viable financial position for area governments is dependent on some minimum size of population and, if so, what that minimum should be. The link between autonomy and finance is explicitly dealt with here.

The financial aspects of federalism and devolution are considered jointly here because both constitutional systems experience comparable problems. Once it is acknowledged that, in practice, the central and constituent governments of federations are not co-ordinate and independent in their jurisdictions and in their fiscal arrangements, it becomes clear that they are required to take comparable decisions to unitary states about area finance. Federations and unitary states both have to decide on the allocation of revenue powers, on the sharing of government revenues between territorial levels, and on the management of grant flows from national to constituent governments (Foster, Jackman and Perlman, 1980, pp. 31–4).

Sources of Revenue

The main sources of revenue available to local and regional governments are taxes, charges, grants and loans. Tables 6.1 and 6.2 show the contribution made by the main categories of revenue to the incomes of subnational governments in European states.

Table 6.1 *Sources of Local Government Revenue in Western European States (%).*

	Taxes	Grants	Interest*	Charges	Other
Austria (1977)	50·0	12·8	4·0	15·1	18·1
Belgium (1978)	29·3	58·1	9·7	2·8	0·1
Denmark (1978)	32·8	52·6	1·9	—	12·7
France (1976)	41·1	43·4	1·5	14·0	—
Ireland (1978)	21·0	59·0	—	20·0	—
Italy (1978)	10·1	31·3	3·7	46·3	8·6
Luxembourg (1976)	47·2	51·3	—	—	1·5
Netherlands (1978)	5·7	79·2	9·3	5·0	0·8
Norway (1972)	54·0	14·9	1·0	26·7	3·4
Portugal (1976)	48·9	51·1	—	—	—
Sweden (1979)	42·4	26·4	1·4	16·8	13·0
Switzerland (1972)	58·0	17·9	7·0	16·5	0·6
West Germany (1976)	34·0	29·3	2·9	24·6	9·2
UK (1978)	28·1	57·0	1·3	13·6†	—

* Including dividends and shares.
† Includes sundry other income.
Source: Council of Europe (1981b).

Taxes

Taxes include local income tax, property taxes, poll taxes (either on persons or households), corporation tax (based on profits or output), local sales tax and a local payroll tax. Most taxes levied by local and regional governments are direct, as there are special difficulties for local governments in levying indirect taxes. For example, Value Added Tax (VAT) is difficult to administer in that transactions may involve a number of different governments. Other indirect taxes face the problem that if neighbouring authorities set different rates, distortions are introduced into an economy operating according to market principles. Also, taxes on consumption have the political disadvantage of generally being regressive. In Western Europe nearly all the countries studied by the Council of Europe's Committee on Regional and Municipal Matters 'rely heavily on direct taxes to finance local and regional authority expenditure, and particularly on taxes based on incomes and on land and property' (Council of Europe, 1981b, p. 53). However, there is immense diversity in the range of activities which are taxed by decentralized governments, including drinking, gambling, advertising, trading, entertainments, building, motoring, polluting, auctioneering, quarrying, and a host of others. Many are low yielding but nevertheless maintained because

Table 6.2   *Sources of Regional Government Revenue in Western European States (%).**

	Taxes	Grants	Interest	Charges	Other
Austria (1977)	43·6	32·0	1·8	9·8	12·8
Belgium (1978)	31·1	63.1	5·8	—	—
Denmark (1978)	51·4	34·1	1·8	—	12·7
France (1976)	74·6	17·0	1·2	7·2	—
Italy (1972)	76·7	5·9	8·6	0·7	8·1
Netherlands (1978)	4·4	83·3	8·3	2·1	1·4
Norway (1972)	38·3	19·1	0·6	36·3	5·7
Sweden (1979)	62·2	17·7	2·2	—	17·9
Switzerland (1972)	52·2	30·4	4·6	12·6	0·2
West Germany (1976)	67·9	19·0	0·9	5·7	6·5

* This table does not strictly compare like with like (for example, German *Länder* with French regions and Swedish *landsting*).
Source: Council of Europe (1981b).

of tradition or to serve the political objective of keeping the tax system as wide-ranging as possible (Council of Europe, 1981b, pp. 62–4).

Taxes on incomes are particularly significant in the decentralized systems of some Scandinavian and European states. In Denmark, for example, 80.6 per cent of county revenues came from taxes on individual incomes. In Sweden 99 per cent of local tax revenue comes from taxes on individual and corporate incomes. The Swiss cantons raise 70 per cent of their revenues from income tax, and the communes 80 per cent. It is no accident that these countries are among those in which the fiscal crisis of local government has been experienced least, a point returned to below.

Taxes on land and property are extensively used by local government systems throughout the world, despite the financial problems to which they undoubtedly contribute. The basis of assessment for such taxes is the taxable or 'rateable' value of land and property as determined by rental or capital values. A frequency of revaluation that is rarely achieved is required if the inelasticity of these taxes is to be minimized. Rates on property may also include movable property, such as stock in trade. Property taxes may be restricted to one type of property (land, for example) or may apply to all property, such as the rating system in the UK (Foster, Jackman and Perlman, 1980, p. 231). Table 6.3 shows the proportional contribution to the tax receipts

Table 6.3   *Receipts from Land and Property Taxes in European Local Government (% of Total Tax Receipts).*

	Regional Authorities	Local Authorities
Austria	—	15·0
Belgium	73·5	48·5
Denmark	19·4	8·8
France	44·0	44·0
Ireland	—	100·0
Luxembourg	—	6·0
Netherlands	74·0	68·0
Norway	—	6·0
West Germany	3·0	11·0
UK	—	100·0

Source: Council of Europe (1981b).

of regional and local governments in selected European states made by property taxes.

Local and intermediate governments usually have the right to fix the rate of local taxes, though in some cases national legislation lays down minimum rates and sometimes national rates are fixed with municipalities free to decide whether to levy the tax (Council of Europe, 1981b).

Tax revenues may be shared by different levels of government, as in the case of assigned revenues where a proportion of the revenue raised by local governments acting as tax collector is retained by that level of government. Local authorities may or may not be able to set the *rate* of tax. An assigned revenue for which local government sets the rate indicates a more decentralized system than one where the centre does (Foster, Jackman and Perlman, 1980, pp. 129–30). Where the central government determines the base and rate of the tax, collects it, and decides on the proportion to be handed over to subnational governments, an assigned revenue approximates closely to a grant, especially if the assignment is based on some attempt at territorial equalization. However, derivation may form the basis of assignment, as in Denmark where 15 per cent of the proceeds from corporation tax are 'returned' to local authorities according to the location of companies (Council of Europe, 1981b, p. 61).

As an alternative to sharing a tax, two levels of government may tap the same revenue source, perhaps with different rates of tax, tax bases, allowances and methods of assessment. Such 'overlapping' tax jurisdictions (Bennett, 1980, pp. 290–3) have been applied to personal and corporate income tax and duties on deaths, gifts and estates. In Canada, for example, there was joint provincial and federal 'occupancy' of tax fields between 1962 and 1982 with the provinces establishing their own personal and corporate tax rates. Such arrangements inevitably produce conflict and hard bargaining between levels of government, especially when, as in Canada, the federal government had obtained its right to personal and corporation tax under temporary 'tax rental' agreements with the provinces (Wilson, 1979).

Charges

Area governments also raise revenues by charging for services which they provide. They may build or acquire property to rent. They may earn income from trading activities and by providing public utilities such as water, gas, electricity and transport. They may charge fees for some of the communal facilities they provide.

Charging users for municipal or regional services brings the mechanisms of the market into municipal and regional government. Charges are generally regarded as an appropriate source of revenue only when the service offered to the community is divisible and when the benefits go mainly to the payer. They are inappropriate for services aimed at poorer sections of society, or which are intended to be redistributive, or which constitute pure public goods, or which produce general as well as individual benefits. Charging may also encourage an inefficient underuse of public facilities (Bennett, 1980, p. 292).

Grants

Grants from higher-level governments to regions, provinces and municipalities may be categorized in different ways. The commonest division is into specific or general. Specific grants are related to particular services and are calculated according to the expenditure incurred on a particular function such as police or roads. The revenue from such a source may only be used for the function specified and often there are strings attached, such that the money will only be paid over if certain conditions laid down by the donor government are met. General or block grants can, in contrast, be spent on whatever functions local authorities are legally empowered to provide.

There appears to be a widespread trend towards general grants, both to achieve territorial equality and to provide for greater decentralization. However, the process of shifting from specific to general grants has been taken much further in some states than in others. In the Netherlands, for example 64·3 per cent of grant income is made up of specific grants for police, public works, public transport, industry and commerce, education, culture, social services, public health, housing and civil defence. In England and Wales, on the other hand, over 85 per cent of grant income to local authorities is accounted for by a block grant (Council of Europe, 1981b, pp. 74–6).

Both general and specific grants may have 'matching' requirements attached to them, whereby local governments are required to match all or some proportion of the grant allocated by the centre. The aim here is usually 'to induce a degree of local involvement, commitment, accountability and responsibility for that particular expenditure programme' (Bennett, 1980, p. 325).

Unconditional grants merge into general revenue sharing, under which a proportion of the revenue most efficiently raised by central government is assigned to territorial jurisdictions. As was noted earlier, in practice 'revenue-sharing performs like a block grant programme but with guarantees' and may have similar motives – equalization, national minimum standards, improving the elasticity of local finances, and so on (Bennett, 1980, p. 330).

Alternative categorization of grants is possible since every kind of expenditure incurred by a local level of government could in principle, be grant-aided. Grants might, therefore, be categorized by service (education or roads, for example), by purpose (equalization, to give tax relief, to meet special needs), or by basis of distribution (such as a percentage of local authority expenditure or units of benefit supplied – for example, school attendances or payments per head of population (Foster, Jackman and Perlman, 1980, p. 133).

Grants have certain advantages as a source of subnational revenue as they often allow services to be funded by more progressive forms of taxation than if left to purely local sources. They can also be used as part of national economic stabilization policy. However, they may also induce inefficient expenditure by disguising and distorting the real cost of local services (Bennett, 1980, p. 313). Furthermore, they are widely thought to undermine local autonomy and there is vocal concern in countries where a higher and higher proportion of local revenues come from grants that this trend must inevitably destroy the independence of area governments and reduce them to the status of agents of the centre which is the paymaster.

Grants certainly seem to have transformed the financial position for subnational governments in many contemporary states. In Western Europe, with the exception of West Germany, 'one of the consequences of the rising expenditure of local government has been an increasing financial dependence upon central government' (Newton, 1980a, p. 11). From 1950 to the mid-1970s grants from higher authorities as a source of local income increased from nil to 20 per cent in Denmark, 5 to 25 per cent in Italy, 14 to 19 per cent in Norway, 15 to 24 per cent in Sweden, and 25 to 44 per cent in the UK (Newton, 1980a, p. 10). In the USA federal aid as a percentage of state and local expenditures increased from 18 per cent in 1969 to 28 per cent in 1977. There is also an increasing dependence of local governments on both the states and the federal government. In fact federal money is essential to the continuance of local government in some areas (McKay, 1980).

However, it is important not to exaggerate the dependence of municipalities on higher level of governments. This can happen if the information is presented in certain ways. In the UK, for example, the position looks much worse if grants are presented as a proportion of relevant expenditure, rather than a proportion of total revenues. While the rates have declined as a percentage of local income, and grants have increased, the increase is not as dramatic as it seems when local government income from sales, fees, charges and trade are excluded. So a declining rate revenue has been offset by both increased grant and increased revenues from other sources (Newton, 1980b).

Loans

The significance and cost of loans as a source of local income varies from country to country. So debt repayments and interest charges make varying demands on current expenditure. The financial squeeze is greatest in countries with high interest rates, a high level of capital-intensive operations by local governments, and a propensity to finance capital expenditure by borrowing (Newton, 1980a).

Expenditure

Although it is true to say that a general feature of decentralization in contemporary states is a high level of dependency on 'superior' governments, there are some important exceptions to this. Their significance will be considered below. What has happened in general is that expenditure has outpaced revenue from purely local sources of income. Local expenditure in Western European states, for example, has experienced a higher rate of growth than central government expenditure and GNP. A comparison of Western nations generally shows a convergence of lower-level expenditure in federal states towards approximately 40 per cent of total public expenditure and between 16 to 20 per cent of GDP; and towards 35 per cent of expenditure in unitary states, or between 5 and 7 per cent of GDP (Bennett, 1980, p. 274). In most countries central government expenditure as a proportion of total public spending has fallen since the Second World War. Only a minority of states, including Ireland, Norway, Switzerland and Nigeria, show an opposite trend. Examples of the main trend in unitary and federal states are shown in Table 6.4.

In the UK local expenditure increased in real terms by 900 per cent between 1900 and 1975. Current expenditure per capita increased by about 850 per cent and capital expenditure by about 2,100 per cent. While local expenditure amounted to 3 per cent of GNP in 1870, this had reached 18 per cent in 1975. Over the past hundred years local expenditure as a proportion of total government expenditure has fluctuated, but it rose between 1945 and 1975 to more than 35 per cent (Foster, Jackman and Perlman, 1980, pp. 77–81).

However, since the start of the world recession in 1974–5 there have been changes in local financial trends in many Western states. As public expenditure as a percentage of GNP has grown more slowly or even declined, the higher growth rate of local and regional expenditure compared to GNP or total government spending has been replaced by a stable ratio (as in France) or a decrease (as in Austria, West Germany, Ireland, Italy, Switzerland and the UK). This is mainly the result of a relative reduction in public investment, particularly by local authorities. The faster growth of central government spending compared with earlier periods is explained by the need for programmes to support the economy and for higher social insurance expenditure (Council of Europe, 1981b).

Since the recession, too, there have been changes which have overall tended to reduce the proportion of local expenditure finaced by higher-level authorities. This is still, however, a matter for concern in a number of countries and will be returned to later. In the meantime, what has led to the enormous financial significance of decentralized governments?

The first factor to be noted is the growth of responsibilities falling to subnational governments in all states. There has been an increase in both the quantity and quality of services provided (Newton, 1980a, pp. 27ff.). Local and regional government everywhere is above all the 'handmaiden of the welfare state'

Table 6.4   *National Government Expenditure as a Percentage of Total in Unitary and Federal States.*

	1950	1973
Unitary States		
Austria	73·0	37·1
Belgium	66·9	49·0
France	53·7 (1960)	45·6
Sweden	54·3	32·0
UK	72·5	56·3
Federal States		
Australia	79·9	55·6
Canada	54·7	41·9
USA	54·4	38·3
West Germany	35·2	20·9

Source: Foster, Jackman and Perlman (1980).

coping with the rapid expansion of health, education and welfare services under pressure from changes in the age structure of the population (Sharpe, 1981b, p. 15). At the same time, these governments have been under increasing pressure to provide services at a centrally determined minimum standard. It may be noted, in preparation for the discussion of the imbalance between expenditure and resources below, that when locally provided services are redistributive in character, demand is disproportionately great in the poorest areas, leading to an even greater imbalance between resources and needs (Sharpe, 1981b, p. 16).

Urbanization and the growth in car ownership have also been sources of 'service pressure' on local-level governments. As societies have become more urbanized, local governments have had to cope with the negative externalities created by high population densities and the urban population's disproportionate need for public goods compared with rural populations. There has also been the high cost of urban renewal in the older cities of industrial societies (Sharpe, 1981b; Jackson, Meadows and Taylor, 1982).

Another major source of pressure on area government's financial resources, and a cause of what some regard as a 'fiscal crisis', is inflation. Inflation is often thought to have a disproportionate significance for local governments because of the tendency during periods of inflation for labour costs to increase more rapidly than other factors of production (Newton, 1980a, p. 35). Local government, because of the nature of the services it provides, tends to be labour intensive. The 'productivity' of local services is thus likely to be lower than in the private sector. This combined with the high cost of land and buildings, both important to local government activities, squeeze resources even further. However, there is, in principle, no reason why the prices of goods and services purchased by local government or the wages paid to local government employees should increase more rapidly relative to other prices in times of inflation (Foster, Jackman and Perlman, 1980, p. 383). Indeed, in the UK, wages and salaries decreased as a percentage of local government expenditure between 1963 and 1977 (Newton, 1980a, p. 106). What have increased are debt charges. Steadily increasing interest rates are particularly important when local governments have high borrowing requirements, as when capital expenditure has to be financed by loans.

Overall, the picture is one of subnational government costs rising at a faster rate than national government costs and at a faster rate than local government incomes. The next question, then, is why should local-level governments not simply impose levels of taxation on their populations in line with the costs of the services which are being demanded. Why should it be necessary for a growing proportion of these costs to be met by financial contributions from central governments?

The Financial Dependency of Area Governments

Expenditure Growth
Income from local taxation has increased at a slower rate than expenditure in many countries, resulting in a growth in the level of central government financial assistance. This arouses fears of a reduction in local autonomy, and certainly a number of countries report increasing levels of central control coincident with growing financial dependency. For example, Belguim has witnessed a strengthening in supervisory control by the state. Financial assistance in Luxembourg has been accompanied by central control. In the Netherlands municipalities are required to submit their budgets to the provincial executive for approval. Limits have been placed on the extent to which local taxes in Ireland may be increased from year to year. Other countries have experienced similar trends (Council of Europe, 1981b, p. 89).

Federal states appear to experience 'fiscal mismatch' as much as unitary ones. Federal systems have found it impossible to keep a balance between the distribution of tax resources and the distribution of expenditure responsibilities. It is usually the case that national governments are stronger financially than regional governments which tend to have more functions to perform than their tax resources can cope with. As Reagan and Sanzone (1981) put it for the USA 'the most expensive domestic functions are for the most part the responsibility of the lower levels of government'. Here, as elsewhere, it is generally easier for the national government to increase its revenues each year than for state and local governments to do so, though the burden of increased demand for public services falls on lower-level jurisdictions.

It is not often feasible politically to centralize functions as a possible solution to the problem. Tax powers could be transferred to bring resources into line with commitments, but this option is likely to strengthen the fiscal inequalities between areas which, again, is usually politically unacceptable. The only remaining option is to transfer cash in the form of grants. In Canada, Australia and the USA, among other federations, grants have increased in importance and constitute a major source of subnational revenue (W. Livingstone, 1968, pp. 125–7).

Revenue-raising Capacity

Thus, the first reason for a higher level of financial dependency is that central governments are generally, though not universally, reluctant to devolve adequate revenue powers to lower-level governments. 'Whilst most Western countries have experienced rapid expansion of services which are best organised at local levels, most of the high yielding revenue sources are usually best organised at national level (especially personal and corporate income tax)' (Bennett, 1980, p. 327).

There appears, in fact, to be a 'remarkably similar' pattern of apportionment of revenue-raising capacity between levels of government regardless of the type of constitution. In most states the central share of tax revenues is between 80 and 90 per cent of total revenues. The exceptions to this are Switzerland, West Germany and Canada, where central government's share of revenues falls below 50 per cent. When compared with the expenditure responsibilities of lower-level governments 'there is a marked difference in the apportionment of revenue-raising capacity and expenditure responsibility between different levels of government in all countries'. Hence the need for intergovernmental transfers (Bennett, 1980, p. 275).

Furthermore, central governments may decide that certain of the characteristics of local taxes are politically undesirable and seek to avoid them by imposing restrictions on existing revenue powers and compensating the local government in the form of grants. Revenue sharing and grants in the USA, West Germany, Australia, Switzerland and Canada have, in part, been designed to reduce the burden of regressive local taxes (Bennett, 1980, p. 327). In the UK one of the reasons why local revenues have not kept up with expenditure is that central governments have imposed constraints. For example, the burden of rates on specific groups has been eased at different times: agriculture in the 1890s, industry in 1921, and domestic ratepayers in 1966. 'Since the Second World War an unconscious principle seems to have emerged which has had the effect of increasing grant to maintain an average domestic rate increase as an acceptable proportion of personal disposable income' (Foster, Jackman and Perlman, 1980, p. 142).

Local revenues tend to be limited to a very small number of sources (the USA is exceptional in delegating all or part of nearly every revenue source to local or intermediate levels of government – Bennett, 1980, p. 285). The UK is alone among Western European states in devolving only one local tax. Elsewhere local government systems have up to five major sources of revenue (Newton, 1980a, p. 101). Sweden, Denmark and Norway rely largely on one type of local tax but it provides a high proportion of local income. The Dutch, on the other hand, devolve a considerable range of taxation powers to municipalities but they only contribute between 4·4 and 5·7 per cent of local government income (Council of Europe, 1981b).

It is, in fact, the elasticity of local taxes rather than their number that is the crucial factor. Comparative data confirms that 'in those countries where a tax on incomes is the principal local tax, local and regional authorities receive a large proportion of their total income from local taxation' rather than government grants. Where land and property taxes are the main sources of local revenue the proportion is far smaller (Council of Europe, 1981b, p. 86).

The main problem for local government systems is that while taxes on incomes provide for greater financial self-sufficiency (and some would argue, greater financial independence) because they are bouyant in the face of inflation, the lion's share of such buoyant or income-elastic taxes tend predominantly to be taken by national government and not devolved to local or intermediate levels. Hence the disproportionate effect that inflation has had on local government, in particular, since the early 1970s.

Local government's dependence on inelastic taxes such as property taxes creates the revenue gap between fast-rising expenditure and slowly rising income, a gap which in Britain has been met by both tax-rate increases and increased grants. A further disadvantage to local government is the political visibility of increased tax rates on indirect taxes at a time of high inflation.

The main reason which national governments tend to give for this reluctance to devolve subnational governments more and different tax powers is that to do so would make it difficult to reduce public spending generally when such reduction constitutes part of national macroeconomic policy (Council of Europe, 1981b). Whether local government spending increases the money supply and is therefore inflationary is, however, an open question and one that often cannot be separated out from a government's ideological objective of restraining the public sector in favour of the private (Prest, 1982; Jackman, 1982).

If it is accepted that the major powers of taxation and expenditure control should rest with the central government in order to manage the economy and plan for a reasonable rate of economic growth, a healthy balance of payments, and an equitable distribution of resources between persons and regions, then the financing of local expenditure increasingly by central grants seems inevitable. However, these assumptions may be (and often are) rejected on the grounds that central demand management is not a necessary condition for economic stabilization or growth, or that control of the economy should not be attempted by governments, or that public expenditure and taxation cannot, in fact, control aggregate demand because of the many factors influencing demand which lie outside government control.

Not surprisingly, the low income-elasticity of local revenue sources produces political pressure from time to time for the devolution of new and more buoyant tax powers to local levels of government. It is generally believed that if a government has to support its spending plans with revenues that it raises from the local populace through its own taxes this will mean people are more aware of the costs of what their elected representatives have decided than if the money comes in the form of a block allocation from a higher level of government. Accountability and ultimately democracy are thereby strengthened.

The nature of the tax, however, needs careful consideration, hence the warning from Foster, Jackman and Perlman who argue that pressure to multiply the number of local taxes in order to increase the buoyancy of local revenue sources is 'of very doubtful political morality' (1980, p. 507) because it amounts to making it *more* difficult for the electorate to appreciate the costs of local services and *less* difficult for governments to conceal the costs of their decisions. This is because the revenue raised from buoyant taxes is less contentious as it flows from automatic rises in tax bills rather than from highly publicized increased tax *rates* in the case of less buoyant taxes.

Territorial Equality

A second reason for the growth in financial dependency on higher-level governments is the political pressure on central governments to equalize living conditions from area to area. This has led, at least as far as most countries in Western Europe are concerned, to a growth in the amount of central government aid to local and regional authorities and a marked tendency for grants to become the major source of finance (Council of Europe, 1981b, p. 43).

The political unacceptability of spatial inequalities in expenditure needs, public service costs and fiscal resources has been the main motive for grant allocations and general revenue sharing in most systems of decentralization. The centre may also wish to discriminate positively between areas to improve the standards of service provision, perhaps in pursuit of a national minimum standard below which it is regarded as politically undesirable for any locality to fall (Bennett, 1980, pp. 325–6). Alternatively, the motive may be to stimulate economic growth and development, often through the provision of costly infrastructure which purely local resources are insufficient to fund. The centre may control industrial location, provide investment grants or preferential loans, or adopt fiscal policies aimed at regional development, such as tax relief to industrialists hiring additional labour. The acceptance by national governments of responsibility for territorial equality, either in the provision of services by decentralized government or through regional planning by national governments, makes it more likely that local governments will become dependent on central grants and less likely that economic planning functions will be devolved to newly established regional governments with territories, populations and resources sufficient to operate on a large scale.

Trading Income

Finally, there are constraints upon lower-level governments on the extent to which they can raise revenues through income-earning services. This again has reduced locally raised income relative to centrally provided income. Economies of scale require some trading services to be operated by regional or even national organizations, such as electricity supply. Where a regional scale of operations is required central governments have often been successful in resisting the creation of intermediate governments to take over such municipal enterprises and place them under democratic management. The centre may also pursue its own political objectives by placing constraints on local services which are income earning, by controlling council-house rents, for example. But most important in capitalist economies are the ideological barriers against public involvement in profit-making enterprise. 'Only in a few countries [in Western Europe] are municipalities allowed into those parts of the economy which are capable of making a profit for private business' (Newton, 1980a, p. 149). Another reason why so little thought is given to the potential for municipal enterprise is the formidable legal barriers that have to be overcome before municipalities can embark on such activities, especially in local government systems which operate under the *ultra vires* principle.

Dependency and Autonomy

The conventional wisdom is that the more subnational governments are dependent on central financial allocations, the more centralized the whole system is bound to become. Accountability of local governments to their electorates is thereby undermined, since locally elected representatives no longer control the spending for which they are ultimately held responsible through the ballot box. Although seemingly a common-sense view, this interpretation of the impact of financial arrangements on intergovernmental relations and levels of centralization hardly does justice to the complexity of the problem.

In analysing the impact of grants and other allocations to local and regional governments it is difficult to know what interpretation to place upon the financial behaviour of the recipient governments. It is possible to show that there is considerable variation in the policies and expenditure programmes of local governments in receipt of central grants. This suggests that grants do not undermine autonomy. However, conformity between governments might not necessarily indicate that the centre is calling the tune. There is no way of ensuring that local authorities do not choose to be similar: 'local government could use its freedom to conform' (Foster, Jackman and Perlman, 1980, p. 355). If uniformity of behaviour might be freely chosen, so diversity might be the result of other factors than local choices. Here, too, it is important to disentangle the differential effects of statutory obligations carried out in different circumstances, such as educational provision in areas with different age structures, from more direct central control over specific authorities.

Nor should it be assumed that the level and scope of central control is dependent on the centre performing the role of paymaster. Controls are unlikely to disappear even if subnational governments were somehow to become entirely self-sufficient. This statement probably applies more to unitary than federal states, however. In the latter, it would be far more difficult for the national government to take powers that were completely unrelated to financial contributions to subnational revenues. Since we have no examples of total fiscal separation between territorial levels of government, the most that can be said is that there certainly appears to be no correlation between level of dependency and level of control. In France, for example, we are told that 'a distinctive feature of French subsidies to local government is that they have constantly decreased for the past decade while it is fairly clear that the grip of the administrative structure on communes has not' (Ashford, 1980, p. 207). Similarly, Britain is an example of a state in which central control has increased in recent years as the proportion of grant aid has decreased. At the same time as the rate of grant towards relevant expenditure has fallen from 65·6 per cent in 1976/7 to 56 per cent in 1982/3 the central government has taken statutory powers to determine what each local authority should spend so that ministers can vary the amount of grant according to a 'standard' level of expenditure determined by the centre. Individual authorities who 'overspend' can be penalized so that central government is not merely concerned with the general financial framework of local government but with particular decisions made by particular authorities (Meadows, 1981). The central government has also obtained the statutory power to prevent local authorities increasing their local taxes to compensate for grant which is withheld because the authority is spending more than the centre's expenditure target.

There is a sense in which grants strengthen decentralized governments by enabling them to perform functions that they would otherwise be unable to perform. It might therefore be argued that at least some, if not all, of the centralization that accompanies grant dependency is offset by the wider range of matters in which area governments can intervene. Against this it may be argued that, if 'proper' tax powers were devolved, local governments could operate a wide range of functions under the discipline of their own revenues.

This, however, overlooks the extent to which the functions of area governments have other qualities. A greater dependency on grants may arise from the use of local government for important redistributive purposes, as when a growing proportion of grants in decentralized revenues reflects a centrally imposed uniformity of standards in education, housing, personal social services and similar public provision within the welfare state. If local government is used for redistributive functions without grants, tax-payers with high incomes and low needs for public services will migrate to areas with low levels of public expenditure. In this respect, central government may be said to 'neutralise some of the market-simulating properties that would arise if local authorities were free to express their own preferences' (Foster, Jackman and Perlman, 1980, p. 208).

Financial dependency and any centralization that flows from it may thus be the inevitable consequence (and perhaps contradiction) of using decentralized government in the pursuit of redistributive political objectives. The less the central control and financial support for decentralized government, the less the redistribution that can take place. The USA would seem to bear this out: 'Not only are the central cities aware of the emigration of the more affluent to suburbs that tax them less, but the suburbs employ land-use zoning to keep out those who would be a particular burden on their services' (Foster, Jackman and Perlman, 1980, p. 208).

Central government's 'empowering' of lower-level governments to provide goods and services and make income transfers between sections of the population thus strengthens the tendency for inadequate and unevenly distributed tax bases to be compensated for by central government grants. More than anything, fiscal decentralization reminds us how political the problem is, arising as it does from fundamental choices about material equality and welfare.

When discussing the effect of grants on autonomy it is important to note what appears to be a widespread move away from specific grants in preference for block or general grants. This understandably provides area governments with more freedom in deciding how the money should be spent. Indeed, comparative studies of European systems reveal that financial controls over both current expenditure and borrowing to finance capital expenditure are tending to be relaxed in other ways. 'The general trend is for detailed central control over the current expenditure of local and regional authorities to be replaced by central government recommendations on rates of growth of local and regional expenditure' (Council of Europe, 1981b, p. 90). While in Western Europe the volume of local authority borrowing has become subject to greater central control, there is a tendency for specific controls over individual schemes to be withdrawn. And in a growing number of countries increasingly formalized procedures for consultations between different levels of government on volumes of expenditure and methods to apportion central financial assistance are being introduced. 'The tendency throughout Western Europe is for co-operative decision-making to replace instructions, and for specific directives to be replaced by general directives, agreements and recommendations' (Council of Europe, 1981b, p. 94). The UK may well be swimming against the European tide in this respect.

There are those who would argue that the trend towards block grants is absolutely crucial in the financial arrangements of decentralized government since the need for local autonomy and political responsibility can, in this way, be reconciled with a high level of dependence on central allocations. Grants, or elements of grants, which are 'unhypothecated' are to be welcomed as they allow local authorities to spend their money as they wish. Indeed, in principle, area governments could be financed 100 per cent by higher-level governments and still be free to determine their own spending priorities. If local governments are controlled, it will be because of other kinds of central intervention that are not dependent on financial donations. So unhypothecated grants should not be assumed to draw centralization in their train, as the Layfield Committee on British local finance assumed they would. Cripps and Godley, for example (1976), argued that, leaving aside non-financial controls, 'even if local government were entirely dependent for its income on central government money, provided the grant is not hypothecated, the electorate is in a position to call its elected members to account and replace them with others if they would rather have the money spent in some other way' (p. 11).

Foster, Jackman and Perlman agree that, in theory, unhypothecated grants could leave local authorities almost complete discretion, with elections decided on local issues. They also argue, however, that there is evidence that the higher the proportion of grant in local revenues, the greater the propensity for a local authority to spend. In other words, the grant elasticity of expenditure appears to be positive (1980, pp. 284–302). This, they claim, weakens the Cripps and Godley case and strengthens the Layfield type of argument – that increased grant proportions reduce local incentives to control expenditure.

The argument that the proportion of local revenues coming from block grants is in itself no cause of centralization and loss of local accountability appears strong. Even if local authorities were encouraged to spend more by an increase in their level of dependence on grants this is not incompatible with the local governments deciding on priorities and the local electorate holding their representatives, who constitute that government, accountable for their decisions. Whether the centre decides to control local decisions by other means (such as legislative or administrative direction), or the electorate decides to reward or punish their representatives by reference to other factors than local spending decisions (such as by voting according to national political preferences), depends on other factors than the proportion of local revenues coming from grants.

The centre could also place a ceiling on local expenditure, to be enforced by the sanction of a cut in grant. This would clearly be much more difficult to enforce if local authorities met a substantial part of their expenditure from their own financial sources rather than from grants. This again lends support to the argument that grants (even unhypothecated block grants) facilitate central control and therefore, at least potentially, make dependent governments vulnerable to centralization.

However, comparative experience indicates that even budget ceilings can be enforced by other than financial means if a central government so decides. There is nothing to prevent the central government of a unitary state, if it has the political power, from obtaining the right to approve the budgets of individual authorities and making it illegal for a subordinate government to spend until central executive approval has been received. Again, control in such a situation would be independent of the percentage of decentralized revenue coming from the centre.

A number of other arguments have been put forward to challenge or modify the discussion so far. First, George Jones shows that the fundamental flaw in the 'unhypothecated grant' argument is that it is based on a restricted concept of political responsibility. In discussing the effects of grants on the responsiveness of local decision-makers to their electorates rather than to the central executive, the idea of responsibility must be widened beyond spending decisions to include the financing of those decisions. Local decision-makers might be responsible for allocating grants to priorities which they and not the centre have decided upon. But for local democracy to operate fully they need to be answerable for the raising of taxes to finance their budgets. When they are dependent on grants, local decision-makers will try to place responsibility for their spending decisions on the centre. Rather than facing the electorate for demands for taxes, they will concentrate on pressuring central government with demands for more grant income (Jones, 1978, pp. 71–2).

It might be thought that this problem could be overcome by the so-called 'gearing' effect of grants. A high level of block grant means that local taxes contribute only a small proportion of local revenues. Therefore, a marginal increase in expenditure will have a larger disproportionate effect on taxes, because the larger the contribution to income from local taxes, the smaller the percentage increase needed to provide additional revenue. The conclusion drawn from the 'gearing' effect is that a high percentage of local income from block grants makes local electorates more aware of the financial consequences of expenditure because a relatively large percentage change in local tax rates is required to finance an increase in expenditure.

Against this it has been argued (Jones, 1978) that because a small change in grant allocation made by central government – whether to the total grant, the formula for distribution, or its actual distribution – will produce major consequences locally, such changes mean that it is more difficult for the public and elected members to assess whether the local financial position is the result of local authority decisions, central government decisions, or of 'fortuitous changes in the grant'. So a high level of grant cannot be said to strengthen through the gearing effect the extent to which local taxes reflect local spending decisions. And it is this relationship which, it is held, is crucial to the credibility of local government.

Other qualifications to the picture so far presented of the impact of grants on intergovernmental relations and local accountability include, first, the claim that grants 'buy' the central government the right to audit, inspect, supervise, initiate, criticize and control. Secondly, grants influence the distribution of expenditure between services by lending financial support so that services where local expenditure is matched by grant aid are less likely to be curtailed than those financed wholly locally. Thirdly, grants place particular services more firmly on the political agenda. Proposals for expenditure will be considered more seriously if grant aid is promised. Fourthly, grant systems bring professionals from the different levels of government together to bargain over plans and priorities, so that the influence of grants is never entirely at the discretion of either local or central government. Fifthly, whatever the truth of the matter, central grants encourage the belief among local decision-makers that 'he who pays calls the tune' and such beliefs distort the relationship between the electorate and their elected representatives.

Conclusion

The conclusion that is likely to be arrived at after an examination of how decentralized government is financed, apart, that is, from the view that the relationship between grant characteristics and local autonomy needs research instead of assertion and counter-assertion (Stewart, 1980a) is that financial arrangements, and particularly dependence on grants, cannot be isolated from other intergovernmental relationships.

Within a unitary state the financial involvement of central in local government is likely to be complementary to statutory authority and administrative power (Page, 1981, p. 43). Within federations, the role of the intermediate level of government, with its constitutional status, complicates the relationship of grant-aided expenditure to decentralization even further. In the USA, for example, recent changes in the balance of power between the three levels of government have meant that the power of the states has increased relative to both federal and local governments. State revenues have proved very resilient during the 1970s, coming mainly from sales and income taxes, in contrast with local government's dependence on property taxes. State governments have become increasingly professionalized. Fiscal constraints at the federal level and consequent reductions in federal aid, particularly to local government, means that local authorities will have to seek aid from the states. So while there has been a 'genuine decentralisation of power' from federal to state government, there is centralization from local to state government, an ironic consequence of stronger states (McKay, 1982, pp. 21–2). The effect of grant dependency will be contingent upon other aspects of intergovernmental relations. There is no simple correlation between central funding and central control.

More importantly, the subject of local finance cannot be isolated from politics, either in the sense of dominant ideology or the differential impact of fiscal policies on the interests of different sections of society. When President Reagan attempts to shift power from federal to state governments with accompanying reductions in federal funds to the states, this cannot be disassociated from the political interests behind the transfer of tax burdens from national to local levels and the adverse effects on the welfare system. Similarly, monetarism in the UK and its effects on local government spending are not unrelated to the interests which benefit from reduced public expenditure, particularly in the health, education and welfare spheres, and those which stand to lose by such changes. As with all other aspects of decentralization, final decisions about financial arrangements are political rather than technical.

7
Decentralized Institutions

Introduction

The decentralization of political power within states requires the creation of decision-making institutions. If a region or locality is to be to some degree self-governing, decision-makers will have to be recruited from the area concerned. Once it has been decided that some part of public policy in an area is to be directed by people from the locality rather than by a civil servant posted there from departmental headquarters, an institution has to be created to consititute official and legitimate procedures for arriving at authoritative decisions. This applies equally to federalism and devolution.

National practices vary enormously and generalization is extremely difficult. A useful distinction to start with is between elected and appointed decision-makers. The former obtain office in rule-making institutions by success in electoral competition. The latter are selected from the locality by a central authority and appointed to the managing body of a public service. Both types of institution so created are usually collective and corporate bodies functioning in the manner of committees. Procedures in the elected body are likely to make it approximate more or less closely to a legislature. Procedures in the appointed body, on the other hand, are likely to be closer to those of a board of directors than a legislature. Since both types of office holder will invariably be inhabitants of the area to be governed the potential for local influence is greater than in a system of decentralization through field administration, though political recruitment by election gives scope for greater local autonomy than appointment where selection and dismissal are in the hands of the centre (Smith and Stanyer, 1976, p. 108).

Democratic Decentralization

Within systems of decentralized representative government many other variations may be observed. The type of decision-making body most commonly found is the multifunctional council of elected representatives. Most subnational elected councils form unicameral legislatures. However, the Yugoslav commune has three chambers, one chamber being representative of the population generally, the others representing those employed in economic and agricultural enterprises and co-operatives (see below). The constituent governments of federations are more likely than local governments to have bicameral legislatures. In most unitary states and within the regions of federations, however, it is usually thought unnecessary to provide for functional or territorial representation by means of a second municipal chamber, though a case could quite reasonably be made for such a practice. Since a majority of national governments do without second chambers (Blondel, 1973, p. 32) bicameralism is unlikely to spread to decentralized government.

Secondly, a distinction may be drawn between direct or indirect methods of election (or what Stanyer refers to as a primary or secondary local government: Stanyer, 1976, pp. 30–1). In Britain local councils are all directly elected even though a two-tier system operates. It thus falls to the adult inhabitants of a district not only to elect a district council but also to elect, together with the electorates of other districts, a county or regional council. Under a secondary system the constituent units nominate some of their members to the secondary body. In India, for example, while the village *panchayats* are directly elected, the councils at block and district levels are composed of the chairmen from the lower-level councils. In Britain secondary authorities are not used in the main system of local government, but some special-purpose bodies, such as the Inner London Education Authority, are constituted in this way. Indirect election may also exist alongside appointment by the centre as a method of recruitment to the managing bodies of some local services. Local authorities can nominate members to the water authority set up for their region while other members are appointed by the appropriate minister of the central government. A variation on this which really removes it from the category of indirect election is found in the British national health service in which health authorities contain members appointed by the minister from nominees of the constituent local authorities. Perhaps the most striking use of indirect election is found in the organization of the British police outside London. Two-thirds of the members of the police committees for each force are local councillors and one-third are magistrates who are appointed from among themselves by the magistrates of the area.

The third major distinction which may be drawn is between multifunctional and single-purpose elected governments. The commonest form of local government is the multi-purpose council but in some political systems these share the field of local government with single-purpose elected bodies as well as appointed boards. In the USA, for example, alongside multi-purpose local authorities there are some 30,000 school boards, some elected and some appointed, as well as boards for health, parks, libraries, planning, housing and public utilities. A decentralized socialist system has led in Yugoslavia to the creation of 'a sort of outer zone' to the communes, in which *ad hoc* functions are performed by self-management councils and other institutions for planning, health, social welfare and public utilities (Pusic, 1975). The functions which multi-purpose governments perform are too numerous and varied to permit any safe generalizations. Local government services are sometimes classified for convenience into *protective* (fire protection, police, public health, sanitation, consumer protection, and so on), *welfare* (education, social services for the aged, poor, handicapped and other groups 'at risk', libraries, and so on) and *environmental* (planning, water, roads, transport and other public utilities, parks for example). There is, of course, no set pattern of functions in the states and provinces of federations. The picture is further complicated by the varying location of 'residual powers'.

The case against the use of single-purpose governments is a powerful one. Services which affect the local community as much as others need to be co-ordinated with those to which they relate closely. A single government needs to establish priorities between a range of services depending on local needs. The allocation of resources between services needs to be debated openly and democratically. A special-purpose authority only sees one facet of the citizen's life. It does not see them 'in the round' as the councillors of a general-purpose authority do (Foster, Jackman and Perlman, 1980, p. 585).

Specialization does not necessarily ensure greater expertise than a multi-purpose government. Effectiveness is only improved when one service is left to compete with a multi-service government and would not be a case for specialization if a multitude of *ad hoc* bodies was created. There is no obvious reason why a service should be depoliticized by setting up special agencies even assuming this to be a desirable objective. Nor is the question of optimum areas so easily settled that multi-purpose areas are necessarily bad. Indeed, even if all special-purpose authorities operated to the same geographical areas (a highly unlikely outcome) political and administrative co-ordination is still difficult, economies of management are lost and power shifts from politicians to officers, an important factor to be considered in the context of accountability (Foster, Jackman and Perlman, 1980). Accountability is strengthened when responsibility for priorities, which is what politics is about, is concentrated. Dispersing functions among single-purpose authorities weakens democratic control (Regan, 1977, pp. 235–8).

While it may be thought that public accountability is improved by not having to elect a representative whose stand on some issues is approved but not on others, the multiplication of special-purpose authorities can cause confusion and apathy. Stronger accountability may stem from being able to relate revenue more easily to expenditure and thus identify costs. The preferences of the median voter may be better expressed with single-purpose authoritites, thus bringing the expression of local preferences closer to the Tiebout equilibrium (Foster, Jackman and Perlman, 1980, p. 585). But if the central government's span of control is reduced by having fewer, bigger authorities, central control would be easier.

Privileged socio-economic classes may benefit by removing a service such as education from the jurisdiction of a government that might not give it the priority they want, or develop it in the way they want. To organize services on this basis is to acknowledge the power of vested interests, not the strength of administrative principles. This is precisely the kind of power which determines how such decisions are made. On balance, the multi-purpose government would seem to serve local democracy better than a multiplicity of special-purpose authorities.

The fourth major contrast in systems of devolution is between single-tier and multi-tier systems. A system of local government may be organized on the basis of unitary authorities, whereby a state is divided into areas in which 'all-purpose' local governments exercise all the powers permitted to local authorities by the country's laws. This was the system proposed for Britain by the last Royal Commission on local government. It was the system which Nigeria adopted in 1976. Alternatively, a 'tiered' system is found in which the country is first divided into areas for functions believed to require large populations and territories. These are then further divided, perhaps more than once, to give a Chinese-box effect of areas within areas, each responsible for an appropriate range of services. England and Wales are currently divided into counties and districts. Scotland is divided into regions and districts. Many districts are further subdivided into parishes or communities. The reform of local government often alters the geographical pattern. In Yugoslavia between 1955 and 1966 the system was transformed from a four-tier structure of provinces, districts, communes and local 'people's committees' into a unitary system of communes. Large cities and conurbations increasingly require complex (multi-tiered) structures of metropolitan government (Leemans, 1970, pp. 161–4). Tokyo, London and Toronto are cities which have settled for a two-tier system of municipal government.

Decisions about the territorial structure of local government are highly charged politically. Conflicting interests seek different benefits from structures in which rural, suburban and urban groups, with their different class affiliations, stand to gain or lose depending on how the boundaries are drawn and the powers allocated. In the USA, for example, 'the creation of either a single government or an upper-tier unit with substantial powers is perceived as a threat by strong political interests, who are convinced that a metropolitan government would control sensitive functions, such as housing, land-use and police, and redistribute resources to their disadvantage' (Zimmerman, 1980, p. 58). Reorganization in Britain has similarly reflected the alignment of urban authorities with the Labour Party and rural authorities with the Conservatives. A unitary system proved unacceptable to the Conservatives 'as the emigration of the upper social groups from the city to the country had the effect of making the cities more homogeneously working-class and reinforcing the Conservative leadership in the counties' (Norton, 1980, p. 267). The capacity of urban and metropolitan governments to fall under the control of working-class political organizations is a constant problem for Conservative governments at the centre, as the case of England's metropolitan authorities in 1984 shows.

An alternative to the creation of an intermediate tier of government between centre and locality is co-operation between lower-level governments to co-ordinate the provision of services over large areas when this is deemed necessary. Sometimes such joint arrangements become so important that they constitute, in effect, a new tier of municipal or metropolitan government. They may also be used to draw private interests into municipal government as in the French *syndicats* of communes, *départements*, chambers of commerce, agricultural interests and other non-governmental associations.

Joint action by neighbouring municipalities is usually taken for a specific service in order to provide the optimum catchment area, although joint action for regional economic planning obviously has implications for many local services. Co-operative arrangements may establish purely advisory bodies which make recommendations to their constituent municipalities, especially in the field of planning. But joint authorities may be endowed with corporate status and executive powers. Co-operation is of particular significance in metropolitan areas and joint authorities with power to take decisions binding on their constituent municipalities are found, as in the case of the Rhine Estuary District Authority, Rotterdam, the Greater Hanover Federation and the Greater Stockholm Planning Board (Leemans, 1970, pp. 122–61).

Finally, systems of devolved government and federations vary in respect of the executive institutions found at regional and local levels. In federations the executive arrangements of the constituent governments usually follow those of the national government. In the USA, for example, the gubernatorial system at state level corresponds to the presidential system at national level. However, most states have elected officers other than the governor, and relations between executive and legislature do not replicate those in Washington. In Canada, the provincial executive follows the prime ministerial pattern of Cabinet government. When Nigeria emerged from military rule in 1979 with a federal constitution based on the American model, each state had a gubernatorial executive in contrast to the Cabinet system of the post-independence constitution. In the USSR the praesidia and councils of ministers of the fifteen republics replicate the Praesidium of the USSR Supreme Soviet and the USSR Council of Ministers.

At local level the pattern of executive institutions varies enormously. A version of the gubernatorial system is found when the chief executive of a municipal authority is directly elected and exercises considerable executive powers. In some cities of the USA, for example, the municipal executive is headed by an elected mayor, following the principle of the separation of powers. Mayors have their own powers that can be used against the elected municipal councils, such as veto rights over council ordinances and the right to appoint departmental heads. Such a system seems to be associated with urban areas in which party politics are hard fought and class divisions strong.

In France, too, the mayors of communes are much more than

the figureheads they are in England and some American cities that do not operate the 'strong' mayor–council system. They have independent powers to appoint officials and make by-laws. In addition, they exercise powers on behalf of the state. They are, however, indirectly elected by the council from among its members and to this very limited extent are comparable to the mayors of the English rather than American cities (Ridley and Blondel, 1964, pp. 94–5).

An alternative means of concentrating executive power in municipalities is to professionalize it. In its strongest form this is the 'city manager' system found in the American cities where party politics is weak and where the dominant ideology seeks to depoliticize local government and turn it into a matter of professional judgement and corporate management. Legislative and executive authority resides with the elected council, but the direction and co-ordination of administration is in the hands of a manager appointed by the council. The manager is responsible for all administration, including the appointment of heads of departments and the preparation of budgets. In theory a bureaucrat, in practice the city manager is bound to exercise considerable political power. The distinction between the political (elected) executive and administrative (appointed) one inevitably becomes very blurred: 'the very nature of their positions obliges city managers to formulate policy proposals for council consideration and to guide them through the legislative process the way other public executives do' (Kaufman, 1963, p. 49).

One form of executive, the *commission*, virtually abandons representative democracy in pursuit of executive efficiency. Originating in the USA but going out of fashion the commission which runs the municipality is, in effect, a directly elected Cabinet. A very small number of commissioners are elected to run particular urban services, such as health, public works and finance. Collectively they form the legislative branch of the municipal authority, enacting by-laws, levying taxes and voting expenditure. The decline of this system is accounted for by its failure to achieve the co-ordination required and its lack of representative qualities.

The commissioner system resembles, to some extent, a ministerial form of executive without legislative responsibility. It is natural that some systems of local government should combine the principle of elected representation through large councils with a 'portfolio' councillor arrangement by which individual councillors take responsibility for designated departments and areas of council policy. They thus correspond to the ministers of a parliamentary system. Where party politics is strong, such portfolio councillors are likely to be senior members of the majority party and collectively to form a Cabinet. Such a system has the advantage of clarifying responsibility and providing a role for 'back-benchers'. The portfolio councillor system was used in parts of Nigeria prior to, and immediately following, independence and has survived in the office of supervising councillor, the chairman of a small committee responsible for the political direction of a major department or area of policy. In the Italian 'special' regions the regional councils elect juntas of 'assessors' who are responsible for specific departments. In the ordinary regions responsibility is collective (Evans, 1980).

An alternative to individual responsibility for specific municipal services and departments is collective responsibility through a committee system. This is a characteristic feature of British local government. Each department or group of departments is headed by a committee of councillors. There is thus a clear contrast with the ministerial form of accountability at national level. Council government is, in this respect, quite unlike parliamentary government. However, something approaching ministerial and Cabinet government may emerge under conditions of party control when key committee chairmanships are taken by senior members of the majority party who then dominate the major policy and co-ordinating committees of the council, such as that for finance or corporate policy.

Municipal government moves even closer to Cabinet government with the 'board of control' system as found in the larger cities of Ontario, Canada. Here not only the mayor, but also a small number of controllers are directly elected at large, rather than from wards, by the city's electorate. Mayor and controllers constitute the board and have strong executive and legislative powers. In Montreal and Quebec Cabinet government is also approximated to by giving the mayor power to select members of an executive committee from among members of the elected council.

Hybrid versions of the above models abound, making each system of local government unique. For example, some of the features of the city manager system have been introduced into British local governments by authorities that have appointed chief executives with overall responsibility for the co-ordinated planning of council services. The parallel should not be drawn too strongly, however, not least because the relation between most chief executives and the heads of departments has remained ambiguous and uncertain. Several cities in the USA combine mayoral with managerial forms in a wide range of executive systems that confer varying degrees of power on the mayor and chief administrative officer. All executive arrangements at the municipal level reflect different and often conflicting political values: representation, professionalism, leadership, accountability, and so on. Considerable variation also exists from country to county in respect of electoral systems, the recruitment and powers of chief executives, committee systems, the use of co-opted members, working procedures, the size of elected councils, delegation to officers and even the scope for direct democracy, as in those Swiss cantons in which all citizens entitled to vote constitute a 'municipal assembly' (Council of Europe, 1978).

Appointed Agencies

The use of special-purpose bodies outside the main structure of government has spread to the subnational level in many contemporary states. They represent another attempt to depoliticize government by handing responsibility for specific community services to appointed boards and commissions. Though the members of such managerial bodies are not field officials of the central bureaucracy, and are drawn from the areas receiving the service, their appointment is usually in the hands of the central executive. This undoubtedly strengthens the control which the centre can wield. Rather than de-politicizing area government, *ad hoc* appointed bodies merely substitute the politics of the centre for the politics of the area, as when in January 1983 members of England's 192 health authorities were 'advised' by the Department of Health and Social Security to desist from campaigning against expenditure cuts in the health services or risk losing their seats when their reappointment becomes due. Since the rationale of appointed agencies is that special arrangements are needed for the administration of services which cannot be run jointly with other municipal activities, generalizations are almost by definition impossible.

In the USA, for example, *ad hoc* bodies have proliferated in hostility to forms of general local government. Special agencies are seen as being removed from politics and in the hands of experts (Kaufman, 1963, p. 57). Similarly in Britain the value of local democratic control has been forced to give way to the supposedly greater managerial efficiency of *ad hoc* bodies or the 'need' to take public services out of politics. Between 1946 and

1975 eighty-five organizations were set up to receive powers lost to local government (Dunleavy, 1980b, p. 103). The politics of the ballot box is replaced by the politics of conflicts between vested interests within the *ad hoc* agencies and the central executive. In the national health service, for example, what has been called the syndicalist principle of representation has been adopted at the regional and district levels so that the managing bodies contain representatives of the main medical professions. The other two categories of members are local councillors and lay people with relevant knowledge, experience, or expertise. Decisions are supposed to be arrived at by consensus rather than majority vote. Community representation is limited to toothless community health councils with no executive or managerial functions (Elcock, 1982). Accountability to Parliament through the appropriate minister is a remote possibility, however, as is judical review by the courts. Studies indicate that these particular *ad hoc* bodies serve to protect the interests of the medical professions, rather than the wider public or community interests which ministers or the lay members of health authorities might be said to represent (Haywood and Elcock, 1982).

The water services in England and Wales have similarly been removed from their position within local government and reorganized under regional water authorities in order to 'benefit' from economies of scale and professional management. Reorganization defers to the power of the professionals and adopts a thoroughly managerialist approach to decision-making (Gray, 1982). The managerial rather than the representative role of water authority members has also been emphasized. Though local authorities provide a majority of the members of water authorities, their accountability is more to central than local government, though they are fully accountable to neither. A-political, technical solutions are, in any case, preferred to decisions based on democratic participation.

Britain and the USA are certainly not unique in respect of the values which are sought through the management of community affairs through appointed bodies. They will always be found where dominant sectors of society perceive their interests to be best served by the adoption of a managerialist approach to public services and the location of them at the fringe of the local political arena. However, as far as European and Scandinavian experience is concerned the main use for *ad hoc* boards in recent years has been for advisory or co-ordination functions as a temporary solution to specific administrative problems. It is not all that common to find *ad hoc* executive bodies being set up to run community services (Council of Europe, 1981a, p. 19).

Institutions, Ideology and Decentralization

Something has been shown of the variability of local institutions and practices. The pattern of institutions for decentralized government to be found in a particular state will reflect important aspects of political ideology. These patterns vary when looked at from other perspectives, too – in terms of the day-to-day operation of politics, for example, or relations between the centre and the governmental periphery. Such factors may, at times, conflict with the ideological presuppositions of decentralized government. The following cases show how the pattern of decentralized institutions are shaped by dominant political values within states functioning with different ideological presuppositions. Each pattern of institutions may be said to constitute a model of decentralization.

The Liberal Model
The liberal tradition in local administration is represented by the English model of elected corporate institutions with quasi-autonomous powers, including that of taxation. Overlaid upon a long tradition of borough government having an existence independent of the centre, the reforms of the nineteenth century, which introduced the elective principle, created a distinctive and lasting pattern of institutions for the administration of state functions at the local level. The traditional units of local government – counties, parishes and boroughs – exercised minimal roles, but with a large degree of independence from each other and from the centre (Richards, 1975, p. 11).

Through these historic institutions local governments came to acquire a role in the maintenance of law and order, the administration of justice and the provision of public services, such as highways and poor relief. But their financial and administrative inadequacies in the face of problems created by industrialization and the growth of population led to the establishment of *ad hoc* bodies, such as poor law unions, turnpike trusts and improvement commissioners. The fragmentation of the state at the local level had begun. Additional principles for the organization of local state institutions emerged in the nineteenth century as the power of the new bourgeoisie asserted itself. One was the principle of central control which developed from the supervision of poor relief by a central commission. Another was the election of councillors by ratepayers. The administration of justice was separated from the administration of public services. Consolidated borough funds were established. Multifunctional local authorities subject to a minimum of control were set alongside *ad hoc* bodies under close supervision (Wilson, 1948).

The liberal ideology of local government endows it with two major functions in society: to serve the democratic objectives of participation, education, discussion and consent; and to provide services under such political direction in an efficient manner (Wilson, 1948, p. 12).

These twin objectives persist, not only in the UK but in other developed capitalist states in which democratic local self-government is regarded as consistent with representative government at the national level. However, the emphasis has switched to the criterion of efficiency, and the objectives to be pursued in an efficient manner are not always those laid down by the representatives of local interests. The 1968 Royal Commission on Local Government in England and Wales, for example, argued that the representative quality of local government was as important as its efficiency, though democracy was seen as *dependent* on efficiency.

Canada's programme of municipal reform in the 1960s also, in theory, was seen as consistent with both local democracy and efficiency. The regional municipal programme in Ontario between 1969 and 1974 was designed, according to official statements, to make local government 'as strong and meaningful as possible'. The financial weakness of small authorities had led to the establishment of *ad hoc* bodies which 'obscured accountability'. Local government had to satisfy the two values of 'access' and 'service'. The former meant a system with permitted participation and administration responsive to local needs. Local government should be concerned with more than just 'service delivery problems'. It should be able to deal with 'the quality of life' and environmental conservation. 'Access' clearly required decentralization. Other provincial pronouncements have emphasized this, such as the 1973 budget which referred to the 'goal of enhancing the autonomy of municipalities and broadening the scope for local decision making' (Plunkett, 1980, p. 17). The access principle also indicated the importance of small units of government.

The service principle, however, argued for authorities large enough to perform functions economically and with 'technical adequacy'. This became the dominant principle and the consequent reorganization, it is claimed, 'diminished rather than enhanced citizen access to government' (Plunkett, 1980, p. 16). As in Britain, the municipal reforms were motivated more by technical and bureaucratic criteria reflecting the interests of the central government (the province) than by the local autonomy to which lip-service was paid. The difficulty of balancing 'access' and 'service' criteria in the design of local government systems noted by Plunkett and others in Ontario is directly comparable to the problem encountered in local government reorganization in Britain.

Political ideology in the USA also emphasizes the value of autonomous and viable general-purpose governments at the local level. Such units are supposed to 'be open to citizen participation, achieve accurate representation of citizen interests, and be especially capable of responding to varied local conditions' (Bowen, 1980, p. 241). In the municipalities and townships local autonomy is supported by 'home rule' charters allowing local authorities to exercise all the powers of local self-government, although here, as in the administrative counties, central control by state and federal governments has increased in relation to taxation, borrowing and civic regulations. As we have seen, this presumption in favour of local democracy is tempered in the USA by the existence of numerous special-purpose districts usually with appointed rather than elected governing bodies. The separation of powers is carried over into local government with directly elected mayors in a large number of municipalities. Elsewhere elected councils employ professional city managers as their chief executives.

The Developmental Model
In less-developed countries contemporary ideologies of decentralization have their roots in alien importations. Many parts of the Third World are still visibly affected by their colonial experience, though it would be wrong to think that the imperial powers exported local institutions identical to those employed in the metropolis. While France extended a uniform state apparatus across her empire, Britain experimented with forms of local rule that would never have been tolerated at home.

The British in India, for example, underlined the unitary nature of their rule at the local level by the office of collector in whose hands were concentrated executive, judicial and administrative powers (Subramanian, 1980, p. 584). Centralized rule encouraged a centralist nationalist movement. Democratic self-government on the liberal model in the localities was introduced too late to be regarded as relevant to the new Indian political leadership.

In Africa, local government in the British colonies incorporated traditional authority from administrative and political expediency. Indirect rule first enabled the colonial regime to benefit from the legitimacy assigned to chieftaincy institutions. Later it restricted the development of an indigenous middle class. When independence loomed and local self-government along roughly democratic lines was introduced as a foundation for national democracy, it was again too late to attract the attention of the nationalist leadership. As in India, the framework of the colonial state apparatus was a hierarchy of provincial and district officers which provided the new nationalist governments with as effective an instrument of political control as it had the British.

The French replicated in their colonies the prefectoral system of local administration in the form of *commandants de cercle*. No kind of democratic decentralization was created until the Loi-Cadre of 1956 created an assembly for each territory. After independence the French model of local government was further incorporated, though sometimes without being fully implemented (Subramanian, 1980, p. 587). The educated élite acquired a taste for centralist government from their involvement in French politics.

The general trend since independence has been to ascribe a developmental role to local government and to modify colonial structures to a greater or lesser extent to reflect the ideology of development. Governing bodies often incorporate both local representatives and central nominees (usually government officials). Co-ordination of central field services rather than autonomous policy-making for the locality has become the norm in many post-colonial states. Variations on the colonial prefectoral system persist in Anglophone Africa, though under different guises sometimes as professional chief executives, sometimes as party officials. No distinction is made between central and local functions, funds and staff (Mawhood and Davey, 1980, p. 409). In federal systems the constituent states have lost power to the federal centre.

The French local government tradition has persisted long after independence in Francophone Africa. The continuance of prefectoral systems, responsible for the co-ordination of all state activities, reduces the autonomy of municipal authorities. In some areas, such as some of the urban centres in the Ivory Coast, the role of prefect has been combined with that of mayor, thus reflecting 'the submission of the local responsibility to the national administration' (Cohen, 1980, p. 418). Local elections have not been held and local councils declined and eventually disappeared.

Other innovations adapted from the French, such as centralized regional planning organisations, special district authorities in urban areas and inter-ministerial planning commissions have further reduced the importance of municipal government. As in many other Third World regions, local governments have not been allowed to wield buoyant revenue powers.

Some post-colonial states have attempted to renovate village government in order to secure more widespread popular support for community development and other rural programmes. The most important example is India's system of *panchayati raj*. A two- or three-tier hierarchy has been created with elected institutions at district, block and village level. Only the village *panchayats* are directly elected. The block *panchayat samiti* and district *zila parishad* are indirectly elected. Responsibilities in the fields of agriculture, animal husbandry, the rural infrastructure and social services have been devolved. Many administrative problems have been experienced (Khanna and Bhatnagar, 1980, p. 429). Variations in the distribution of functions between levels, as well as the number of levels used, exist from state to state. But everywhere members of state and federal parliaments are associated with *panchayati raj*, and state governments have retained considerable control over development administration. The *panchayats* are regarded even here more as administrative agents of the state than as politically autonomous bodies. Efforts have been made to de-politicize their activities, but these have not been successful. Political factionalism has been carried over into *panchayati raj* from other parts of the Indian political system. Political consciousness has been strengthened and new élites have created opportunities to further their interests. The rural poor, however, have not experienced much material gain from democratic decentralization.

In the urban areas of India a familiar Western pattern of municipal government is in operation, though characteristically beset with the equally familiar problems of efficiency, honesty, co-ordination and solvency found in all urban sectors of the Third World. Municipal governments consist of elected councils for policy-making and a standing committee for policy planning and the supervision of administration, recognizable to those brought up in the English tradition. The office of commissioner, however, corresponds more to the French prefect than an English chief executive as he is a senior state civil servant responsible for the municipality's administration.

The Communist Model

Although it is an oversimplification to talk of a 'soviet model' of local government, it is possible to identify a number of characteristics which distinguish the local state institutions of socialist societies from those of capitalist and mixed economies.

The first element in the ideology of socialist local organization is the theory of mass participation and control. In principle, all state activities are subject to supervision by democratically elected councils. In the USSR, for example, there are elected soviets for every level in the territorial hierarchy of the state and these are designated by the constitution as the supreme legislative bodies for each level. This 'supremacy' is tempered by a number of factors, not least of which is the large number of deputies who constitute a soviet and their infrequency of meeting.

In the socialist states of Eastern Europe local democracy is an official principle of local state authority (Zawadzka and Zawadski, 1980, p. 362). In Yugoslavia, under the federal constitution of 1974, the commune is designated a self-managing community based on the power of the working class (Pavic, 1980, p. 354). Beneath the communes, at the level of a group of villages or the district of a city, are local community councils for self-managing territorial communities. Representation is on a functional basis. Communal assemblies consist of three chambers: one for 'associated labour' or workers in industry and state agencies; a chamber of local communities; and a socio-political chamber representing workers and citizens in social organizations, youth bodies, the party, trade unions, and so on. The first two chambers are indirectly elected from an electoral college of delegates from constituent organizations. Communal councillors are delegates in that they act 'in conformity with the basic views expressed by their self-managing organisations and communities' and are subject to recall (Pavic, 1980, p. 356). In addition, at the local level, there are self-managing 'communities of interest' for education, science, health, culture, welfare, housing, water, transport and energy.

Proletarian democracy is provided for in China under the 1975 constitution by people's congresses and revolutionary committees at provincial, county, city, district and commune level. According to the constitution 'the local people's congresses at various levels and the local revolutionary committees elected by them ensure the execution of laws and decrees in their respective areas; lead the socialist revolution and socialist construction . . . ; examine and approve local economic plans, budgets and final accounts;

maintain revolutionary order; and safeguard the rights of citizens' (quoted in Bedeski, 1980, p. 451). Representative assemblies exist at all levels even down to production brigades and teams.

The second prominent feature of local government in socialist states is the integration of state and party apparatuses. In the USSR soviets are expected to function under the supervision of the appropriate local party organ. Party members on all elected bodies are required to form a group which is duty bound to carry out the instructions of party committees (Hough, 1980, p. 343). This control extends beyond the administrative departments of the local soviets to the managers of industrial, educational and judicial institutions. In China, especially since the Cultural Revolution, party and government apparatuses at the local level have been indistinguishable. Revolutionary committees have constituted the executive in local government as well as the local leadership of the party. Since 1978 the revolutionary committees have been replaced as organs of local government by local people's congresses, but the main tasks of the congresses are to approve and implement party policy. There is considerable overlapping of membership between party and local government committees. The administration of municipal functions such as political affairs, security, industry, communications, finance, education, culture and planning is accountable to both the revolutionary committee and the party committee.

A third feature of socialist systems to be noted is the extent of government responsibilities and the complex interrelationships between local councils and other state organizations at the local level. In the USSR the practice has grown up of central ministries funding urban developments, especially housing, which would otherwise come under municipal government. Local soviets have to bargain with powerful ministries over public investments in their areas. Party officials are involved in the control of both municipal and non-municipal state activities, particularly industrial. City councils have the difficult job of co-ordination. Central decrees require them to negotiate agreements with enterprises, institutions and organizations located within the city on the joint use of funds for public services, such as housing, roads and education. The local soviet is also entitled to examine the draft plans of such enterprises and can try to influence the decisions of higher-level authorities before including them in the plan for the urban economy (Hough, 1980, p. 350).

In the communist states of Eastern Europe, too, social ownership of the means of production also gives councils a varied role in the economic, social and cultural spheres. For example, the Polish constitution empowers people's councils to 'guide the overall socio-economic and cultural development in their respective areas of responsibility, exercise influence over all administrative and economic units in their areas, inspire and co-ordinate their activities, and exercise supervision over them' (Zawadzka and Zawadzki, 1980, p. 368). Local councils plan development in all spheres of the local economy and can determine organizational forms, though such planning is becoming increasingly centralized. State enterprises are obliged to obtain the agreement of local authorities on their investment and employment policies. All councils have supervisory rights over all state agencies whether 'subordinate' or not. The system of self-management in Yugoslavia also requires council co-ordination of public functions and self-managing socio-political organizations not directly administered by local authority departments.

Economic activity is even more closely integrated within China's local state apparatus, especially in the rural areas. Communes are divided into production brigades which are, in turn, divided into production teams. These provide for collective ownership at each level. Teams can own land, animals and small machinery. They organize the labour of their members, and manage their incomes. They can keep some of the profits. Brigades manage larger projects, such as small irrigation works, processing plant, orchards, schools and clinics. They may also own larger farm machinery. Large-scale enterprises, such as tractor stations, hydroelectric power installations, repair shops, forests, experimental farms, middle schools, and hospitals are run by the communes, (Bedeski, 1980, p. 425). In the larger urban areas, municipalities run factories which are collectively owned, with profits being used for both workers' benefits, such as medical care and nurseries, and capital investment.

The fourth main characteristic of socialist local government is democratic centralism, whereby local administrative agencies are answerable to both the local elected body and the higher-level administration. This is the organizational principle of the Chinese communes. Indeed, it seems as if in China local administration is 'supervised by elected committees while policy is laid down in central ministries' (Bedeski, 1980, pp. 452–3). In the USSR democratic centralism applies to both party and state apparatus. At the local level each party committee is subordinate to the control of the party committee at the territorial level above. The executive committee of a soviet is subordinate to the higher executive committee. And the departments of a local soviet for such matters as health, education and trade are answerable to both the soviet and the department or ministry at the level above them in the territorial hierarchy by which the local departments are largely funded (Hough, 1980, p. 345). However, the degree of integration of local departments into higher-level ministries varies from one function to another.

The official version of democratic centralism in Eastern Europe is as follows: 'to assure uniform state guidance in fundamental matters of general national significance and to provide broad opportunities for the development of local initiative and activity'. The constitutions of Hungary, Czechoslovakia and East Germany 'guarantee' the autonomy of local councils. However, central supervision is close from both representative and bureaucratic institutions at a higher territorial level. A local council's decision may be annulled by a council at a higher level if it is 'contrary to the fundamental line of state policy'. Supervision by central departments is even more direct and detailed (Zawadzka and Zawadski, 1980, p. 371).

Decentralization under state socialism appears as something of a façade behind which lies the total centralization which the single-party state, above all other devices, makes possible. This centralization rests on the logic of the single-party system which ensures that no organ of the state is controlled by any opposition group (Kulski, 1959, p. 117). The control resting in the hands of the party's central leadership over the lower levels of the organization means that not only is policy-making centralized but also that the central leadership itself will be self-perpetuating. The leadership guarantees its own political base by its control over crucial positions in the party hierarchy. Centralization is thus inseparable from dictatorship. The whole society becomes blanketed by the oppressive force of the centre. This allows no room for variability in public policy at any level. It produces a stifling and cumbersome bureaucracy whose only response to criticism is repression. Constitutionally the state apparatus may appear extremely decentralized (the federal constitution of the USSR, for example), but party and state bureaucracies ensure conformity to central direction (McAuley, 1977, p. 211). Any variability in policy to suit particular regions comes from the centre rather than from an expression, through political action, of regional interests. In so far as any element of decentralized power exists it can hope to do little more than impede the implementation of centrally determined policies (Kulski, 1959, p. 117).

Conclusion

This survey does not exhaust the institutional possibilities for decentralization, but it indicates the main political choices which have to be made in states with levels of subnational government. Such choices are made in political circumstances – that is, when interests are in conflict. They are made within an ideological framework which sets certain, albeit flexible, limits on what can be done. Such a framework has to contain changing policies towards local institutions, such as 'participation', 'efficiency', or 'economy', emanating from the centre and reflecting conflicts being worked out there. A particular ideology may be able to accommodate a wide diversity of institutions at the local level (as in the USA) or a fundamental change in structure (as in France with the democratization of the regions and the abolition of the prefects).

8
Field Administration

The Definition of Field Administration

In Chapter 1 field administration was distinguished from
devolution in three important respects. First, the kind of authority
delegated to field officers of central ministries and agencies is
bureaucratic rather than political, in the sense that field officers
are part of an organizational structure and hierarchy with spheres
of competence formally defined by superior officials at
headquarters. For example, in the UK, the Department of the
Environment's (DoE) field staff perform a wide range of
administrative functions delegated from headquarters in London.
Regional officials of the Department of Transport advise local
highways authorities on submissions for transport grants, and
provide advice to headquarters on the best way to allocate funds
within the region. DoE regional offices similarly advise local
authorities on their applications to the Department for capital
allocations from the centre to local housing programmes. Again,
recommendations are made to headquarters on how to allocate
funds within the region. Such recommendations are very
influential and often amount to decisions rather than just advice
(Young, 1982, pp. 76–7).

Secondly, field administrators are usually civil servants
recruited according to the normal selection procedures used in
the appropriate department or ministry. They are then posted
to a province, region, or district, usually for a limited period
before being moved on to another area or back to headquarters.
A spell in the field may be regarded as a necessary stage in the
career of an official destined for seniority. It may also constitute
a significant political gesture, indicating that the government is
responding to demands for more flexible and accessible central
administration.

Political factors may affect recruitment to field offices in other
ways. In some systems of government certain field officers

perform such important political roles, relating to the security of the state and the enforcement of government policy, that their selection is based on political as well as administrative criteria. Political loyalty and skills may be as important as administrative skills, if not more so, in the selection of key field officials.

Thirdly, the areas within which field officers operate will be delimited by the administrative requirements of their functions rather than by local community characteristics, unless these happen to be relevant to the administrative tasks of the field staff. This is likely to mean a proliferation of area boundaries and perhaps periodic attempts to institute a set of 'standard' areas to which all field services are required to correspond in the interest of better co-ordination. But the logic of field administration, especially of the 'functional' variety (see below), leads inevitably to territorial jurisdictions which reflect the particular and unique tasks of different central departments and agencies. For example, in Britain the boundaries of the Ministry of Agriculture regions reflect a combination of factors, some of which would be considerations for other departments, too. First, there is the problem of span of control, arising in part from the two-tiered field structure of regions and divisions, and in part from the need to provide a reasonable amount of work at the regional level without damaging lines of communication within the ministry or between the ministry and the agricultural industry. Here, clearly, the nature of the work being performed has its impact on territorial structure. Secondly, the established pattern of the agricultural and food industries should determine where boundaries are drawn. The kind of agriculture practised in a locality will determine whether it is included in one region or another. Thirdly, co-ordination is important and as far as possible ministry regions are drawn so as to deviate as little as possible from the government's standard regions (B. C. Smith, 1967, pp. 36–7).

The Role of Field Administration

The need for decentralization in the state was considered in general terms in Chapter 3, and some of the factors identified there were more relevant to the determination of field administration than devolution. There are a number of quite specific reasons why a state should require its central administrative bodies to operate a system of field administration.

Access

First, day-to-day management may require a local presence and point of contact with the public and client groups. Many central ministries are, in some sense, concerned with service delivery and must have their officials accessible locally to deal with claims made by members of the public on those services. The enforcement of state policy may similarly require officials to be given specific territorial jurisdictions in order to manage the contact with individuals and groups which such enforcement requires. In the UK, for example, regional offices of the Department of Industry are the 'access points' for financial assistance to industry (Hogwood, 1982b, p. 9). Local offices of the Department of Health and Social Security are the access points for claimants to a range of statutory welfare and social security benefits. Revenue collection everywhere requires the presence locally of central officials with powers of assessment and collection.

Such administrative responsibilities may have a considerable political content. In India the executive work of the district officers has included the rehabilitation and resettlement of refugees, the supply and distribution of essential commodities in times of rationing and shortages, and the welfare and advancement of members of the *harijan* caste. They have discharged special responsibilities in connection with the conduct and management of elections. The district officer is returning officer and is responsible for the peaceful and impartial conduct of elections. He is responsible for holding elections to local councils such as *gram panchayats*. The decennial census also requires his close supervision (Rai, 1967, p. 25). Agricultural extension work requires close and frequent contact between government personnel and farmers. Such contacts between field offices and the public do not necessarily imply great discretion on the part of the officials concerned. The power to exercise discretion and adapt government policy to the 'needs' of a specific region or locality as perceived by the field offices is a separate issue and will be dealt with below. The range of functions allocated by the state to central rather than local or provincial governments, and thereby requiring localized administration through field services, is also a highly variable factor, depending on the central governments' policy objectives. This will also be returned to below.

Supervising the Machinery of Government

Field administration may be needed to ensure that other parts of the machinery of government are supervised and controlled to the satisfaction of the central authorities. This places the field officer in a very special relationship to municipal authorities in his territory. In France the prefect, a representative of the state, the government and the Ministry of the Interior, has until recently been the chief executive of the local authority at the level of the *département*. The prefect also exercises *tutelle* over the communes within a *département* (Ridley and Blondel, 1964, pp. 93, 104). French local and regional administration is currently undergoing a period of reorganization in the interest of greater democratization. However, the legality of communal decisions is checked by the new commissioners of the republic (formerly the prefects) and for budgetary matters by the president of the regional audit chamber. The commissioner may refer any action he considers illegal to the administrative court. Administrative and jurisdictional control of the *départements* and regions is exercised in a similar way.

In the UK local authorities are subject to varying degrees of control and influence from specialist branches of the central administration. District auditors are appointed by the Secretary of State for the Environment (the central department with overall responsibility for the local government system) to ensure that local authority spending is within the powers assigned to them by law. An auditor can apply to the courts for a declaration if he believes any item of expenditure is illegal.

Field officers are also given the power of inspection over state institutions such as prisons, schools, courts, police forces and co-operatives. Inspection often involves a good deal of advisory work rather than the enforcement of sanctions in pursuit of efficiency. Nevertheless, Griffith found from his study of central–local relations in Britain that inspection was 'one of the most powerful means whereby government departments are able to exercise influence over local authorities' (Griffith, 1966, p. 56). Sometimes the special status of inspectors is underlined by distinctive methods of appointment, such as having inspectors of schools, police forces and fire services in the UK appointed by the Crown, rather than the appropriate minister (Griffith, 1966, p. 56).

Field officers also become influential in the policy formation processes of local governments. In the 1970s in England the regional offices of the DoE became increasingly involved in local land-use planning, with fewer authorities to deal with after the reorganization of 1972 (Young, 1982, p. 84). The regional office gives advice as plans are prepared and determines what issues will be discussed at the statutory public meeting. Regional officials advise the minister on the results of this meeting. Links between regional offices and local authorities are both formal and informal. Regional planning strategies have also enabled civil servants to control the content of local plans. The borderline between advice and control in such cases is blurred (Young, 1982, p. 86).

Control may also merge into sponsorship, when field officers lend assistance to enable subordinate bodies to do what they want to do more effectively. In many less-developed countries local authorities are heavily dependent on central cadres of officials to administer the services which in law the authorities themselves are empowered to provide. Field officers elsewhere also give encouragement and assistance. In England some of the smaller district councils, lacking the necessary professional skills and experience, have been assisted in making applications for the EEC Regional Development Fund grants for projects in economically disadvantaged areas. Field officers may have to overcome resistance to innovation on the part of local authorities.

Supervision can mean arbitration between agencies in conflict. Regional officials in Britain concerned with housing have engaged in diplomatic negotiations between local authorities seeking land for new development and others resisting incursions into green land. Officials have a certain amount of discretion as to how far they become involved in such arbitration (Young, 1982, p. 83).

Communications

A third function of field administration is to act as the 'eyes and ears' of headquarters, assessing public reactions to policies and evaluating their effect on whatever sector they were aimed at (Young, 1982, p. 90). Field officers also act as the mouthpieces of headquarters, informing public and private agencies of their rights and duties under new policies. For example, DoE officials in the 1970s were active in explaining the complexities of policies for housing action and improvements and of the 1975 Community Land Act. Department of Industry regional offices have a similar role to perform with firms over central government's industrial and energy conservation policies. This role enables some offices to become promotional and interventionist (Young, 1982, p. 79).

Field staff are also part of the 'feed-back' which headquarters need in assessing the impact of policy on target groups. In the functional system field officials probably have more influence on implementation methods than major policy initiatives, though the two are not all that easy to distinguish between (Cross, 1970, p. 433). Prefectoral field officers are more likely to have an influence on major policies since they are usually responsible for peace, order and good government. There is little that the centre might wish to initiate that will not have some significance for these objectives.

Departmental Management

Field administration sometimes requires a hierarchy of field offices outside headquarters. A state may be divided into regions which are then further subdivided into areas or districts. Field officers at the regional level may then be mainly concerned with managing a network of subordinates rather than providing a substantive service on behalf of the state or supervising other state institutions such as local authorities. Field administration, in other words, may constitute a miniature administrative system in its own right, with its own internal chains of command and spans of control, and the co-ordination of different specialisms (B. C. Smith, 1967, pp. 39–40).

The management role often extends to involvement in co-ordinating mechanisms and negotiations with the field representatives of other departments with related responsibilities. From 1964 to 1979 the regional controllers of the DoE or its predecessors chaired the meetings of regional economic planning boards, interdepartmental committees of senior regional civil servants. Through these committees, regional officials tried to co-ordinate the different policies of ministries and other agencies (such as health authorities and development commissions) concerned with regional planning in its broadest sense. Some field officers are more concerned with negotiations within and between field hierarchies than with contacts with target groups.

Political Roles

Political Stability

In addition to these administrative roles a number of more explicitly political functions has been identified. The first is that of maintaining political stability. Sources of political instability that have been countered by field administration, particularly of the prefectoral variety, include indigenous opposition to colonial government and government based on conquest; geographical or ethnic 'disaffection'; and locally based opposition to central government policy. Historical evidence suggests that, unless sources of instability are contained and consensus strengthened by devolution to localized minorities, 'rulers tend to invoke a patently or latently authoritarian politico-administrative structure' and 'an important component of such a structure is a prefectoral field-administration system' (Fesler, 1962, p. 129).

Colonial and post-colonial regimes have employed field

administration for the political objective of containing sources of instability. In colonial India, for example, district officers were responsible for maintaining the peace and preventing disorder. The maintenance of order involved political artistry as well as administrative skills (Blunt, 1937, p. 116). Under colonialism the district officer was required to locate sources of internal conflict and to settle disputes that might threaten the stability of the regime (B. C. Smith, 1967, p. 96).

Containing Political Opposition

Field administration may be used to obstruct opposition to the government as well as threats to the regime. Threats to the current holders of political power can be contained by manipulating the machinery for the peaceful transfer of power, notably elections. The history of the French prefects is perhaps the best example of this. Richardson's history of the French prefectoral corps under the restored Bourbon monarchy shows how the prefects played 'a crucial political role' in the system of parliamentary government which evolved after 1815. Their primary function was electoral. They subjected voters to various pressures on behalf of pro-government candidates. Richardson claims that during the Restoration the political role of the prefects came to 'pre-empt all others' and that 'politics intruded at every stage and level of an administrative career' (Richardson, 1966). In fact, the predominant characteristic of the French prefectoral system during the nineteenth century was the manipulation of the prefects' legal and administrative powers, as well as the adoption of extra-legal methods to ensure electoral support for the incumbent government (Chapman, 1955). It is widely believed that the prefects still act as electoral agents for government candidates, though there is disagreement among observers as to whether such accusations are part of the ritual and mythology of French politics. Prefects undoubtedly advise pro-government candidates but there is little evidence that this is a crucial factor in election results. Prefects are probably aware that excessive electoral bias would cause too many administrative problems subsequently. Machin concluded that ministers value prefects more as administrators, persuaders and conciliators than as electoral agents, though they are not discouraged from assisting government candidates if doing so will not lead to problems (Machin, 1977, pp. 173–5).

The history of Italian administration also provides ample evidence of this role of field administration. During the period of constitutional monarchy from 1848 to 1859, when the executive branch of the central government was dependent on a parliamentary majority, the prefectoral administration was employed to build and maintain electoral support for government deputies. Administrative skill in keeping the central ministries informed of political manoeuvres was part of the prefects' supportive role. Under the Liberal regime of 1870 to 1922, however, the prefects employed much more direct methods in mobilizing support in the provinces and localities on behalf of the central government. By bringing pressure to bear on public servants and local notables, by using patronage, bribery, intimidation and sometimes violence, by manipulating legal powers to discriminate against opposition elements, the prefects played a leading role in constructing and supporting parliamentary majorities (Fried, 1963).

Policy Control

The political support of government majorities by field administration may be supplemented by the control of political institutions to ensure their 'responsiveness' to the centre. This was an outstandingly important role in colonial regimes. The function of 'political' officers, as they were often called, was to exert influence over local chiefs and their advisers so that the decisions they made were consistent with European concepts of justice and morality and with colonial policy (B. C. Smith, 1967, p. 96).

Field officers have often been used in openly partisan ways to control the localities. By the exercise of administrative powers, such as over local budgets, *ultra vires*, inspection and policy approval, field officers can impede the operation of local authorities in political conflict with the government. Italian politics has produced numerous cases of harassment of communist municipalities by prefects, a factor which draws the prefects deep into local politics (Fried, 1963).

The Political Loyalty of Field Staff

The use of field administration in maintaining political support for regimes and governments in potentially dissident areas carries with it problems for the regime itself in its relations with its field personnel, particularly that of ensuring that its field representatives themselves remain loyal. Numerous examples of this problem can be cited. Fried shows how in seventeenth-century Piedmont prefects and *intendants* were appointed from among lawyers and magistrates to ensure class loyalty to the regime. Savoyards suspected of sympathy with the French were discriminated against. The problem of loyalty occurred again in Italian politics during the early years of the twentieth century when the prefects were called upon to promote the social welfare of classes which had hitherto been subject to repression by policies executed by the prefects. In such a situation strains are imposed on field officers who identify with a class whose privileges are threatened by a government to which they are supposed to respond loyally.

The importance of the responsiveness of field administration to national governments is the central theme of Jacob's study of German administration since Bismarck (Jacob, 1963). In the Second Reich responsiveness was not a problem because of the class background and attitudes of field officials. In the Weimar Republic strict hierarchical controls were enforced. Purges were used in the Third Reich. Nevertheless, the history of German administration provides examples of all the problems of loyalty and responsiveness: ideological conflict between field staff and government; strong local loyalties and attachments; inadequate communication with the centre; interference from local assemblies; confusions, contradictions and inefficiencies caused by over-centralization.

All political systems have to manipulate administrative and political controls to effect a balance between responsiveness to central policies and discretion in the exercise of field responsibilities. Kaufman's study of the US Forest Service describes how the autonomy of its field officers, the forest rangers, is supported by a number of organizational factors which have to be countered by integrating devices initiated from headquarters. Deviation from national policies can occur when rangers exercise discretion in interpreting and applying general regulations and instructions. Choices have to be made between conflicting directives. The 'distance' − sociologically as well as geographically − between field officers and headquarters encourages diversity. Informal patterns of behaviour can develop and are not always compatible with national policy. Field officers can be 'captured' by local interests, cowed by local pressures and identify more with local communities than with the organization. The personal predilections and prejudices of field staff sometimes clash with the policies of the forest service. The service itself actually supports an ideology of decentralization which delegates as much responsibility as possible to forest supervisors and rangers. There is, then, an 'impulse towards disintegration' in the forest service which has to be neutralized to ensure the existence of an integrated organization. Three techniques of integration are used. First, action is predetermined by the authorizations, direction and prohibitions contained in statutes, executive orders and departmental rules. Some decisions need headquarters clearance. Disputes are settled by referral upwards. The centre also controls the allocation of funds to some 800 ranger districts. Secondly, deviation is exposed and discouraged by reporting, inspections, sanctions and the frequent transfer of personnel. Finally, the right kind of motivation is encouraged by recruitment, training and the creation of an organizational environment, including promotion, transfer, the use of symbols and frequent consultations by headquarters with field officers, conducive to identification with the goals of the service and 'voluntary conformity' (Kaufman, 1960).

In the soviet administrative system political factors operate so as to permit considerable deconcentration of decision-making in an otherwise highly centralized state. The soviet case shows that the politicization of field administration can actually relax central control and allow discretion to be exercised in the field, especially in industrial administration, when efficiency demands it (Hough, 1971). The fact that in the one-party system party members hold important administrative posts allows the leadership some confidence in areal deconcentration. Party membership ensures a common value system for central and field officials. The centre's control and incentive systems encourage confidence in field administration on the part of the leadership. The existence of a co-ordinating 'prefect' in the party organization at provincial level has facilitated area deconcentration by placing responsibility for deviations from the rules in the hands of provincial party organs.

Political Change
A final political role of field administration, particularly for colonial and post-colonial states, is the instigation of political change in the structure of authority and the processes of decision-making. (B. C. Smith, 1972a, p. 101). Field administration in less-developed countries also contributes to the change of economic and social structures.

Varieties of Field Administration

Mention has been made of such diverse field officers as French prefects and regional directors of UK government departments. Generalizations about such state officials are difficult to make, but a broad distinction between functional and prefectoral types is useful in (a) understanding the role of field officers in relations between the centre and the localities and (b) in understanding contemporary trends within systems of field administration.

Functional Systems

In a 'functional' system of field administration (Fried, 1963; B. C. Smith, 1967) the senior representatives of the state bureaucracy in the provinces are in charge of functionally specific state services, such as education, health, industrial development, or agricultural extension work. Administration in the field falls into almost watertight compartments. Co-ordination is arranged centrally or through interdepartmental committees at the provincial or regional levels. In a purely functional system there will be no general representative of the state and central government – no provincial governor or prefect. The territories which each department delimits for its field operations will not necessarily be shared by other functional departments but will be suited to the particular and to a large extent unique administrative requirements of a particular government policy.

Some systems of field administration, such as those of the UK and USA, are entirely functional, though in the UK the existence of Secretaries of State for Scotland, Wales and Northern Ireland introduce an unusual co-ordinating device for certain special 'regions' of the country, namely those with distinctive national characteristics. However, there are strong political pressures towards uniformity with the rest of Britain (Randall, 1972). In Scotland the pressures for administrative uniformity, economic and political, have not produced a distinctive style of decentralized administration (Mackintosh, 1964, p. 272). These secretaries of state are Cabinet ministers not field officers. The political significance of having selected areas represented by politicians at Cabinet level is great, as are the administrative implications of the co-ordination provided by the Scottish, Welsh and Northern Ireland Offices. But these arrangements serve to separate certain (not all) aspects of central administration out on an area basis (a division of functions by place) for a limited number of specified regions. So there is a clear difference between this and the appointment of a government minister to every region of a state with regional responsibilities which are overlaid on those of functional ministries.

Functional systems are found everywhere. They may or may not be accompanied by the prefectoral variety. In France, for example, the 'external services' of government are responsible for their ministries' work in the provinces. The Corps des Ponts et Chaussées acts as the external service for a number of ministries requiring public works projects to be carried out. It is responsible for the fieldwork of the technical divisions of the Ministry of Public Works. The Ministry of Agriculture has a number of specialized external services, often based on different sets of administrative areas. The Ministry of Construction has a director in each *département* and a regional organization for town planning. The external services of the Ministry of Education are also organized at both regional and departmental levels. Departmental directors of the Ministry of Labour and Social Security supervise the enforcement of labour regulations and direct the employment services. The external services for social security have a regional organization. Regional directors supervise the social security institutions and are assisted by inspectors and medical advisers. All these 'functional' field services are associated with a prefectoral system. In some other states the same kind of system operates without a superior co-ordinating and controlling official.

Prefectoral Systems

A prefectoral system of field administration involves the appointment of a general representative of the central executive to a subnational territory (the province in Italy, the *département* in France, for example). The prefect is the senior government officer in the area. Prefectoral officials usually have broadly defined responsibilities for 'good government'. Two broad categories of prefectoral system may be identified, depending on the relationships between the prefect, on the one hand, and local government and the external services or functional field offices, on the other.

In the 'integrated' system the prefect is the superior field officer to whom the officials of other ministries are subordinate. The prefect represents the national interest, the state and the government. He embodies the authority of all central ministries. In relation to local government the prefect is the senior executive officer of the higher-tier local authority and exercises control over lower-tier authorities. The role of the prefect in French local government has already been mentioned. They are 'the representatives of the state, delegates of the whole government, agents of the Minister of the Interior and executive officers of the General Councils' (Machin, 1977, p. 110). Ridley has identified eight roles performed by a prefectoral official in an integrated system. There is the formal representative of the state – the 'lord lieutenant' role. As 'regional commissioner' the prefect is executive authority of last resort responsible for internal and external security. As 'political agent' the prefect is delegate of the government ultimately responsible for all central administration in the area. As 'director general' the prefect heads all central government field services in the area. Responsibility for law, order and public safety falls to the prefect as representative of the Ministry of the Interior and thus 'chief of police'. As 'tutor of local government' the prefect supervises the local authorities in his area. Government intervention to stimulate local and regional economic growth may make the prefect a 'planning commissioner'. And as 'county manager' he acts as chief executive of the elected local authority at county level (Ridley, 1973).

In the unintegrated system the area under the prefect's jurisdiction is less likely to be adopted by the field services of functional departments than in the integrated system. The prefect is only one among many channels of communication between the localities and the capital. Each ministerial representative in the field maintains independent links with its own headquarters. They are not subordinate to the authority of the prefect. In Italy (Fried, 1963) the prefects represent, as in France, both the Ministry of the Interior and the national executive. The ministries in Rome, however, have a degree of functional autonomy which restricts the power of the prefect to co-ordinate field administration at the provincial level. The prefects are responsible for co-ordinating the different services within the portfolio of the Ministry of the Interior, such as police and fire services. But the management of services coming under the ministries is their own responsibility. Italian law and administrative practice does not allow for any overall direction of the state's provincial administration. The prefecture can, however, provide co-ordination if it is necessary. It is a system which is both politically and administratively convenient.

As regards local government, while the prefect exercises administrative supervision and control, local authorities appoint their own chief executives. In this respect the unintegrated prefectoral system reflects political tradition. It is a compromise between conflicting political demands for provincial autonomy and centralized control (B. C. Smith, 1967, p. 82). It may satisfy ideological requirements for provincial autonomy while supporting weak provincial and local institutions.

Many Third World regimes have found it useful to continue with a prefectoral form of field administration introduced under colonialism. The role of the prefect has changed, however, with emphasis placed on the co-ordination of specifically developmental activities, that is, administration aimed at improvements in production (especially in agriculture), marketing, distribution and social welfare. The old-style district officer, government agent, collector, or district commissioner have all but disappeared but a prefectoral system still appears to be needed. Central government agents for inspection, advice, supervision and co-ordination are widely regarded as essential elements of local or provincial administration.

The prefectoral system of field administration, whether of the integrated or unintegrated variety, is a significant factor in decision-making by devolved governments at every level. Even the decision by the Socialist government in France to democratize the regional level of government did not envisage it operating without the involvement of the central government's main agent in the field. A commissioner of the republic, representing the state at regional level, will exercise a role similar to that of the departmental commissioner and *a posteriori* control of administrative action will be exercised under the same conditions as for communities and *départements*.

Local or regional authorities are, however, by no means solely in contact with representatives of the state. They also find that the functional field officers of the government's 'external' services are involved with their administrative activities. It has already been noted how regional officials in the UK participate in local decision-making. In France local authorities have been heavily dependent not only on the prefects but also on the external services of central government. Field officers of the central ministries, in addition to performing the executive work of the ministry, also act as officials of the *département* and supervise administration by the communes. Field officers have had to encourage the adoption of communal policies and then implement them in the smaller communes. Larger communes may have their own professional and technical staff, but even here officials of the central ministries are very influential, especially in town planning (Ridley and Blondel, 1964, pp. 109–11).

The Delegation of Authority

If field administration is placed within the context of decentralization generally, one thing is very clear. The picture one has of the level of decentralization depends on whether one stands in the community or in the organization. The organization (in this case a central government department) may be highly decentralized, with extensive powers delegated to its field staff. As far as the area in which the field staff operate, however, the system will appear very centralized, with no power residing in locally based institutions. A highly decentralized system of field administration will only be territorially decentralized to the extent that groups and interests within the local community can exert influence over the way field officers exercise their discretion.

Levels of Delegation

So decentralization within a field hierarchy must be measured in a very different way to political decentralization from central to area governments whether on a local or regional scale.

The *responsibilities* assigned to field personnel will influence the level of decentralization in the system. Field officers will have different *tasks* (approval of schemes, executive powers, inspectoral functions, and so on) with varying degrees of *autonomy* within them (approval of schemes under a certain cost, the inspection of specified institutions). Decentralization can thus be increased by expanding the range of decision areas (the official's jurisdiction) or by increasing the level of autonomy within a decision area. For example, before 1970 in the UK the field officers of the successive ministries responsible for industrial policy only processed applications for loans and grants. Some discretion was allowed in the issuing of development certificates approving new industrial developments, defined in terms of size of factory or factory extensions, though it was kept 'strictly in accordance with centrally determined policy' (Hogwood, 1982b, pp. 103–4). After 1972 the regional offices of the Department of Trade and Industry were authorized to approve assistance up to £2 million. Decentralization will also be affected by the willingness and ability of individual officers to push their discretion to the limit. Their own judgements and values are vitally important when, as is evidently the case in British housing policy, 'there is some evidence that money gets pushed at the most efficient spenders by regional civil servants' (Young, 1982, p. 92). It may, however, be very difficult to compare levels of discretion between field services because of the heterogeneity of the work performed (Cross, 1970).

The form of *interdepartmental co-ordination* used will also have an impact on decentralization within field hierarchies. A prefectoral system will reduce decentralization since it adds to the degree of central control over the field agents of functional departments. Where an administrative system employs no field co-ordinator, interagency co-ordination will be achieved by combinations of the following practices: identity of regional boundaries; identity of regional office location; information flows; discrete and specific objectives of co-ordination; equality of status among field officers; and interagency committees (see below).

How a field organization handles the problem of conflict between functional experts and general administrators is also indicative of the level of decentralization operating in that organization. Decentralization is partly dependent on the degree to which all an agency's field activities within a geographical area are directed by a single official. Whether or not a multifunctional government department allows each division to direct its own field staff, or brings each of them under the control of a field director depends on such factors as the relations between the members of the headquarters organization and the extent to which the department's functions are subservient to a single purpose. Where a field director is set up there is always the possibility of variation in the control which such an official can exercise over the field representatives of functional divisions within the ministry or department.

Policies of transferring personnel between headquarters and field stations, and between the districts of the field organization will affect the degree of decentralization. The vertical movements of personnel counter the tendency for field service to be assigned low status within the organization. The horizontal movement of personnel prevents provincialism from developing within the field service. Other personnel policies, such as training, can influence the behaviour of field staff. Socialization may encourage loyalty to, and identification with, the goals of the centre. However, the centre may have to weigh its deployment decisions against political factors, such as acceptability of field officers, especially those with political roles, to local political notables, as in France (Machin, 1977, p. 176).

Communication between headquarters and the field for planning and control will affect the level of decentralization within a ministry or other central government agency. Organizations have to decide how advice and orders should flow from headquarters to field; how to keep regional directors fully informed of the ministry's work; how field offices should feed information to headquarters; and how field officers can be involved in policy planning.

The methods used for supervising the work of field offices also vary. Some are more remote than others. 'Advance review' hardly leaves anything to the field office except gathering information prior to referring matters to headquarters for decision.

'Reporting', at the other extreme, leaves the field officer to justify decisions after they have been taken. This maximizes the discretion of the official unless there are objective, measurable tests of performance. 'Inspection' falls between the two other methods of supervision and often enhances field discretion by including professional advice (Fesler, 1959).

Influences on Delegation

Since the forms of field administration, and the contexts within which they are found, vary so much it is very difficult to generalize about the factors which affect decisions about how much authority an organization should delegate to its field staff. The following factors, identified by Fesler, are obviously important.

Political responsibility will affect delegation within organizations. If the political heads of government departments are held accountable to the legislature, president, or party for their department's performance they may be reluctant to allow too much discretion to be used in their name, and too much deviation from national policies. However, central politicians may prefer to leave field officers to take responsibility in some difficult political cases which happens, on occasion, in France, for example (Machin, 1977, p. 170). This is yet another factor which makes the measurement of delegated powers to field officers extremely difficult. Answerability to the courts may also restrict the delegation of authority to field officers (Fesler, 1959). The development of representative and responsible government in the Third World with the end of colonialism heralded a significant reduction in the authority of field staff.

Time may be an important factor in the delegation of authority. The organization and staffing of a field system, and the delegation of authority within it, may have to await the establishment of authority and stability at the centre (Fesler, 1959, p. 271). The more routine the work, the easier it is to decentralize (though decentralization may confer little more than the right to check how the regulations apply to a particular case for, say, a welfare benefit or pension, and entail little discretion or judgement).

However, the opposite may hold true in conditions of underdevelopment, where programmes for rural development, employment, irrigation, and so on are so novel as to make it undesirable for the centre to exercise too much control. When there is great uncertainty and no precedents, as is the case with many development programmes, it may be necessary to allow considerable discretion to the officials on the spot.

Another administrative factor limiting decentralization to field staff is the competence of the personnel available. This has to be weighed against the need for speed and economy. Developing countries are not only particularly conscious of shortages of skilled manpower but also of the need to relieve congestion at the centre. The type of decision-making will also affect the level of decentralization: whether an organization has a narrow or broad range of functions to perform; whether there is a large degree of technical specialization required in the agency's work; whether the functions require national uniformity or provincial diversity (Fesler, 1959, p. 273).

Factors external to the organization can be important. Decentralization may be promoted if there is a need to engage citizen participation in the administrative process. (As will be shown in Chapter 9, administrative decentralization may be carried out to create an impression of citizen participation without any release of power.) Secondly, if two agencies engage in joint activities and there is a need for provincial co-ordination, there may have to be roughly equal levels of delegated authority within each so that field officers can collaborate on equal terms. Thirdly, levels of decentralization will be affected by the likelihood that field officers, especially when empowered to appoint staff, award contracts, or issue grants and loans, will come under political pressure from local interests (Fesler, 1959, p. 275). This will not necessarily entail a withdrawal of authority by headquarters. It may entail a voluntary relinquishing of discretionary power by the field staff themselves. In new states field officers have experienced pressure from local political leaders (some of whom are very influential in the capital) to mould national or state policy to suit their interests. The field officer may have no option but to retreat into bureaucratic formalism as protection against conflicting pressures and demands. A 'formal stance of neutrality and instrumentality' is necessary in the administrator's dealings with politicians and leaders of powerful social classes, especially if the policies to be implemented go against the interests of the dominant rural classes (G. D. Wood, 1977).

Pressures and Conflicts within Field Administration

As administrative systems, field organizations are susceptible to all the management problems that are likely to beset any large-scale, complex organization at some stage. There are personnel problems that have to be settled, such as the grading of field staff relative to headquarters and the deployment of staff between headquarters and the field and among the districts. Counteracting provincialism may be a major preoccupation of the centre, and field staff may need to be posted frequently if they are not to be 'captured' by local interests. Against this, it might be politically and administratively expedient to have local people posted to their own regions to provide sensitivity to local problems. Lines of communication between headquarters and the field also pose problems. Three organizational choices are singled out for examination here as being particularly significant for the organization of central bodies at the subnational level. They are: the role of the generalist administrative officer both within and between government departments; the politicization of field administration; and methods of interdepartmental co-ordination in the field.

The Role of the Generalist

The apparent need for both general administrators and specialist staff in field organizations presents problems both within and between field hierarchies. There are pressures towards specialization which call into question the role of the generalist in both cases. Within a field organization there may be many professional staff performing specialist functions for the department, as well as an area director or controller who is likely to be from the administrative rather than the professional cadres of the civil service. This complicates the process of communication and control between headquarters and the area offices. It has to be decided whether all communications should be channelled through the area director, or whether an attempt should be made to separate technical and professional matters from administrative decisions, leaving professional staff with direct access to headquarters in cases of the former. It is usually desirable for responsibility for the efficient management of the whole field operation to be located in a single area controller, but the decision as to whether this post should be filled by a specialist or generalist is subject to all the considerations relevant to this general issue throughout the public service.

The relationships between field hierarchies are particularly affected by this distinction when the prefectoral form of co-ordination is used. The more the state has developed an interventionist role, the greater the pressures on the prefectoral official to withdraw from involvement in decision-making requiring specialist knowledge (B. C. Smith, 1967, p. 88). In France, for example, the proliferation of field services under the Third and Fourth Republics reduced the powers of the prefects who lacked technical knowledge, formal powers (delegated to the directors of the field services rather than the prefect), and information. Attempts to strengthen the authority of the prefects under the Fifth Republic had little effect. The functional field services regard themselves as technical specialists and the prefects as politically biased generalist administrators. Even the formal powers of the prefects placed organizational and technical matters outside their jurisdiction (Machin, 1977, pp. 139–41). Professionalism, administrative convenience and *ésprit de corps* within specialized field services undermine the co-ordinating role of the prefect and lead to 'vertical separatism' in field administration (Ridley, 1973).

In field administration the prefectoral system has been saved by its political rather than administrative advantages. Threats to the regime or government from provincial political movements make the prefectoral form of field administration an indispensable instrument of control. However, there will always be tension between the administrative requirements of technical operations, including relatively large areas, and the political need for a generalist representative of the state operating within small, more historic jurisdictions. This is a feature of the political system that has serious implications both for recruitment to key field offices and for forms of co-ordination in the field.

Partisanization

Since most field administration is part of the political process it is necessary to refer to the 'partisanization' rather than politicization of field administration. This is because field staff have been particularly affected by the rejection, notably in socialist states, of the myth of civil service neutrality. Decisions to create a civil service that is politically committed to the ideology and policies of the government have had serious implications for field administration, particularly the prefectoral variety. It has sometimes meant that civil servants in the field have had to demonstrate political loyalty as well as administrative competence (by membership of the party, for example). Or politicians have been given area portfolios, with functions hitherto performed by administrative staff being transferred to them. Or party officials locally have become integrated into the state apparatus by being assigned administrative responsibilities on behalf of one or more central departments. The distinction between politician and administrator becomes completely blurred (Picard, 1980). Field administration often works as a projection of the party, particularly in one-party states. Regional and local officials will have to be experienced and loyal party members selected as much for their political reliability and sensitivity as for their administrative ability.

The USSR, as Hough has shown, is an example of a state in which local party officials perform the role of 'prefects' in the administrative system. They perform typical prefectoral roles, maintaining political stability, co-ordinating the field services of central ministries, and directing economic development programmes. The first secretaries of the party organizations at republic, *oblast* (region), city and *raion* (district) levels have extremely broad responsibilities for 'every kind of political, economic and cultural activity within their area' (Hough, 1969, p. 124). The party secretary serves as chief industrial executive and head of the trade union council, as well as political boss. He is responsible for the safety of both the party and the state. He must mobilize support for the regime through agitation, propaganda and a concern for the welfare of workers. The secretary plays a key role in the selection of supervisory personnel in party organs and administrative agencies. He acts as an ombudsman, defending citizens against the administrative apparatus of which he is the head. The role of the secretaries in industrial decision-making and planning is particularly distinctive. They check on the performance of industrial managers, enforce legality, issue policy guidance and promote technological progress. In industrial plants the secretaries of the primary party organizations share in the management of the enterprise with the industrial directors. As well as ensuring that central policies are implemented in the localities 'local Party officials have been vigorous spokesmen for the needs and interests of their areas' (Hough, 1969, p. 256). Hough concludes that in the USSR 'the local Party organs really are a textbook example of the classic prefect in a modern setting' (p. 303).

Co-Ordination
The political significance attached to field administration by the state will have an obvious effect on the way interagency co-ordination is dealt with at area level. References have already been made to the co-ordinating role of prefectoral systems. There are other devices that can be used, though they all encounter the inner logic of field administration which leads towards specialization of function and area (Fesler, 1959, p. 284).

One device is to establish a standard pattern of area boundaries to which all field organizations should conform. Co-ordination is obviously eased if the officials involved in joint discussions, planning and action have identical territorial jurisdictions. However, there are technical problems with this, even in an administrative system where there is a strong tradition of pragmatism. In the UK, after wartime experience of regional administration, the Treasury attempted to continue with a set of standard regions to which all central departments with regional organizations would conform unless staffing economies and administrative 'convenience' required deviations from this pattern. Gradually regional boundaries proliferated. When regional planning was introduced in the early 1960s departments with relevant responsibilities were encouraged to adopt a new set of standard planning regions for their field organizations. This, however, had little impact. In some cases a single departmental controller is responsible for field personnel operating within different patterns of areas, though field offices represented on the regional planning boards tended to conform to the standard regions. Boundaries, in fact, are determined more by departmental functions, the area director's span of control, the optimum population to be served and organizational history than by the demands of co-ordination, though some departments are influenced by pressures to conform to standard areas (Hogwood and Lindley, 1982).

Other co-ordinating devices include locating offices in the same towns or even the same buildings, and pooling common services such as equipment, storage facilities and audit. Socialization and communication can help interagency relations and make co-operation easier. Filling field posts with officers of equal status aids the deliberative side of co-ordination, though ensuring action following a decision may require differentiation of status between officials. Departmental needs, with different levels of delegated discretion and greater emphasis on vertical relations with headquarters than horizontal relations with other field offices, are likely to make comparability of status of secondary importance, particularly in the functional system.

Committees are a ubiquitous feature of field administration, even when the system centres around a prefectoral co-ordinator. Misunderstandings often arise with this type of institution, particularly over whether such committees are purely for consultation between officials or have an independent executive status. For example, in the UK it was originally envisaged that the regional economic planning boards would draw up regional plans which would reflect government commitments. This function was eventually transferred to advisory councils, but this did not prevent the resulting interdepartmental committees being interpreted as some kind of Continental, prefectoral system or a reversal to pre-democratic forms of administration by agents of the Crown. The interdepartmental committee was interpreted as a new level of government, despite the fact that relations between civil servants and their departments were not changed (B. C. Smith, 1969, pp. 115–17). In other states, committees combining interdepartmental functions with consultation have been set up. Field officers and representatives of local interests sit on the same committees, as in the case of Tanzania's development committees. Here lip service is being paid to local democracy without releasing power from the central authorities to be exercised by representative governments at the local level (see Chapter 10).

Finally, there is the option of adopting, continuing, or resurrecting some kind of prefectoral official: prefect, district officer, regional commissioner, government agent, and the like. But, as we have seen, such methods of co-ordination are under pressure from a number of different directions, all involving levels of specialization and divisions of labour which render the traditional administrative variant obsolete. First, there is the need for specialist cadres of officials to act for the state in an expanding range of policy areas. Secondly, this specialization has spread beyond the substantive areas of public policy, such as health, rural development and social welfare, to include the machinery of government itself. The official responsible for 'good government' has had to give way to inspectorates, auditors and other professionals employed by the state to supervise the operation of its executive, legislative and judicial institutions. Thirdly, field administration has witnessed the intrusion of what might be called the 'specialist in politics'. It can no longer be assumed that the administrative officer in charge of an area will have an adequate perception of politics. Hence the assignment of provincial responsibilities to ministers of state, politicians and party officials recruited into the administrative apparatus. Finally, and again particularly in the Third World, there are the specialists in development. The colonial emphasis on revenue collection and the preservation of law and order has given way since independence to development administration and an emphasis on co-ordination designed to achieve the regime's developmental goals. The area co-ordinator is likely to be seen as leader of a team rather than as an enforcer of regulations. 'Extension' work takes precedence over law and order, now the responsibility of the courts and the police. Chairmanship of district development committees replaces supervision of local authorities.

This is by no means exclusively a Third World phenomenon, as the example of France shows. Under the Fifth Republic the prefectoral corps was assigned the task of co-ordinating, promoting and 'encouraging' the economic development of the *départements*. New decision-making powers were added to their relations with field services, local authorities and pressure groups to ensure co-operation in the making and implementation of development plans. The French example, however, also shows that it is not easy for this type of field officer to break out of the traditional mould of maintaining public order, political harmony and consensus, and administrative co-ordination (Machin, 1977, pp. 127–9).

Conclusion

Field administration exists in a political environment. Field staff are part of the political system of their respective areas. They stand in varying relationship to other political and administrative institutions and to non-governmental organizations which make up the local political and economic structure. The formal relationships with such bodies (executive control of local authorities or regulation of industrial activity, for example) will be modified by informal relationships based on personal and group power. The full significance of the field officer's role in local politics is a function of formal powers and other political resources which the official can muster. The main ones are personality, social status, political connections, information and political acumen. The political environment of field administration also includes the tensions at national level between the need for political control of the provinces and professionalism in the delivery of public services.

9

Decentralization, Participation and Neighbourhood

Introduction

Clearest evidence that decentralization can be a political hurrah word, given whatever meaning suits the government of the day, is found in the experiments in neighbourhood government that have formed part of so many different programmes for urban redevelopment and social welfare in recent years. Neighbourhood decentralization, a label that has been attached to very different kinds of institution, is designed to shift power, or to give the appearance of such a shift, to smaller jurisdictions than those which constitute the formal structure of municipal government. The aim of neighbourhood government is to decentralize within municipalities.

Such decentralization has formed part of the administrative reforms initiated by a very large number of modern states. Decentralization to urban communities within large urban areas was recommended by the Council of Europe in 1966. Elected neighbourhood councils were proposed by the US Advisory Commission on Intergovernmental Relations in 1967. The decentralization of appropriate municipal services to the neighbourhood level was urged by the American National Commission on Urban Problems a year later. Various commissions in European and Scandinavian states have proposed neighbourhood decentralization to strengthen communal democracy (Kjellberg, 1979, p. 82).

Municipal decentralization has often revealed basic inconsistencies in official programmes for administrative reform. In Britain, for example, the reorganization of local government proceeded on the assumption that larger areas were needed to ensure effective provision of services. Local democracy, too, was thought to need larger units since democracy and effectiveness were seen as interdependent values (Royal Commission on Local Government in England, 1969, para. 28). Both Royal Commissions on local government in Britain recognized the need for representative institutions to express the interests and sense of identity of smaller communities. New 'local councils' were recommended to do for urban areas what parishes had long done for the rural.

Community councils were eventually set up in Scotland, but not in England and Wales, and the restructuring of local government proceeded on the basis of enlarged areas. However, no sooner had the legislation been implemented than it was being argued in government circles that both democracy and effectiveness required a much more localized orientation *within* local governments. Decentralization to the neighbourhood level, to a greater or lesser extent and in differing guises, was contained in a large number of the urban experiments of the 1970s designed to reduce poverty and deprivation by 'positive discrimination'. Educational priority areas, community development projects, planning action areas, the urban programme, general improvement areas, housing action areas, and comprehensive community programmes have all, in varying degrees, seen urban problems in terms of decentralization. Similarily, it was argued that two major local government functions, planning and the personal social services, should decentralize in order to encourage participation.

Motivations

Neighbourhood decentralization has been closely associated with the vogue for 'participation'. Most of the programmes for urban reform in the USA and Britain were designed to encourage citizen participation in decision-making in the belief that communities could overcome their own problems if the involvement of community members could be engaged. Indeed, decentralization to neighbourhoods and other small communities has been prompted by a particular view of the nature of social problems in the urban context.

In Britain the attempts in the late 1960s and early 1970s to decentralize municipal services were closely associated with the conviction that the problems of urban deprivation and decay — bad housing, poverty, poor environment and the absence of social provision — could be solved by positive discrimination. When poverty was 'rediscovered' in the 1960s the poor were officially regarded as a cultural group characterized by low standards of education, child care, social amenities, public health and environment. Positive discrimination was intended to break the cultural 'cycle' of poverty. Related to this was the belief that deprivation could be combated by an area-based approach to selected neighbourhoods. Poverty was assumed to be concentrated in small geographical areas, to be tackled by administrative adjustments (Flynn, 1978). This was reflected in the Plowden Committee's report on primary education (Wells, 1981) and was implemented not only in educational priority areas, but also in general improvement areas and action areas under the Housing Acts of 1969 and 1974. Poverty, it was confidently expected, could be dealt with by better administrative co-ordination, improved communication between the poor and the public services of the welfare state, self-help and changed attitudes among the poor themselves. In this way, a marginal group who, because of administrative failure, personal inadequacy and cultural position, had slipped through the welfare net in an otherwise affluent country could be retrieved (Mayo, 1975, p. 7).

Another impulse for neighbourhood decentralization was the growing belief in the desirability of participation and the need to find some way of representing interests and needs that did not find expression in the normal run of party politics. It is likely that the ambiguity of the participation idea increased its appeal to politicians (Hatch, Fox and Legg, 1977, p. 2). Participation is certainly a concept that has been employed in widely differing contexts – industry, education, town planning, social services – and, as with so many political concepts, there is no shortage of politicians willing to import the favourable connotations of one meaning into an area where the reality will be completely different. Where participation has been associated with municipal or neighbourhood decentralization it has usually appeared to mean influencing policy-making and implementation by expanding democracy at the local level (W. H. Cox, 1976, p. 171).

Disillusionment with party politics in the 1960s and 1970s turned activists towards grass-roots politics, community action and community work. It was at this time that the Liberal Party's ideology of community politics seemed successful (L. Smith, 1981, pp. 4–5). Social alienation on council housing estates had led to tenant participation in estate management as local authorities attempted to develop a community spirit. Other official responses to the participatory and community ideology included parental participation in school management, a community-based youth service and community-run, pre-school play groups (L. Smith,

1981, p. 7). It was hoped that communication and participation could reduce feelings of powerlessness and produce a better-informed and more-involved citizenry. The vogue for participation undoubtedly reflected frustration at powerlessness, remoteness and a consequent 'crisis of authority' (Sharpe, 1976, pp. 122–3). Such pressures, though not always the opportunities, for participation have been experienced in cities throughout the USA, Canada and Europe (Magnusson, 1979).

The reorganization of local institutions and changes in locally oriented policies must be seen in the context of managerial and technocratic values which were influential within British government in the 1960s. It was widely assumed that improvements in administrative performance could be achieved by greater professional competence. Many political issues were regarded as technical problems which merely needed to be exposed to the right level of expertise. In local government this meant taking advantage of economies of scale and creating organizations large enough and rich enough to deploy the knowledge required for the solution of the problems which local authorities faced.

The vogue for participation and the rise of the neighbourhood or community in the political consciousness was thus confronted by a seemingly irreversible trend towards centralization and larger, more remote units of government resulting in a demand for some recognition of smaller entities within the local government system. The neighbourhood council movement contributed to the pressure on the reformers for a truly local level of government, such as the urban parish, while the idea of integrated community care seemed to demand the adaptation of corporate approaches to the community level, especially in deprived areas. The notion of action teams for a co-ordinated approach, as initiated in the personal social services by Seebohm (Committee on Local Authority and Allied Social Services, 1968), gradually spread to other local government services as part of the attack on urban deprivation. In the USA dissatisfaction among deprived sectors with existing institutions for the representation of interests led to a demand for 'extreme administrative decentralization, frequently coupled with insistence on local-clientele domination of the decentralized organizations' especially within the anti-poverty programmes and in education (Kaufman, 1969).

The 1960s had also seen a growth in community work as a branch of social work and the development of a community approach to social problems. The appointment of community workers in new towns and some other local authorities, the formation of councils of social service and community relations councils, and the formulation of theories about 'community care' all represented a more integrated approach to policies designed to meet social needs. They were aimed at problem families and communities rather than individual clients. Another aspect of this was a growing concern that welfare services were becoming more impersonal and bureaucratic (Corkey and Craig, 1978, p. 45). A related development was the growth of community activism involving protest, squatting, and other forms of direct action. Action groups drew attention to the plight of the homeless, and tried to defend neighbourhoods against the impact of urban renewal. National pressure groups, such as Shelter, sponsored local projects, while the Child Poverty Action Group (CPAG) and claimants' unions urged the poor to claim their right to welfare (Smith and Anderson, 1972, p. 307). Community action had important implications for participation by focusing on the poor's lack of power, and by rejecting the electoral system and the politicians it produced in favour of 'continuing involvement of all the people all of the time in the decision-making process' (Baine, 1975, p. 17). The growth of community action produced a new breed of pressure groups representing people whose interests had not been articulated before. However, to a large extent, schemes for neighbourhood decentralization in Britain and elsewhere have been designed to absorb such local activism in ways which are supportive of the state (Kjellberg, 1979).

A related factor here was the emergence of voluntary associations concerned with the physical environment, as more people experienced the impact of urban planning (Damer and Hague, 1971, p. 221). The planning profession itself had developed an ethical concern for the quality of urban life and, to some degree, was sympathetic to the idea of public participation, which in Britain in the 1960s seemed more relevant to town planning than any other public service. There was also a growing involvement of social scientists in social policy, not only conducting research for top-level advisory bodies, but also combining action research with local experimental programmes, such as the educational priority areas and community development projects. On both sides of the Atlantic a new style of social planning emerged, involving consultation, surveys, public hearings and other participative means of information gathering (Magnusson, 1979).

Racial tension was a further contributory factor in Britain as in the USA. Concern about race relations was growing in the older industrial cities containing concentrations of immigrants. This forced a response from government in the form of special resources for urban aid. Fear of social disorganization and violence arising from immigration became significant in party politics (Flynn, 1978, p. 40). The central government may also have felt the need to allay local authority fears that it was not interested in the urban problem, especially as racial tension was accompanied by a growing tendency for dissidence to be articulated by protest and direct action (Corkey and Craig, 1978). Social stability was a major concern of governments at this time. In the USA, to an even greater extent than in Britain, containing urban political instability was a powerful motive for neighbourhood decentralization. Neighbourhood democracy was a preferred alternative to the more radical demands being made in black ghettos for community autonomy (Magnusson, 1979). Indeed, Britain drew on American experience and the lessons to be learnt from the US anti-poverty programmes initiated by President Kennedy, programmes combining positive discrimination, community development, participation and social science research. It is significant that American government support for community action and participation had begun in the early 1960s to restrain violent protest and appease the poor (Magnusson, 1979, p. 133).

Types of Neighbourhood Government

The experiments in neighbourhood government, decentralization and participation produced very different kinds of institutions and procedures which by no means all permitted the same form or level of citizen involvement and influence. The following ideal-types may be identified, though it is important to remember that, in reality, the dominant function of one type may also be a secondary function of another.

Neighbourhood Consultation

First, there have been many experiments in neighbourhood decentralization that have simply involved procedures for consulting individuals and organized interests about neighbourhood projects, such as housing schemes, urban renewal and roads. Such procedures did not involve delegating authority to assemblies representing the inhabitants of a community or neighbourhood, but constituted part of the information-gathering process in existing bureaucracies, such as municipal planning departments. The 'participation' allowed for and officially encouraged tends to be more a formality than a genuine opportunity for people to control their own environments. Land-use planning and the personal social services were the local government functions most affected by the fashion for participation at the time of local government reorganization in Britain. Local authorities were urged to set up community forums for a dialogue with the public and its activist groups, and appoint community development officers for communication between citizens and local planning departments. Land-use planning was overwhelmingly concerned with the participation side of neighbourhood decentralization, although improving the administration of planning applications and plan implementation to reduce delays was also a major objective in the late 1960s and early 1970s, and encouraged administrative decentralization (see below) to enable matters to be settled locally (Damer and Hague, 1971).

Participation and responsiveness were also argued to be crucial in the administration of the personal social services. The Seebohm Committee (Committee on Local Authority and Allied Personal Social Services, 1968) argued that the maximum participation of the community in the planning and delivery of social services was central to the idea of a community-oriented family service. The identification of need, the mobilization of new resources and the exposure of defects were all seen as dependent on public participation. This was required at all stages: service planning, service provision and publicity. Consumer control of professional and bureaucratic power was advocated. Participation was also to reduce the stigma attached to being a client of the social services by blurring the distinction between 'givers' and 'takers'. Services would also be made more responsive and effective by the formation of area teams of social workers providing a co-ordinated family service (administrative decentralization). Part of the task would be community development: assisting local groups to express their needs by collective action.

Though the language of participation in these contexts often appeared to imply a measure of neighbourhood control, the debate about participation in planning soon revealed the limitations imposed on the concept by official ideology. The Skeffington Report of 1969 adopted an ideological stance on behalf of the professional prerogatives of planners (Damer and Hague, 1971, p. 223). It also assumed planning to be a-political, taking place in a politically homogeneous society. Participation was largely seen as a means of educating the public in professional values. It was perceived as a way of ensuring that the planners obtained public endorsement rather than strengthening the citizen's role (Dennis, 1972, p. 223).

Participation in the making of strategic plans has consequently, in practice, amounted to little more than councillors answering constituents' questions. Local residents are not involved in dialogues about alternatives. Participants' comments have no more than a marginal influence. The public are involved too late in a procedure where they are as aware of their own inability to provide clear alternatives to the planners as they are of the unlikelihood of them having any influence (Hatch, Fox and Legg, 1977, pp. 193–6). The authorities are able to abandon consultation when hostility is shown to the policy-makers (Rossetti, 1978; Room, 1979). Some authorities have set up area committees of councillors to deal with planning applications. This has made planning more sensitive to local interests and less dependent on officers. However, there is no evidence that it has achieved significantly greater public awareness or interest in planning, or managed to promote local democracy and participation in planning matters (T. J. Phillips, 1979, p. 331).

Recently there has been a retreat from the commitment to public participation and the range of issues upon which the public can have a direct influence remains unchanged (Vielba, 1979, p. 57). Participation in planning, as in other parts of the system, has been a search for legitimacy rather than a means of power-sharing or democratic public involvement. In so far as it has benefited the public it has been those with expertise or the resources to command it (Sharpe, 1976, p. 125).

Participation in the context of the urban programme and individual local government services has also amounted to little more than consultation with affected interests. The community development projects set up in selected urban locations in the early 1970s for action and research to alleviate deprivation received a mixed response from their parent local authorities (Smith, Lees and Topping, 1977). Participation was restricted to the admittedly valuable role of organizing tenants' and residents' associations and raising the political consciousness of dependent groups (see below).

Additional governmental hostility was experienced when it emerged in some areas that participation and community action, both endorsed by the government, were producing a very different interpretation of poverty and deprivation to that of the authorities, one hostile to the assumptions on which state intervention rested.

Field Administration
Another reformist device which has enabled governments to take

advantage of the fashion for decentralization and participation is field administration within municipal bureaucracies. Posting officials to neighbourhood or 'street-level' offices of the city administration is one way of making communication between citizen and the administration easier. This essentially bureaucratic device can thus pass for a form of decentralization and participation, though very little authority may be delegated to the neighbourhood officials involved. Under the American Model Cities Scheme, for example, neighbourhood service centres and 'little city halls' were opened where municipal officials were available for consultation (Magnusson, 1979, p. 134). The decentralization of municipal bureaucracies is practised in varying degrees in most European states, especially in the larger cities (Council of Europe, 1978, p. 33).

In Britain, although local government was reorganized on the basis of enlarged areas it was decided that both participation and administrative effectiveness required internal administrative decentralization within local authorities. Hence the 'area management' device urged upon local government by the DoE in 1974. The objectives here were to extend the corporate approach to an area level, make services more sensitive to local needs, provide a convenient channel of communication between the local authority and community groups, such as neighbourhood councils and residents' associations, and relate council policy more closely to local casework, particularly in the personal social services (Miller, 1981). Area management was to improve co-ordination, reduce remoteness and revitalize local democracy.

Such decentralization within the local authority administrative structure also attempted to counteract the remoteness of local government caused by the shifting of important community services, particularly education and personal social services, to upper-tier authorities outside the conurbations. The various urban experiments to tackle deprivation also included measures to improve the management of local services by better co-ordination between departments at the community or neighbourhood level (Lawless, 1979, p. 18). Field officers have been appointed, professional services have been co-ordinated, and area committees of councillors have been set up. Action teams of community workers have been appointed to stimulate community involvement and improve the accessibility of services to needy client groups (Corkey and Craig, 1978). Many different schemes of internal decentralization have been devised as individual authorities moulded their innovations to local political and administrative values. The inner area studies initiated by the DoE in 1972 sought improvements in co-ordination through area committees and 'mini' town halls. The comprehensive community programmes introduced in 1974 were another attempt to give local authority corporate planning an area dimension.

Area management, however, has generally not meant that power to decide on the allocation of resources has been delegated even to area administrators or area committees. There has also been only very limited public involvement in any of the schemes (Lawless, 1979, pp. 100–2). The existence of representative government at council level and powerful bureaucratic hierarchies in large departments meant that delegation to area offices was difficult to achieve (Hambleton, 1977, p. 26; Mason, 1978, p. 18; Hadley and Hatch, 1981, pp. 75, 104).

However, bringing local authority management to the neighbourhood or housing estate level has, in some cases, reduced costs and improved standards. Some area management schemes have influenced council policy-making and have improved service delivery. Small-scale projects have been initiated to supplement existing authority services. Local councillors have found area committees a useful forum in which to debate the impact of council policies on a specific locality. Some public involvement has been generated where members of the public have been allowed to attend area committee meetings and join in discussion. In some places area committees have established a formal relationship with community councils (Webster, 1979, p. 50). None of this, however, adds up to neighbourhood government or decentralization of the kind hinted at in official statements.

Functional Decentralization

A third type of neighbourhood government occurs when representatives from small communities sit on management boards appointed by the parent authority. Such bodies are usually single-purpose entities, rather than multifunctional governments. Examples are the short-lived community school boards set up in New York in the late 1960s and the 'co-operation committees' and 'parent councils' of the Norwegian schools system (Kjellberg, 1979). Boards of institutions such as nurseries, recreation centres and homes for the elderly have been set up in Sweden. In the American War on Poverty Programme the Office of Economic Opportunity organized the election of representatives from poor neighbourhoods to the boards of the planning agencies set up to administer the poverty programmes (Magnusson, 1979). This form of decentralization to neighbourhoods is analogous to the use of *ad hoc* appointed bodies for municipal services discussed in Chapter 7. In many countries the practice extends down to the level of specific public institutions, such as schools, hospitals, recreation centres, homes for the aged and day nurseries which are provided with boards of lay and professional people to share in management (Council of Europe, 1978, pp. 32–3). Depending on how such institutions are funded, they serve the important political function of passing responsibility for community services to groups most in need of collective provision.

Ombudsmen

Yet another institution at neighbourhood level is the ombudsman device, for seeking redress when citizens feel aggrieved at the decisions of the authorities and thereby improving access to local services. In Britain the 1972 reform legislation brought this procedure into the local government world, though not at the neighbourhood level. On the contrary, the country has been divided into three large regions each with a commissioner responsible for investigating complaints against all the local authorities in the region.

However, in the USA there have been experiments with the ombudsman function at neighbourhood level. This function overlaps with that of providing a neighbourhood-level field service within appropriate municipal bureaucracies, since area officials can channel grievances. This happened almost by accident in New York City when municipal officials, having established a network of contacts with neighbourhood leaders, began to receive complaints. This developed into the Mayor's Urban Action Task Force. By 1970 there were task force officials in twenty-five neighbourhoods. Each task force office was led by a senior city official appointed by the mayor with a staff of city employees to handle citizen complaints and maintain channels of communication with neighbourhood groups (Yates, 1974, p. 364).

Neighbourhood Action Groups

Neighbourhood decentralization has often meant the initiation by higher authorities of community action and self-help. Funds have been allocated for the development of community organizations, often under the guidance of centrally appointed community workers. This type of neighbourhood decentralization clearly overlaps with others referred to, since it involves assumptions about both participation and the need to improve service delivery by means of better co-ordination between departments at the neighbourhood level and greater responsiveness to citizens' needs.

In Britain the community development projects (CDPs), under the urban programme inaugurated in 1968, rested on the belief that urban deprivation could be resolved, in part, by self-help. People were to be encouraged to express their needs and views effectively (Lees and Smith, eds, 1975). Participation in the determination of need and action was a clear objective (Lawless, 1979, p. 111).

However, experience of the urban programme in British cities shows that the stimulation of community action will not always produce results acceptable to its initiators. Indeed, it was the emphasis in some CDPs on relating the problems of deprived groups to their position within the working class and its relationship to the state and private markets that led to them being wound up by the Home Office, sometimes to the relief of their parent local authorities. As the CDP teams moved away from self-help projects, from tinkering with the administration of local government services and from the idea of deprivation being caused by personal inadequacies and institutional malfunctioning towards demands for radical democratic intervention, stronger working-class organizations campaigning for public control and accountability, and an emphasis on the need for structural changes to the labour and housing markets, so both the Home Office and local authorities withdrew their support and co-operation (Lawless, 1979). When the central and local bureaucrats and politicians showed a lack of interest in the advice which the CDP workers channelled to them, CDP attention turned back to their local audiences and groups, such as trades councils, trade union branches and shop stewards committees, to stimulate interest in the wider economic context in which the problems of urban deprivation could be understood (Corkey and Craig, 1978). The local participation sponsored by the CDPs thus tended to entail conflict rather than co-operation with the local authority (A. W. Cox, 1979).

The fact that participation in the urban programme has not amounted to neighbourhood self-government should not detract from the real achievements in stimulating the articulation of political demands. Local organizations for political pressure have been built up, albeit in the context of an administrative approach to deprivation. Neighbourhood community workers have been employed to assist groups in setting up and running their own advice centres. Local authorities have been persuaded to decentralize their administrative organizations. Affiliated community groups have sometimes developed into neighbourhood councils. Issues were kept alive through the support given to pressure-group action. Participation in local government elections was often increased in project areas. The formal CDP structures gave continuity to the otherwise more fleeting and sporadic activism of community groups (Smith, Lees and Topping, 1977). Such community activism can be a vital source of information for political parties in precisely those areas where the grass-roots organizations of the parties tend to be weakest at debating vital issues (Green, 1974, p. 13).

However, these things were achieved in the face of official pressure to use participation as a manipulative and incorporating device (Higgins, 1978, p. 122). Official community workers in most schemes for neighbourhood decentralization have attempted to integrate their clients into the social and political system (Magnusson, 1979, p. 131). Those citizens who most need institutions by which they can promote their interests lack the political resources of money, organization and expertise to engage in 'interest-oriented participation' on their own initiative, having to make do with 'cooptative participation' whereby their activism is channelled towards goals set by the political authorities (W. H. Cox, 1976, p. 180; Bachrach and Baratz, 1970).

Neighbourhood Government

Finally, there is neighbourhood government of a type that comes closest to deserving the name. This is where an elected body with executive powers and financial resources is set up for a small locality. Unlike other kinds of neighbourhood decentralization, this entails the creation of a new tier of local government with functions of its own, either delegated by the central government or by the municipality of which it is a subdivision. Cologne, Madrid and Barcelona are examples of cities which have set up neighbourhood bodies with independent decision-making powers. However, the general picture which we have of municipal decentralization in Europe and Scandinavia is one of limited delegation, indirect election and limited financial and administrative resources. Neighbourhood councils have enabled a larger number of citizens to participate in local politics but have not produced more statistically representative assemblies. They have mainly been concerned with planning, traffic regulation, schools and cultural activities (Council of Europe, 1981a, pp. 19–20). Often neighbourhood councils are given purely advisory powers. They are sponsored by city governments to ease the process of consultation. In this respect they constitute a territorial version of the neighbourhood action group policy. An important variable here is whether territorial councils or committees emerge spontaneously, or are inaugurated from above.

In Britain the reorganized system of local government provided for the retention of rural parishes and the creation of urban units in some of the new districts. In order to compensate for the preference shown for efficiency as the dominant value in local government reform and the subsequent choice of large areas and populations as the basis of the new system, participation at a more local level is allowed. The first attempt to provide an institution for community-based participation was the role assigned to parishes and community councils under the new local government structure.

Parishes have few powers and often those they exercise are contributions to facilities provided mainly by other authorities. Such powers include the provision of allotments and community halls, litter control, cleaning and draining ponds, maintaining and lighting footpaths, and the provision of bus shelters. Most of the powers relating to footpaths, roads and traffic can only be exercised with the consent of the county council. The other activities of parishes are to advise, and be kept informed, on planning applications, minor by-laws, sewerage works and footpath surveys. Parishes are thus peripheral influences on the forces which shape local society (Rowe, 1975, p. 104). They are also larger units than would normally be associated with 'neighbourhoods'. This is true of other countries, such as Italy where the neighbourhood government movement is well established (Dente and Regonini, 1980). There has been little extension of the parish role into Britain's urban areas beyond the successor parishes, even with their limited powers. Most district councils in urban areas are hostile to the establishment of statutory bodies for small localities, an hostility related to the belief that elected representation at municipal level is incompatible with more local participation. The Association of Neighbourhood Councils has pressed the government for a statutory status to be given to urban parishes (Humble, 1979). The district authorities have taken the line that new statutory bodies would add complications, costs, work, confusion and delay to local government services. They are seen as weakening the influence of the elected member and creating a further source of confrontation between the public and the authorities. At most, district authorities have been prepared to acknowledge neighbourhood councils as voluntary bodies (Association of Municipal Authorities, 1975).

Voluntary neighbourhood councils have, however, flourished

in some urban areas. They have acted as territorial interest groups pressuring the local authority for improved housing conditions, better traffic control, more play space, or against school closures, compulsory purchase orders, and the like. Some have employed community workers to stimulate group formation and action. Their main function has been to provide a vehicle for voluntary activity in setting up advice centres, providing special facilities such as play groups, youth clubs, craft centres and pensioners' clubs, and generally sponsoring self-help projects, sometimes with financial support from the local authority. They are comparable to the organizations in the Swedish 'neighbourhood movement', the Dutch 'district organisations for social development' of the 1950s and the Norwegian 'community associations' (Kjellberg, 1979).

Neighbourhood councils in Britain must, at best, be seen as pressure groups rather than democratic bodies providing opportunities for participation in the planning and management of services. They generally have limited resources. They have no authority in the sense of statutory jurisdictions. They are on a par with the many other kinds of interest groups – residents' associations, tenants' associations, street committees, community action groups and ratepayers' associations – that populate the local political system. Most observers appear to doubt that neighbourhood councils can ever have more than the right to be informed and consulted, to comment on the plans of higher authorities, to extract justifications from decision-makers, to act as a sounding board and to exert influence on the way services are run (Senior, 1969; A. W. Cox, 1979, p. 212). They may be able to increase community activism and strengthen the politicization of the community. To that extent they are valuable institutions for improving access.

A slightly stronger version of the parish was given to Scotland. Here community councils have both executive and consultative functions (Rowe, 1975; Burnett, 1976; Clarke, 1977). They receive financial and administrative support from regional and district councils. Some regional councils have made funds available in an attempt to allay fears that regional government would be remote and unresponsive to needs (Burnett, 1976). However, the central government decided against giving community councils any statutory powers and rejected a proposal that they should administer some services on behalf of regional or district authorities. Their role is thus restricted to 'expressing and representing local opinion' and 'safeguarding and improving local amenity' (Scottish Office, 1971).

The Scottish community councils have thus not proved convincing institutions for local participation. Electoral participation has been slight (Masterson, 1978; Masterson and Masterman, 1980). The districts have manipulated the organization of community councils to exclude radical approaches to local problems. Party politics has been barred, either explicitly or through social pressure. Ideological discussion has been suppressed. The councils have become reactive, defensive institutions rather than innovating ones (Clarke, 1977).

The reluctance to devolve significant powers to the neighbourhood level is widespread. It is noticeable that, in Italy for example, the smaller and more participatory the neighbourhood councils, the weaker the powers which they are granted. The Italian municipalities have also managed to integrate neighbourhood councils into their administrative structures where they serve as an important legitimizing device in areas of limited economic and political significance (Dente and Regonini, 1980).

Participation, Neighbourhood and Reform

Experiments in neighbourhood decentralization, with their emphasis on community participation, reveal a great deal about official perceptions of power as well as poverty in those areas where deprivation was a major concern. In Britain decisions about the structure of the local government system were based on the assumption that political power derives from the right to vote in periodic elections. Equal rights would mean equal power. The stronger administratively the local government, the more meaningful is the power exercised in local elections. Voting and other forms of participation have, in most of the schemes for neighbourhood decentralization, been seen as viable political actions regardless of the socio-economic circumstances of the participants and whether the institutions in which they participated could ever hope to have a jurisdiction over the forces that shaped their lives. The agenda for participation was hardly ever officially acknowledged as problematic.

Where participation has been designed to alleviate multiple deprivation and poverty, the assumption has generally been that the poor only need to be mobilized to protect their interests more successfully. The theory of participation upon which urban initiatives and schemes for decentralization have been based is thus flawed by the assumptions that lie behind the 'cycle of deprivation' view of poverty. Just as the poor were to lift themselves out of their poverty by self-help, better communication with the administration, and technical improvements to the welfare apparatus, so their political power was to be enhanced by group mobilization. But just as poverty was shown not to be a problem of educational underachievement, family inadequacy, personal incompetence and administrative malfunctioning, but of low incomes, poor housing, planning blight, high unemployment, migration and other structural changes in urban society brought about by the investment and employment decisions of national and international corporate interests (Room, 1979, pp. 184–7) and the policy decisions of governments, so political impotence is not a function of group disorganization but of the multiple deprivation out of which the poor are supposed to organize themselves. Consequently, the poor see themselves as powerless because of their poverty. Poverty and powerlessness are inseparable. Both spring from causes extending far beyond the neighbourhoods in whose regeneration the poor are supposed to participate.

When the consciousness of the poor is raised to a recognition of the material base of power, they tend to participate in ways not contemplated by the theory of participation with which governments operate – through claimants' unions, the welfare rights movement, trade unions, and so on. Communities may then move towards action on the wider issues of deprivation, such as public and private investment decisions. Participation as seen by the authorities is supposed to control deviants within the community, not the external forces producing deprivation. The consensus model of 'community' participation in Britain envisaged no real change in the power relations between policy-makers and client groups (Smith and Anderson, 1972, p. 314). Inequalities of power as an explanation of deprivation were as neglected as were inequalities of income and social status (Cleworth, 1977, pp. 24–5).

Participation in neighbourhood government has largely meant providing the authorities with information on the attitudes of deprived groups (L. Smith, 1981, p. 9). It has often meant absorbing dissent by involving activists in time-consuming bureaucratic delays. It has been a means for politicians and planners to educate the public in an appreciation of the resource constraints on local authorities. Ultimate control has remained with the existing authorities. Participation has not involved a delegated power of decision (Lawless, 1979), nor has it changed the pattern of dominant influences on council policy (Paris and Blackaby, 1979, p. 155).

American experience also suggests that the purpose of

neighbourhood decentralization and participation is to defuse radical demands for reform and reduce urban tension as the gulf between promise and delivery by municipal bureaucracies widens. Neighbourhood decentralization is a form of state intervention on behalf of the social consensus which appears to offer subordinate classes more self-government. Reformist decentralization in the USA has been described as 'repression by inauthentic participation' (Katznelson, 1972, p. 329). Local institutions have been created to ensure that participating citizens cannot challenge the existing distribution of power, only legitimize it. Citizen participation under such schemes as the US Community Action Programme tended to benefit the less disadvantaged sections of society as those with more economic power extracted greater co-operation from officials. Though the official goal was to attack poverty no real resources were offered to the poor. Nor is there evidence that decentralization has led to improvement in the standard of municipal services. It may even have had an adverse effect (Yin and Lucas, 1973, p. 336). The mentality of the poor, not their material condition, was to be changed, implying that they were responsible for their own deprivation. The institutions in which they could participate had no more than token power. Participation and decentralization are, in effect, convenient ways of obscuring class conflict behind the myth of 'community'. Compromise and conciliation are extracted from disadvantaged groups by the granting of minor concessions. Local leaders are neutralized politically by co-option into an extension of the state administration (Coit, 1978, p. 302).

Conclusion

European and North American experience of neighbourhood government, with its attendant objectives of participation and improved administration, provides a number of useful lessons in the operation of power in the contemporary state.

First, concentration on the grass-roots or street-level community obscures the interdependence of power between different levels of government. Effective power at neighbourhood level may depend upon holding power at district, regional, or even national levels. Power at community level may be no more than a token if the power to make the important decisions lies elsewhere, either with higher levels of government or private corporations. Power needs to be won at whatever level effective decisions to change things must be taken (Sharpe, 1976, p. 121). The small, local community, if such an entity can be envisaged, may be on too small a scale to cope with deprivation which is related to economic structures (Lawless, 1979, p. 209). Participation could impede the achievement of important political objectives if it meant delegating power to units of government too small to be effective (Parry, ed., 1972; see also Schmandt, 1972). There is more to participation than grass-root or neighbourhood activism.

Secondly, neighbourhood politics and participation can take many different forms, not all of which need to be accommodated within formal institutions of neighbourhood government.

Participation can mean direct action, rather than co-option into consensus-seeking administration. It can mean self-management, whereby institutions run within the policy framework of a local authority – such as housing estates, play groups, nurseries, advice centres, or old people's clubs – are managed by those who live or work in them. It can mean voluntary work to compensate for the shortcomings of official institutions. It can mean having a formal consultative role in some stage of public policy-making, such as land-use planning. It can mean group representation on a statutory body: functional representation supplementing territorial representation. All such forms of participation may help different sections of society protect their interests. In the USA, for example, the experiments in decentralization improved people's understanding of neighbourhood institutions, strengthened the human-service orientation in urban policy, and helped counteract the tendency for service bureaucracies to be accountable solely to themselves (Yin and Yates, 1974).

Thirdly, the concept of community or neighbourhood has a powerful ideological role in modern states. It presupposes harmony and consensus within a social entity defined exclusively in spatial rather than class or ethnic terms. A common territorial interest is asserted and an absence of conflict assumed. The appropriate political action within such communities is limited, short-term, sporadic and piecemeal. It is reformist and defensive. It takes place within a framework of values and objectives determined by dominant interests within the state. Community action within the confines of state-sponsored schemes of neighbourhood decentralization assists in the reproduction of the system of domination represented by the state itself (Saunders, 1980, pp. 128–30). Neighbourhood decentralization may become a form of repressive tolerance.

10

Decentralization and Development

Throughout the Third World decentralization has long been regarded as a necessary condition of economic, social and political development. The concept has, however, been used extremely loosely, permitting many different kinds of institutional arrangements to be presented in its name. Indeed, this variety underlines the political importance attached to decentralization in less-developed countries. Ideologically, it has proved an indispensable concept. Perhaps not surprisingly, the developmental burden which has been placed on the idea of decentralization has been too great for it to bear. Third World states find much promise in decentralization. The performance of decentralized government all too often falls disappointingly short of these expectations.

The emphasis in decentralist programmes and reforms has generally been on democratic decentralization, that is, development is seen as requiring a measure of political autonomy to be devolved to institutions which local people may participate in and control. It is, then – as W. Hardy Wickwar recognized when writing about the idea of local government in political theory – democratic decentralization, or local government that has been the object of much optimistic attention in the Third World, particularly since the Second World War. Wickwar, in fact, identifies an 'unbroken thread' running through the history of modern local government – a tradition of 'corporate patrimony'. Democratic decentralization in the Third World, he argues, is a continuation of this (Wickwar, 1970, pp. 80–93).

It must be understood from the outset that the roles described for local-level democracy by Wickwar and others constitute expectations, objectives and aspirations rather than outcomes. Before assessing the record of democratic decentralization in the

Third World it is necessary to be more precise about these roles. These can be separated out to a certain extent for the purposes of analysis, though there is much interdependence between them (Rondinelli, 1981b; Rondinelli and Cheema, 1983).

The Promise of Decentralization

First, there is the idea that democratic decentralization is a more effective way of meeting local needs than central planning. It provides a mechanism responsive to the variety of circumstances encountered from place to place (H. S. Phillips, 1963, p. 12). It has been shown that in Zambia, Tanzania and Papua New Guinea, among other new states, decentralization, especially in rural development programmes, has been set the objective of making decisions more relevant to local needs and conditions by having them taken by local people (Conyers, 1981). Nigeria's return to civilian rule after thirteen years of military government was preceded by a fundamental reform of the country's local government system, itself a testimony to the importance still attached by Third World regimes to viable local-level institutions. A principle aim of the reform was again to make appropriate services and development activities responsive to local wishes and initiatives by devolving or delegating them to local representative bodies (Smith and Owojaiye, 1981). Thus decentralization is designed to reflect unique local circumstances in development plans and their implementation (Maddick, 1981, p. 1).

Secondly, decentralization has been seen as particularly relevant to meeting the needs of the poor. It is argued that if development is to mean the eradication of poverty, inequality and material deprivation it must engage the involvement and mobilization of the poor (Rondinelli, 1983). Decentralization is especially needed to enable the rural poor to participate in politics. Their political as well as their material position would thus be strengthened (United Nations, 1979). Democratic decentralization should place local power in the hands of the majority (Rondinelli, 1981a, p. 598). In socialist regimes, such as the Sudan's, decentralization has become a fundamental ideological principle and essential for creating a system of government in which power is vested in the masses (Rondinelli, 1981a, pp. 600–1; see also Rondinelli, 1981b, p. 133). Local-level participation has been seen as necessary to the elimination of poverty, particularly in Tanzania. From his study of Tanzania, Samoff concluded that 'Participation is far more important to increasing production and productive capacity than are expertise and technology' (Samoff, 1979, p. 33; see also Rondinelli, 1983).

Thirdly, decentralization is said to improve access to administrative agencies (de Mello, 1981). Fourthly, forms of decentralization in which people can participate are said to soften resistance to the profound social changes which development entails. Participation in local institutions should help overcome the indifference, pessimism and passivity of rural people. Decentralization can secure commitment to developments needing a change of attitudes (Conyers, 1981). National development may produce social disorganization and political instability by encouraging industrialization, urbanization, mobility, education, mass communication and meritocracy. Local government can ease the process of change by providing local leadership to win support for change by involvement. Conflict can be turned in constructive directions (Gorvine, 1965). Decentralization is seen as a means of 'penetrating' rural areas. Support for development can be mobilized by decentralization (Rondinelli, 1981b, p. 597).

Fifthly, decentralization should reduce congestion at the centre. It provides for greater speed and flexibility of decision-making by reducing the level of central direction and control. Rural development, in particular, requires such flexibility during implementation when policy changes may be needed at short notice. The kind of initiative and effort required for flexible development administration is stifled by over-centralization (Conyers, 1981). In Tanzania, for example, decentralization has been used in an attempt to overcome the defects of centralization, identified as declining production, growing opposition to remote bureaucrats and a falling-off in levels of self-help (Samoff, 1979, p. 31).

Sixthly, there is a persistent belief that local democracy is necessary for national unity. In large countries with great social and economic diversity it is felt necessary to satisfy the legitimate political aspirations of subgroups, particularly those which are ethnically distinct (Maddick, 1981, p. 2). The Third World provides many examples of decentralization policies designed to satisfy the demands, discussed in Chapter 3, for the recognition of communal identity (Rondinelli, 1981a; Alassam, 1981; Aliyu, 1978; Tordoff, 1981; Conyers, 1981; Bonney, 1982).

Another major theme in arguments in support of democratic decentralization, and one which clearly reflects the nineteenth-century roots of much contemporary theorizing on the subject, is the educative effect of participation in local government.

Participation in such institutions is supposed to enhance civic consciousness and political maturity. People learn more quickly when they have to take responsibility for the decisions of local officials. They obtain an invaluable training in resource allocation. Thus a close association is perceived between local political institutions and political development. Through experience in local government people learn to choose between priorities and leaders. They gain experience in holding those in office accountable. After all, only local people 'know where the shoe pinches'. Such an education should ultimately enrich government at the centre as better-trained politicians emerge from the grass roots (Maddick, 1963, p. 106; Bonney, 1982; Smith and Owojaiye, 1981).

Finally, the state needs to mobilize support for development plans. Popular energies need to be harnessed to the task of economic regeneration. Plans and objectives have to be communicated under difficult physical and cultural conditions. Local institutions can provide local data, interpretations of local needs, indoctrination (into the benefits of health programmes, for example), inputs (such as savings and direct labour) and community self-help projects. Advantage can be taken of what is believed to be a greater willingness to pay local rather than central taxes. Local government allows the maximum utilization of local resources which has an efficiency value quite apart from the other benefits, such as political education, which it may bring to society (Maddick, 1963; Bonney, 1982). Hence the close association between democratic decentralization and community development which tries to harness a capacity for self-help to the aim of improving the economic and social well-being of 'communities'. Governments have to persuade people that they can achieve more by relying on their own contributions of labour and money than by relying on state interventions. Community development has often entailed mobilization by the government of community resources and institutions.

Performance

Experience of decentralization in less-developed countries has almost everywhere fallen far short of expectations and the declared objectives of policy-makers.

The participative quality of decentralized institutions has been especially prone to erosion from above. There is a pronounced and widespread tendency to replace elected bodies with decision-makers nominated by the centre. This occurs even when there is a strong ideological commitment to decentralization on the part of the regime, as in the Sudan, Tanzania, Thailand, Nigeria and Zambia, for example (Rondinelli, 1981a, pp. 601–2; Samoff, 1979; Conyers, 1981; Chikulo, 1981; Roth, 1975; Saxena, ed., 1980).

It has also been evident that when institutions for local participation and control have been created it is rare for significant powers to be devolved to them. The scope of local government functions in Africa, Asia and Latin America has rarely amounted to much more than tax collection. Field agencies tend to be empowered with developmental functions, not local or provincial governments (Humes, 1973; Reddy, ed., 1978; Stubbings, 1975; B. C. Smith, 1981b; Tennant, 1973). Approaches to decentralization, contrary to official rhetoric, have tended to be highly paternalistic and élitist. Studies of India, the Sudan, Kenya, Zambia and Venezuela all indicate that local governments are generally not endowed with adequate powers and autonomy to take effective decisions or mobilize local resources. They have failed to enlist the co-operation of the people and to stimulate participation in development (Reddy, 1981). Low levels of autonomy and participation are thus mutually reinforcing.

A third discrepancy between policy and practice is the level of centralized control which is maintained over so-called decentralized institutions. Despite the rhetoric of politicians and senior civil servants and the official support given to decentralized power and participation, the trend has been towards greater central control, particularly in financial and personnel matters (Howell, 1977, p. 113). It has been noted how unwilling central decision-makers are to strengthen local institutions for fear of losing their own power (Henderson, 1967). Throughout Latin America, Africa and Asia intergovernmental relations have been characterized by widespread centralization, reinforcing a client-patron relationship between the central government and the rural areas (Barraclough, 1964; Ramusson, 1975; Chikulo, 1981; Samoff, 1979; Folson, 1981; Rondinelli and Mandell, 1981; Friedman, 1983; Mathur, 1983).

In most new states field administration has been used as a substitute for local government (Cheema and Rondinelli, 1983). Field administration has its own rationale and protagonists. It is not uncommon for arguments advocating decentralization within central departments and development agencies to be conveniently confused with arguments for the devolution of power to localized governments. It may be politically useful for a government to create the impression that it is strengthening the autonomy of a local community when, in reality, it is strengthening the hand of its own bureaucrats in the field.

Administrative decentralization is said to sharpen the planner's awareness of developmental problems (Rondinelli, 1981b, p. 596). It is also said to increase the efficiency of officials at the centre by relieving them of routine decisions. It facilitates the co-ordination of specialized programmes at the point of implementation. This has been a particular objective of regional deconcentration in a number of Latin American states (Harris, 1983). However, the experience of the Third World with this form of decentralization has not been altogether successful. Waste and duplication of effort have resulted (Wiswawarnapala, 1972, p. 135; Stubbings, 1975; I. Livingstone, 1975; Gopal, 1980). There is also no guarantee that field officers themselves will be delegated sufficient powers. Over-centralization can be as much a feature of field administration as of devolution, as a recent study of Zambia showed (Chikulo, 1981, pp. 61–2). Field administration also encounters problems of communication. The status hierarchy built into bureaucratic structures impedes the flow of information upward (Saxena, ed., 1980, p. 16).

Decentralization programmes have not been noted for smooth relations between bureaucrats and elected representatives. The dependence of local authorities on secondments from higher levels of governments for their administrative personnel has often led to conflicts of values between officials stationed in the localities and local politicians (Reddy, 1967; Tordoff, 1967; Folson, 1981, p. 16; Rondinelli, 1981a).

Two other factors relating to the performance of decentralization in the Third World needs to be considered. One in the poor level of administrative performance by local authorities. Most studies of decentralization include a catalogue of defects in budgeting, staffing, revenue collection, maintenance work, financial control, information and honesty. Shortages of trained personnel, difficulties in intergovernmental co-ordination and low levels of managerial and professional capability combine to minimize the effectiveness of local-level institutions (Rondinelli and Mandell, 1981; Reilly, 1981; Bonney, 1982). Substantial amounts of local expenditure in Third World states are absorbed by administrative costs and debt repayments. Administrative incapacity is, however, by no means a uniquely local problem. Central governments are often unable to support decentralist experiments with competent personnel, efficient administration and other badly needed resources (Rondinelli, 1983).

Finally, decentralization seems unable to function without fiscal dependency. Local authorities in less-developed countries seem increasingly to be dependent for revenue on higher levels of government. Studies of Korea, the Philippines, India and Taiwan all show local governments with weak tax powers and tax effort becoming financially dependent on grants and other forms of transfer (Rondinelli and Mandell, 1981, p. 196). Few local authority systems have been given an autonomous financial base (Bonney, 1982; Rondinelli, 1981b, p. 621; Smith, 1982). The financial problems of subnational governments examined in Chapter 6 are most acute in the Third World.

Myths of Decentralization

In order to understand why decentralization fails to make the contribution to democracy and development that is promised by its protagonists, it is necessary to question some of the fundamental assumptions on which programmes of decentralization so often seem to be based. Decentralization in the Third World needs to be placed in a broader political and economic context than is commonly found in most academic discussions and governmental plans. This means avoiding some of the more obvious pitfalls of liberal democratic theory. It also entails rejecting a manageralist interpretation of local governments' problems. It should then be possible to avoid explanations which are merely restatements of the problem, as when the viability of local institutions is said to be undermined by inadequate independent revenues. We need to know why the central authorities are apparently so reluctant to devolve adequate revenue-raising powers to subnational governments. The remaining parts of this chapter attempt to sketch out the elements of a new approach to the relationship between decentralization and development. The context within which decentralized institutions typically have to operate in less-developed countries is considered first. Then some attention is given to the problem of relationships with the centre.

First, it is important to reject a romantic view of decentralization. It is not an absolute good in its own right. Decentralized administration and local government may be used for a variety of ends, just as central government can be. How decentralization is evaluated should depend on the purpose for which it is employed. Centralization may be a preferable strategy if it leads to territorial justice or the redistribution of wealth.

The response to this line of argument is likely to insist that at least local self-government, if organized according to democratic principles, gives power equally to the people. The more that state activities are decentralized, the greater the chance for the masses, through their elected leaders, to begin to redress the socio-economic imbalance between rich and poor. The principle of one person, one vote places all on a politically equal footing enabling the majority, who are the less privileged members of society, to prevail. They should be able to use their majority to effect changes for the better.

Such a view of decentralization takes a narrowly institutional and procedural view of democracy. To the extent that power resides elsewhere than in the right to vote this model of decentralized democracy is unrealistic. An ability to influence local policy-making and gain access to the decentralized services of the state depend on many factors other than the right to vote, even if that right can be exercised.

Take, for example, the picture which Alavi presents of village politics in Pakistan. Political contestants focus their attention on their lineages composed of independent peasant proprietors working through, and politically organized by, their elders and the lineage council. Thus the local lineage segment rather than the individual citizen is the significant unit of political participation. An individual household's political actions are subject to the authority of the lineage. Contestants for political office focus on the elders of the lineage.

Political alliances and support depend on economic status and particularly access to land. The political power of the poor and landless is reduced by their dependence on wealthier landowners and patrons rather than increased by the right to vote. Economic dependency is so pervasive that it is generally useless for a political rival to try to win support by intervening on behalf of badly treated tenants. Those who command the community's economic resources, mainly land, have access to the sources of power other than a patron-client relationship with those economically dependent on them. They can employ intimidation by cattle thieves and police to guarantee political support for their chosen candidates for political office in the institutions of 'basic democracy'. Even the small amount of power which the poor might possess depends on activities outside the formal machinery of government, such as the ability to organize a successful strike among hired labourers. Political parties tend to be caucuses of influential persons operating at the district level and are not organized to articulate the demands of ordinary peasants. Peasant unions are badly needed to mediate between the poorer peasants and officialdom, especially since officials tend to behave in an arbitrary and corrupt manner amid highly complex administrative procedures.

The less-privileged members of society are thus unable to form electoral majorities based on their common class interests. Rather they are divided into factions based on transactional relationships with a powerful individual. The poorer the members of the faction, the less choice they have in offering their allegiance. The bases of factional support combine kinship, caste, neighbourhood, economic dependence and mutual enmity towards some third party. Horizontal alignment (such as class interest) gives way to vertical alignments which have no ideological purpose and so do nothing to reduce dependence. The political choice for the majority of villagers is between factions which reinforce their dependent position in society (Alavi, 1971; see also H. Hart, 1971).

In India, too, the distribution of power within local institutions reflects the distribution of wealth within society. The economic power of landowners and employers influences the voting behaviour of the poor. Patron-client relationships undermine the freedom of lower classes to vote against their landlords. Even election to office is no guarantee that a member from a lower class or lower caste will obtain effective power (Schulz, 1979, pp. 71–2). Thus decentralization to representative and majoritarian rural institutions under the system of *panchayati raj* has simply strengthened the position of wealthy farmers *vis-à-vis* landlords and money-lenders.

Decentralist reforms, then, must not be divorced from the power structure of the community, particularly in the rural areas. Decentralizing power may simply play into hands already powerful because of wealth or hereditary status (Howell, 1977; Rondinelli, 1981a). A romanticized perception of 'community' often lay behind programmes of democratic decentralization and community development in the Third World as it has done in the industrialized democracies (see Chapter 9).

Centralization and Underdevelopment

Students of local government everywhere are acutely conscious of the centralizing tendencies which are such a ubiquitous feature of contemporary states. Explanations of such centralization, particuarly in relation to local democracy, tend to be technocratic and managerialist. The central authorities are seen as performing 'rationalizing', 'improving' and 'servicing' roles for local government. Their task is to maintain standards, rationalize the allocation of resources and 'programme' local socio-economic development within the framework of a national plan. Centralization is thus seen as a consequence of the greater technical and administrative competence of central government and is designed, in part, to overcome the 'excesses' of decentralization (United Nations, 1962; van Putten, 1971, p. 226).

The disadvantages of over-centralization are acknowledged in such interpretations, but a major role for central government at the local level is seen as arising inevitably from the need for nationally planned services, the control of scarce resources, territorial equality, implementation problems and centrally provided funds (Maddick, 1963; van Putten, 1971, p. 227).

Such a formulation begs as many questions as it answers, not least whether central agencies are better at managing finance and other resources than local, and whether they are also administratively stronger and aloof from the 'excesses' so often ascribed to local authorities. Centralization may be more realistically explained by reference to the configuration of political forces emerging in the new state as new relations of production develop with the support of state intervention. Local government powers, revenues and subordination, and the contradictions between ideological commitments and institutional practices, are the consequence of class interests represented by higher-level governments, the fiscal effects of economies dependent on export commodities, and shifts of power towards the national level of government in response to political instability. These features of underdevelopment will be briefly considered.

Ideology and Class Interests
Emerging class interests, articulated increasingly through levels of government which command the largest volume of state resources, will inevitably be hostile to the fragmentation and decentralization of power. In less-developed countries the emerging bourgeoisie is often dependent for its growth on national, not municipal, political power (Reilly, 1981; Bonney, 1982). There is thus likely to be conflict between a regime's ideological commitment to decentralization and the needs of new socio-economic interests. Participation at the local level may be an important concession to be offered to the lower classes if they are to be incorporated into a system of government and an economy which permits such classes very little individual

autonomy or personal power. Local democracy can offer the appearance of self-determination without its substance. But local autonomy may have to be contained on behalf of classes whose interests are most effectively articulated elsewhere.

The crucial issue for decentralization in developing countries is what level of government is seen by the political representatives of the dominant class as the most appropriate for deploying the economic resources at the disposal of the state and for managing conflicts with competing classes. In Nigeria, for example, the interests of the newly emerging indigenous propertied classes are increasingly articulated through the states of the federation. Powerful elements in the countryside which threatened the dominance of the new state-level political élites have had to be contained. Local government was reorganized to underline its subordinate position.

The state-level governments have become the instruments through which the growing indigenous entrepreneurial class gains access to capital for private investment. Political office at the level of the states provides many kinds of reward. There are lucrative positions in the administrative apparatus itself to be deployed for political and material advantage. There are contracts to be obtained by companies supplying goods and services to the large infrastructural projects in which state governments are involved. The states control access to the important goods which are the basis of commercial and industrial activity in the federation. They play a vital role in the development of capitalist enterprise by providing access to capital, often in combination with foreign investors. Credit schemes, public works, partnerships between state agencies and foreign business concerns, public ownership and control of land are the main ways in which state governments are currently promoting a diverse range of economic activities including prestige property developments and manufacturing industries.

Private enterprise in agriculture is also being sponsored by state intervention. Attempts to revive agriculture and improve productivity have taken the form of interventions by both state and federal governments to encourage large-scale private agriculture. Irrigation schemes have been initiated by thirteen parastatal river basin development authorities. Ownership of all land has been vested in state governments, thus opening up access to land for large-scale agriculture to outsiders. The right to allocate urban land has been transferred from local government to the state. This has helped private entrepreneurs overcome obstacles to the accumulation of land holdings presented by traditional land-tenure systems.

The significance of state government to commercial, industrial and agricultural development thus has serious implications for local government autonomy. Education, practically the only major function left to local government, is a necessary stage on the road to a bureaucratic position. The expanding state bureaucracies and their dependent entrepreneurs have a vested interest in controlling policies for educational provision. Local authorities have been left with very limited functions relating to agricultural development, land-use planning and the physical infrastructure. What few powers they have are bound to be closely controlled to ensure integration into the plans and projects which support capitalist developments initiated by state governmental agencies. The powers devolved to local government reflect the interests of those who control the state level and the extent to which they are prepared to loosen control over important inputs provided by the government to a growing industrial, commercial and agricultural business class.

In a socialist state such as Tanzania the emerging class structure will obviously be different. The consequences for decentralization may be similar, however.

Initially at independence the Tanzanian political élite believed that to overcome poverty and constrain regional, religious and ethnic divisiveness it was necessary to centralize the direction of the economy and co-ordinate nationally the deployment of extremely scarce resources, especially capital, technology and skilled personnel. They were encouraged in this by the aid donors who required long-range plans which only centralized institutions could produce.

Subsequently it was decided that decentralization was necessary for the achievement of the regime's political and economic objectives. However, this decentralization has been administrative rather than political. Plans are formulated centrally. Administrators dominate representative institutions. 'Participation' has been an instrument to instruct, guide and legitimize rather than to locate decision-making powers in the hands of local people (Samoff, 1979, p. 43). Participation is incompatible with the bureaucratic and technocratic values held by the newly emerging bureaucratic bourgeoisie and necessary to their continuing dominance. While other classes might benefit from representative institutions and high levels of participation, a bureaucratic bourgeoisie does not. Participation is further precluded by the ideology of 'government as expertise' through which the bureaucracy claims authority based on knowledge. To the extent that increased productive capacity in the countryside depends on local-level participation and self-government, it is unlikely to be achieved when a programme of decentralization is 'undertaken within the setting of a ruling bureaucratic class and a dominant ideology of technology' (Samoff, 1979, p. 57).

The kind of class analysis which has been applied to Tanzania has also been applied to the Maghreb states of Algeria, Tunisia, Morocco and Libya. Again, centralization is seen as, in part, a consequence of that coalition between bureaucrats and petty bourgeois populists which benefits from expansion of the central state machine. Bureaucrats and petty bourgeoisie control the means of production through the state apparatus and resist the devolution of power to peasants, workers, or the bourgeoisie through competitive politics either at national or local levels. The decentralization of political and administrative activity is thus part of the process by which the bureaucracy and petty bourgeoisie control the post-colonial state (Nellis, 1983).

The power of the bureaucracy in Third World states thus has serious implications for decentralization (Rondinelli, 1983). This makes it all the more necessary to use theoretical equipment which can account for bureaucratic dominance when analysing decentralist experiments in the Third World.

Fiscal Dependence
Financial weakness is among the severest obstacles to viable political decentralization. Underdevelopment may mean, among other things, that it is structurally difficult to organize sources of revenue which would strengthen financial independence at the local level. If an economy is based on a small number of revenue-earning export commodities there may be few alternative tax bases that can be developed and little political interest among the dominant classes in exploiting them.

In Nigeria, for example, intergovernmental relations are dominated by persistent and overwhelming dependence on resources allocated by higher levels of government. A major problems for local government, as for other levels of government in Nigeria, is the level of dependence on revenues from a single source, oil. Governments at both state and local levels have, in recent years, become increasingly dependent on allocations from federal revenues deriving from petroleum exploitation.

Little is being done to diversify the country's revenue source, despite the immediate impact on all governments of any downturn in oil revenue and the vulnerability of revenues to the decisions of foreign companies regarding exploration and development. Local government is now even more vulnerable to fluctuations in the price or quantity sold of the nation's most important resource. Nigeria is by no means the only country to find a lack of local revenues compounded by the inability of central government to provide allocations, an inability brought about by balance-of-payments problems, high rates of inflation and dependence on scarce foreign capital (Rondinelli, 1983).

It will be some years before it is known whether the policies inaugurated in the late 1970s to transform oil revenues into industrial and agricultural production capacity will produce wealth which the state can tax to diversify its revenue base. However, alternative sources of local revenue are unlikely to be utilized when dominant political groups have a vested interest in funding government expenditure at all levels through duties on export commodities. The centralist approach to local government is thus reinforced by a fiscal system which benefits those who might otherwise be expected to consider alternatives to central allocation for the financing of local government. Those who control government at the federal and state levels are more likely to seek resources to be allocated by the state in duties on import and export goods rather than in taxes on individual or corporate wealth.

The lack of political pressure for an autonomous local revenue can be traced back to colonial times when property rating was only introduced in those urban areas designated as townships (Home, 1976, p. 68). The structure of interests represented in post-colonial municipal government was not likely to extend the system. In developing countries the funding of local government cannot be separated from the general system of public funding and that system's usual dependence on export commodities in the absence of alternative revenue capacity. This is not just a question of whether there is a political will amongst the propertied interests which control state institutions to create alternatives. It is also a question of whether the structure of the economy, inhibiting diversification and the development of indigenous enterprise, allows the development of alternative sources of wealth which can be taxed by the state at any level other than the national. When rural incomes in a predominantly agricultural society are under pressure from falling export crop prices and high inflation, it is politically difficult both to increase taxes on incomes and maintain law and order, as some rural protest movements in Nigeria have shown.

There are other severe political obstacles to the expansion of locally raised revenues. There is a long history of reluctance among tax collectors to impose the full rate on wealthier groups with whose class interests they identify. Tax assessment has been used as a political weapon, with members of opposition parties over-assessed and government supporters exempt. It will be difficult to overcome hostility to the extension of property rating even when local councils are politically motivated to do so. The property owners of the urban areas have been well represented in both state assemblies and local councils, a factor likely to impede the expansion of property rating and, indeed, other forms of taxation.

Political Stability

Contrary to conventional wisdom, the threat of political instability seems to lead to centralization and measures to weaken, rather than strengthen, local centres of primordial political identity. The destabilizing effects of underdevelopment set up centralizing tendencies throughout the Third World. Ethnic and religious divisions, regional disparities, rural stagnation, dependency, dissidence, pervasive scarcity and the volatile international scene lead to a situation in which centralization is almost inevitable. The war against underdevelopment is seen by élites as demanding a government of national unity as much as a war against a foreign aggressor. Third World states inevitably take steps to 'impose a modicum of national integrity on their weak and fragile polities' (Nellis, 1983, p. 136).

Conclusion

An explanation of centralization in underdeveloped countries in terms of the *administrative competence* of local authorities compared with central agencies will almost inevitably overlook important features of underdevelopment which impinge upon intergovernmental relations in Third World states. The location of policy-making activities, the allocation of financial resources and the deployment of central control and influence are not managerial decisions based on considerations of manpower, finance and administrative competence.

An analysis of local democracy, participation and community self-government which ignores local inequalities of wealth and power will be similarly deficient. Decentralization may be judged differently, depending on whether it reinforces the position of those already dominant in local society or serves to increase the political power of classes hitherto subjected to exploitation. Writers and reformers concerned with decentralization and development would do well to heed James Fesler's warning about the romantic and doctrinal approach to local self-government:

In many countries and many communities village government is conservative government. In villages and towns where economic and social power is strongly hierarchical, the local government tends to be dominated by landlords and other possessors of economic power. If, as is often the case, they do not hold governmental office, they effectively influence the choice of officials . . . Being conservative government, village government is likely to resist opportunities to expand its services to the common people and increase regulation of those having economic power or traditionally high status. (Fesler, 1965, p. 543; see also Griffin, 1981)

11
Conclusion: The Politics of Decentralization

In discussing the different elements of the decentralized structures of nation-states it has become clear that the decisions that need to be made about those structures are political rather than technical. The study of decentralization reminds us yet again that any distinction between politics and administration can only be false. It might be conventional to consider decentralization as an administrative concept, and even evaluate it and discuss change as if it is a matter to be settled by technical arguments about optimum areas, administrative efficiency and managerial performance. But the outcomes in the form of working federations or systems of regional and local government are the result of political forces in conflict.

The pressures on the modern state to decentralize seem, at first glance, to fall into two quite distinct categories, one apparently administrative, the other political. The managerial needs of national organizations can only be met by delegating authority to field officers. Politically, threats to integration from culturally distinct communities can only be met by a measure of devolution. The two processes seem quite separate. However, having decided that an administrative presence in the regions and localities is needed does not conclude the process of political choice. A decision still has to be made on how the administration is to be carried on, and whether it is to be politicized. There are too many cases of state intervention in the fields of income maintenance, transportation, public utilities and health care that have been centralized after a period during which they were the responsibility of regional or local governments, and too many instances of government functions which are under central administration in one state and local in another, to believe that there is some politically neutral formula for the territorial allocation of governmental powers. The distribution of power between levels of government, as well as the choice of institutions for decentralization, are the outcomes of political conflicts at the centre which originate in group and class interests which sometimes have a territorial identity but which also unite and mobilize people regardless of region.

Perceptions of decentralization, and any normative stance to be taken on it, will be coloured by whatever theory is held, implicitly or explicitly, of the state. A liberal view of the state will attach considerable significance to localized government as part of a foundation for political equality and liberty as well as a political training ground and source of stability. It will be seen as supporting democracy in the narrow sense of competitive, representative and majoritarian government. This perception may be associated with an economic model of the citizen who seeks to maximize personal utility by way of locational decisions and voting behaviour.

There are two types of critique of this view of decentralization. One operates within the liberal paradigm, but questions the utility of a concept of democracy which ignores the economic and social bases of political power. It draws attention to the oligarchic nature of local communities which is reinforced rather than neutralized by the workings of democratic self-government. It emphasizes material equality as a necessary condition for political equality, and acknowledges that centralization may be required for progressively redistributive ends, whether between regions or social classes. A somewhat weaker critique simply asks whether actual political behaviour, in so far as we have adequate indicators of it, confirms the expectations held by democratic decentralists.

Marxists, in contrast, start from fundamentally different assumptions about liberal democratic states and their capitalist foundations. The local level is seen as contributing to the state's function under capitalism of renewing the forces and relations of production and maintaining the legitimacy of the social order. In so doing, however, it generates new socio-economic interests for whom the local political system acts as an important mediator. The state at the local level is far from being a mere extension or replication of the state in its national manifestation. Different conflicts are played out at the local level, not least over the issue of decentralization itself and what power the centre is entitled to wield over its subordinate jurisdictions. This approach to the state thus leads to a radically different view of intergovernmental relations to that implicit in liberalism and pluralism.

Relationships between territorial levels of government are thus further evidence of how political conflicts are managed in contemporary states. Changes in intergovernmental relations are not merely the outcomes of political conflicts at the national level; and they result in further conflict within, as well as between, levels of government. National and local political arenas are integrated. One way in which local interests can increase their political strength locally is to work through national institutions to alter the territorial distribution of power. National decision-makers have their local allies when seeking to control lower levels of government, whether it be for progressive or regressive redistribution.

Such an interpretation of intergovernmental relations suggests that a dialectical approach is needed. Changes in the territorial distribution of power in favour of central authorities will be resisted by regional or local interests for whom there are advantages in decentralization. One phase of public policy-making and state intervention may need the legitimation of decentralization and participation. A subsequent, centralist phase will need to challenge or even contradict this legitimacy. In all such phases of state intervention there will be changing alliances between political interests at the different geographical levels of the state.

Hence the importance of the distinction between decentralization and autonomy. By considering decentralization within the context of a wider structure of power it is possible to see the autonomy of regional and local levels of government as partly the consequence of central decisions to restrict local jurisdictions, partly of a power structure which limits the agenda of legitimate political action, and partly of a structure of social relations which state institutions are designed to sustain. Subnational levels of government may develop degrees of autonomy which contradict these structures of social and political relations. The extent to which local institutions might be used to challenge these structures will probably depend on whether they have allies in control of higher levels of government, as was suggested in the discussion of neighbourhood participation in Chapter 9. This is not to deny that local and regional governments are viable arenas for political participation on the part of underprivileged groups. It is simply to assert that any formal constraints on the use of governmental authority will reflect wider and more complex patterns of domination.

The diverse experiments with neighbourhood decentralization and community participation undertaken by many industrialized states in recent decades reveal most clearly the contradictions of decentralization that have somehow to be resolved politically. Participation in neighbourhood institutions may be encouraged to create the impression that urban communities, particularly in deprived areas, have the political power to ameliorate their social and economic conditions and redress their grievances. But such attempts at decentralization soon encounter two major obstacles. The scale of operations at neighbourhood level is far too small for effective governmental intervention to counter social and economic deprivation. Indeed, it is ironic that in the 'war' on poverty many of the objectives that have been set for the smallest geographical levels of government can only be tackled at national or even international levels. Only by ignoring the significance of work and incomes for poverty is it possible seriously to suggest that neighbourhood decentralization can provide a political arena in which the poor can effectively combat their deprivation. Emphasizing the contribution which the social services and other forms of state intervention make to the relief of deprivation may create the impression that, through political participation and self-help, depressed urban communities can lift themselves out of their deprivation. But it also adds a new dimension to conflict within municipalities experimenting with neighbourhood decentralization. Elected representatives at the level of municipality are obviously reluctant to create too strong an impression that authority has been devolved beyond them to the neighbourhood or street level, when they know that responsibility for providing services to the neighbourhoods and communities within their areas must ultimately be taken at that level which commands the necessary resources.

The second contradiction arises directly out of the first. Neighbourhood decentralization is supposed to channel community activism and participation towards existing patterns of state intervention. It is not supposed to mobilize social movements to agitate against those sources of deprivation that the state may have no wish to control, such as wage levels, factory closures, prices and property speculation. When the activism encouraged by schemes of neighbourhood decentralization and participation turns in these directions, states tend to resort to more orthodox forms of urban planning and management, if not to outright repression.

The financial decisions affecting decentralization also reveal the political nature of the conflicts between levels of government which stem from divisions of socio-economic interest which cut across territorial political arrangements. National political objectives will determine the level and type of revenue-raising capability delegated to subordinate governments. These objectives will be the source of conflicts within the local political system as well as between local and central authorities. Other political decisions will have fiscal implications for decentralized government: whether there are ideological and consequently legal constraints on municipal enterprise and therefore the capacity to raise revenues from sales; whether the advocacy of large-scale organization and professionalism is successful, thereby making the democratization of regionalized services politically impossible; and so on. One abiding political paradox for some decentralists is that central government grants may at one and the same time provide a financial basis for progressively redistributive policies and reduce the autonomy of local political authorities. The fiscal relationship shows again how an evaluation of decentralization will depend on the objectives being pursued. A transfer of power from one level of government to another may simply be a way of shifting the tax burden to political arenas in which those with an interest in low levels of public expenditure predominate.

The area question can only be resolved politically because the interplay of political forces determines both the choice of institutions and the choice of principles for the drawing of boundaries. A choice of technical criteria for the delimitation of areas may reflect the political influence of the professional groups involved in service delivery, as may the choice of institutions (area boards rather than area governments, for example). But the ascendancy of managerial and professional values may be reinforced by pressures to neutralize the political salience of issues, as in the case of water supply when the water of one region (Wales or Normandy) is tapped to supply the needs of another (the English Midlands or Paris).

The delimitation of areas depends on more than the resolution of conflict between the technical and democratic qualities of administration. Even if a democratic form of decentralized government is opted for there is still room for political conflict over the scale of operations represented by the geographical structure of the system. Classes and other social groups with an interest in egalitarian policies and objectives may benefit from large jurisdictions and consolidation, while those who benefit from inequality and low levels of public provision will favour smaller jurisdictions and fragmentation. However, the extent to which such conflict of interest is expressed in overt political action will depend upon the level of consciousness among different groups of the relationship between the scale of decentralized government and their material interests and political efficacy.

The politics of territorial structure and reform can only be artificially separated from the question of areas. The theory of decentralization suggests that different interests will perceive different structures of decentralized government as being to their advantage materially and therefore politically. Different political alignments will favour fragmentation or consolidation, particularly in the metropolitan areas, depending on the expectations they have of redistributive outcomes. The internal organization of local governments will reflect the political interests that are currently dominant, such as alliances between the professionals employed by the state and social classes whose material interests benefit from a depoliticized, managerialist approach to local decision-making. The overall structure of a decentralized system and the possibilities for reorganization will be conditioned by prevalent values articulated through the choices of national governments. Quite considerable compromises may have to be made with the values inherent in the pre-reform structures on behalf of the interests seeking a political advantage from change.

Political interests are equally important in the choice of field administration for the government of regions, districts and localities, and in the way field personnel perform the tasks assigned to them. Decentralizing to bureaucrats by no means removes administration from politics. It simply alters the opportunities for different groups to wield power. Whether decision-making authority has been devolved to democratically organized collectivities or delegated to civil servants will have far-reaching consequences for the access which different groups will gain to the various benefits distributed through state intervention. Central control through field administration is not an end in itself. It is a means by which specific interests ensure that their needs are met with adequate resources and that their priorities are not subsumed under the broader range of interests competing for resources through some form of area government. There is, of course, politics of an organizational kind within any structure of field administration. But the field officer is also a political animal within the community in which he serves. The socio-economic groups which he encounters there will not only test his loyalty to headquarters. They will have different kinds of interest in maintaining that form of decentralized administration intact.

Decentralized structures of government in contemporary states do not only require political choices to be made by political élites and activists. They also require social scientists to make crucial choices of method, approach and underlying assumptions about power and the state. These, too, are political choices.

Bibliography

Alassam, M. (1981), 'Decentralisation for development: the Sudanese experience', paper to UN Interregional Seminar on Decentralization for Development, Khartoum, September.

Alavi, H. (1971), 'The politics of dependence: a village in West Punjab', *South Asian Review*, vol. 4, no. 2.

Aliyu, A. Y. (1978), 'Local government reform: as seen in Kaduna', in K. Panter-Brick (ed.), *Soldiers and Oil* (London: Frank Cass).

Ashford, D. E. (1974), 'The effects of central finance on the British local government system', *British Journal of Political Science*, vol. 4, no. 3.

Ashford, D. E. (1975), 'Theories of local government. Some comparative considerations', *Comparative Political Studies*, vol. 8, no. 2.

Ashford, D. E. (1979), 'Territorial politics and equality: decentralization and the modern state', *Political Studies*, vol. 27, no. 1.

Ashford, D. E. (1980), 'Central-local financial exchange in the welfare state', in D. E. Ashford (ed.), *Financing Urban Government in the Welfare State*. (London: Croom Helm).

Ashton, P. J. (1978), 'The political economy of suburban development', in W. K. Tabb and L. Sawers (eds), *Marxism and the Metropolis. New Perspectives in Urban Political Economy* (New York: Oxford University Press).

Association of Municipal Authorities (1975), 'Policy Committee Report. Appendix B', supplement to *Municipal Review*, no. 541 (January).

Bachrach, P., and Baratz, M. S. (1970), *Power and Poverty, Theory and Practice* (New York: Oxford University Press).

Baestlein, A. *et al.* (1978), 'State grants and local development planning in the Federal Republic of Germany', in K. Hanf and F. W. Scharpf (eds) *Interorganizational Policy-Making, Limits to Co-ordination and Central Control* (Beverly Hills, Calif.: Sage).

Baine, S. (1975), *Community Action and Local Government*, Occasional Papers on Social Administration, no. 59 (London: Bell).

Barraclough, S. L. (1964), 'Interaction between agrarian structure and public policies in Latin America', in G. Hunter *et al.* (eds), *Policy and Practice in Rural Development* (London: Overseas Development Institute).

Beard, C. (1965), *An Economic Interpretation of the Constitution of the United States*, 3rd edn (New York: The Free Press).

Beaumont, P. B., and Heald, D. A. (1981), 'Public employment', in P. M. Jackson (ed.), *Government Policy Initiatives 1979–80: Some Case Studies in Public Administration* (London: Royal Institute of Public Administration).

Bedeski, R. E. (1980), 'People's Republic of China', in D. C. Rowat (ed.), *International Handbook on Local Government Reorganisation. Contemporary Developments* (London: Aldwych Press).

Bennett, R. J. (1980), *The Geography of Public Finance* (London: Methuen).

Birch, A. H. (1955), *Federalism, Finance and Social Legislation in Canada, Australia and the United States* (London: Oxford University Press).

Birch, A. H. (1956), 'A note on devolution', *Political Studies*, vol. 4, no. 1.

Birch, A. H. (1964), *Representative and Responsible Government* (London: Allen & Unwin).

Birch, A. H. (1977), *Political Integration and Disintegration in the British Isles* (London: Allen & Unwin).

Birch, A. H. (1978), 'Minority nationalist movements and theories of political integration', *World Politics*, vol. 30.

Bish, R. L. (1978), 'Intergovernmental relations in the USA: some concepts and implications from a public choice perspective', in K. Hanf and F. W. Scharpf (eds), *Interorganizational Policy-Making. Limits to Co-ordination and Central Control* (Beverly Hills, Calif.: Sage).

Bish, R. L. and Ostrom, V. (1973), *Understanding Urban Government* (Washington DC: American Enterprise Institute for Public Policy Research).

Blondel, J. (1973), *Comparative Legislatures* (Englewood Cliffs, N J: Prentice-Hall).

Blunt, E. (1937), *The Indian Civil Service* (London: Faber).

Boaden, N. (1970), 'Central departments and local authorities: the relationship examined', *Political Studies*, vol. 18, no. 2.

Boaden, N. (1971), *Urban Policy-Making. Influences on County Boroughs in England and Wales* (Cambridge: Cambridge University Press).

Bonney, N. (1982), 'Local government and political development in Papua New Guinea', *Public Administration and Development*, vol. 2, no. 2.

Bowen, E. R. (1980), 'United States', in D. C. Rowat (ed.), *International Handbook on Local Government Reorganisation. Contemporary Developments* (London: Aldwych Press).

Brand, J. (1965), 'Ministerial control and local autonomy in education', *Political Quarterly*, vol. 36, no. 2.

Brand, J. (1976), 'Reforming local government: Sweden and England compared', in R. Rose (ed.), *The Dynamics of Public Policy: A Comparative Analysis* (Beverly Hills, Calif.: Sage).

Brown, T., Vile, M. J. C., and Whitemore, M. (1972), 'Community studies and decision-taking', *British Journal of Political Science*, vol. 2, no. 2.

Burnett, A. D. (1976), 'Legislation for neighbourhood councils in England', *Local Government Studies*, vol. 2, no. 4.

Castells, M. (1978), *City, Class and Power* (London: Macmillan).

Cawson, A., and Saunders, P. (1983), 'Corporatism, competitive politics and class struggle', in R. King (ed.), *Capital, Ideology and Politics* (London: Routledge & Kegan Paul).

Chapman, B. (1955), *The Prefects and Provincial France* (London: Allen & Unwin).

Cheema, G. S., and Rondinelli, D. A. (1983), *Implementing Decentralisation Programmes in Asia. Local Capacity for Rural Development* (Nagoya, Japan: United Nations Centre for Regional Development).

Chikulo, B. C. (1981), 'The Zambian administrative reforms: an alternative view', *Public Administration and Development*, vol. 1, no. 1.

Clark, T. N. (1973), 'Community autonomy in the national system: federalism, localism and decentralization', *Social Service Information*, vol. 12, no. 4 (August).

Clarke, C. (1977), 'Community Councils: power to the people?', in C. Crouch (ed.), *Participation in Politics* (London: Croom Helm).

Cleworth, P. (1977), 'Positive discrimination and urban deprivation', *Local Government Studies*, vol. 3, no. 3.

Cockburn, C. (1977), *The Local State. Management of Cities and People* (London: Pluto Press).

Cohen, M. A. (1980), 'Francophone Africa', in D. C. Rowat (ed.), *International Handbook on Local Government Reorganisation* (London: Aldwych Press).

Coit, K. (1978), 'Local action, not citizen participation', in W. K. Tabb and L. Sawers (eds), *Marxism and the Metropolis. New Perspectives in Urban Political Economy* (New York: Oxford University Press).

Cole, G. D. H. (1947), *Local and Regional Government* (London: Cassell).

Committee of Inquiry into Local Government Finance (Layfield Committee) (1976), *Local Government Finance*, Cmnd 6453 (London: HMSO).

Committee on Local Authority and Allied Personal Social Services (Seebohm Committee) (1968), *Report*, Cmnd 3703 (London: HMSO).

Connor, W. (1973), 'The politics of ethnonationalism', *Journal of International Affairs*, vol. 27, no. 1.

Conyers, D. (1981), 'Decentralization for regional development: a comparative study of Tanzania, Zambia and Papua New Guinea', *Public Administration and Development*, vol. 1, no. 2.

Corkey, D. and Craig, G. (1978), 'CDP: community work or class politics', in P. Curno (ed.), *Political Issues and Community Work* (London: Routledge & Kegan Paul).

Council of Europe (1978), *Conditions of Local Democracy and Citizen Participation in Europe*, Study Series on Local and Regional Authorities in Europe, no. 15 (Strasbourg: Council of Europe).

Council of Europe (1980), *The Strengthening of Local Structures, with Special Reference to Amalgamation and Co-operation between Municipalities in Council of Europe Member States*, Study Series on Local and Regional Authorities in Europe, no. 10 (Strasbourg: Council of Europe).

Council of Europe (1981a), *Decentralisation of Local Government at Neighbourhood Level*, Study Series on Local and Regional Authorities in Europe, no. 27 (Strasbourg: Council of Europe).

Council of Europe (1981b), *Financial Apportionment and Equalisation*, Study Series on Local and Regional Authorities in Europe, no. 24 (Strasbourg: Council of Europe).

Council of Europe (1981c), *Functional Decentralisation at Local and Regional Level*, Study Series on Local and Regional Authorities in Europe, no. 26 (Strasbourg: Council of Europe).

Cox, A. W. (1979), 'Administrative inertia and inner city policy', *Public Administration Bulletin*, no. 29 (April).

Cox, W. Harvey (1976), *Cities: The Public Dimension* (Harmondsworth, Middx.: Penguin).

Cripps, F., and Godley, W. (1976), *Local Government Finance and its Reform: A Critique of the Layfield Committee's Report* (Cambridge: Cambridge University Press).

Cross, J. A. (1970), 'The regional decentralization of British government departments', *Public Administration*, vol. 48 (Winter).

Dahl, R. A. (1981), 'The city in the future of democracy', in L. D. Feldman (ed.), *Politics and Government of Urban Canada*, 4th edn (London: Methuen).

Dahl, R. A., and Tufte, E. R. (1974), *Size and Democracy* (London: Oxford University Press).

Damer, S., and Hague, C. (1971), 'Public participation in planning: a review', *Town Planning Review*, vol. 42, no. 3.

Davey, K. J. (1971), 'Local autonomy and independent revenues', *Public Administration*, vol. 49 (Spring).

Dawson, A. H. (1981), 'The idea of the region and the 1975 reorganization of Scottish local government', *Public Administration*, vol. 59 (Autumn).

Dearlove, J. (1979), *The Reorganization of British Local Government* (Cambridge: Cambridge University Press).

de Mello, D. L. (1981), 'Strategies and problems of public accountability under decentralisation', paper to UN Interregional Seminar on Decentralization for Development, Khartoum, September.

Dennis, N. (1972), *Public Participation and Planners' Blight* (London: Faber).

Dente, B., and Regonini, G. (1980), 'Urban policy and political legitimation: the case of Italian neighbourhood councils', *International Political Science Review*, vol. 1, no. 2.

de Tocqueville, Alexis (1835), *Democracy in America* (New York: Vintage Books edn, 1945).

Dickinson, R. E. (1964), *City and Region. A Geographical Interpretation* (London: Routledge & Kegan Paul).

Dikshit, R. (1975), *The Political Geography of Federalism* (London: Macmillan).

Downs, A. (1967), *Inside Bureaucracy* (Boston, Mass.: Little, Brown).

Duchacek, I. D. (1970), *Comparative Federalism. The Territorial Dimension of Politics* (New York: Holt, Rinehart & Winston).

Dunleavy, P. (1979), 'The urban basis of political alignment', *British Journal of Political Science*, vol. 9, no. 4.

Dunleavy, P. (1980a), 'Social and political theory and the issues in central–local relations', in G. W. Jones (ed.), *New Approaches to the Study of Central–Local Government Relationships* (Aldershot, Hants: Gower and SSRC).

Dunleavy, P. (1980b), *Urban Political Analysis. The Politics of Collective Consumption* (London: Macmillan).

Dunleavy, P. (1981), 'Professions and policy change: notes towards a model of ideological corporatism', *Public Administration Bulletin*, no. 36 (August).

Dupré, J. Stefan (1969), 'Inter-governmental relations and the metropolitan area', in L. D. Feldman and M. D. Goldrick (eds), *Politics and Government of Urban Canada* (London: Methuen).

Durkheim, E. (1893), *The Division of Labour in Society*, translated by George Simpson (New York: The Free Press edn, 1964).

Earle, V. (ed.) (1968), *Federalism. Infinite Variety in Theory and Practice* (Itasca, Ill.: Peacock).

Elcock, H. (1982), *Local Government. Politicians, Professionals and the Public in Local Authorities* (London: Methuen).

Evans, R. H. (1980), 'Italy' in D. C. Rowat (ed.), *International Handbook on Local Government Reorganisation. Contemporary Developments* (London: Aldwych Press).

Fesler, J. W. (1949), *Area and Administration* (Montgomery, Ala: University of Alabama Press).

Fesler, J. W. (1959), 'Field Organisation', in F. M. Marx (ed.), *Elements of Public Administration* (Englewood Cliffs, NJ: Prentice-Hall).

Fesler, J. W. (1962), 'The political role of field administration', in F. Heady and S. L. Stokes (eds), *Papers in Comparative Public Administration* (Ann Arbor, Mich.: Institute of Public Administration, Michigan University).

Fesler, J. W. (1965), 'Approaches to the understanding of decentralization', *Journal of Politics*, vol. 27, no. 4.

Fesler, J. W. (1973), 'The basic theoretical question: how to relate area to function', in L. E. Grosenick (ed.), *The Administration of New Federalism* (Washington DC: American Society for Public Administration).

Finer, S. (1957), *A Primer of Public Administration* (London: Muller).

Flynn, N. (1978), 'Urban experiments limited: lessons from the Community Development Project and Inner Area Studies', in M. Harloe (ed.), *Urban Change and Conflict* (London: Centre for Environmental Studies).

Folson, K. G. (1981), 'Mobilising and managing financial and physical resources under decentralisation schemes', paper to UN Interregional Seminar on Decentralization for Development, Khartoum, September.

Foster, C. D., Jackman, R. A., and Osborn, M. S. (1976), 'Centralization and local discretion in educational expenditure', app. 10 to Layfield Committee of Inquiry into Local Government Finance, *Report*, Cmnd 6453 (London: HMSO).

Foster, C. D., Jackman, R. A., and Perlman, M. (1980), *Local Government Finance in a Unitary State* (London: Allen & Unwin).

Fried, R. C. (1963), *The Italian Prefects* (New Haven, Conn.: Yale University Press).

Fried, R. C. (1974), 'Politics, economics and federalism: aspects of urban government in Austria, Germany and Switzerland', in T. N. Clark (ed.), *Comparative Community Politics* (Beverly Hills, Calif.: Sage).

Friedman, H. J. (1983), 'Decentralized development in Asia: local policy alternatives', in G. S. Cheema and D. A. Rondinelli (eds), *Decentralization and Development. Policy Implementation in Developing Countries* (Beverly Hills, Calif.: Sage).

Friedrich, C. J. (1968), *Trends of Federalism in Theory and Practice* (New York: Praeger).

Frognier, A. P., Quevit, M., and Stenbock, M. (1982), 'Regional imbalances and centre–periphery relationships in Belgium', in S. Rokkan and D. Urwin (eds), *The Politics of Territorial Identity* (Beverly Hills, Calif.: Sage).

Furniss, N. (1974), 'The practical significance of decentralization', *Journal of Politics*, vol. 36, no. 4.

Garlichs, D., and Hull, C. (1978), 'Central control and information dependence: highway planning in the Federal Republic of Germany', in K. Hanf and F. W. Sharpf (eds), *Interorganizational Policy-Making. Limits to Co-ordination and Central Control* (Beverly Hills, Calif.: Sage).

Gilbert, E. W. (1948), 'Boundaries of local government areas', *Geographical Journal*, vol. 3, nos 4–6 (April–June).

Glasson, J. (1974), *An Introduction to Regional Planning* (London: Hutchinson).

Gold, J. R. (1976), 'Neighbourhood, territory and identity in the city', in J. R. Gold (ed.), *Neighbourhood Planning and Politics*, Discussion Papers in Geography (Oxford: Oxford Polytechnic).

Gopal, G. H. (1980), 'Administration of anti-poverty programmes in rural Andhra Pradesh', in T. H. Chaturvedi and S. Kohli (eds), *Social Administration* (Delhi: Indian Institute of Public Administration).

Gorvine, A. (1965), 'The utilisation of local government for national development', *Journal of Local Administration Overseas*, vol. 4, no. 4.

Gough, I. (1979), *The Political Economy of the Welfare State* (London: Macmillan).

Gray, C. (1982), 'The regional water authorities', in B. W. Hogwood and M. Keating (eds), *Regional Government in England* (Oxford: Clarendon Press).

Green, G. (1974), 'Politics, local government and the community', *Local Government Studies* (June).

Greenwood, R., Jones, G., and Stewart, J. (1982), 'Making government more local', *New Society*, 25 February.

Griffin, K. (1981), 'Economic development in a changing world', *World Development*, vol. 9, no. 3.

Griffith, J. A. G. (1966), *Central Departments and Local Authorities* (London: Allen & Unwin).

Grodzins, M. (1960), 'The federal system' in American Assembly (ed.), *Goals for Americans* (Englewood Cliffs, NJ: Prentice-Hall).

Grumm, J. G., and Murphy, R. D. (1974), 'Dillon's rule reconsidered', *Annals of the American Academy of Political and Social Science*, vol. 416.

Gyford, J. (1980), 'Political parties and central–local relations', in G. W. Jones (ed.), *New Approaches to the Study of Central–Local Government Relationships* (Aldershot, Hants: Gower and SSRC).

Hackett, J., and Hackett, A.-M. (1963), *Economic Planning in France* (London: Allen & Unwin).

Hadley, R., and Hatch, S. (1981), *Social Welfare and the Failure of the State* (London: Allen & Unwin).

Hambleton, R. (1977), 'Policies for areas', *Local Government Studies*, vol. 3, no. 2.

Hanf, K., and Scharpf, F. W. (eds) (1978), *Interorganizational Policy-Making. Limits to Co-ordination and Central Control* (Beverly Hills, Calif.: Sage).

Hansen, T. (1981), 'The dynamics of local expenditure growth', in L. J Sharpe (ed.), *The Local Fiscal Crisis in Western Europe* (Beverly Hills, Calif.: Sage).

Harris, R. (1978), 'Communications and the rate support grant process', *Linkage* (July).

Harris, R. L. (1983), 'Centralization and decentralization in Latin America', in G. S. Cheema and D. A. Rondinelli (eds), *Decentralization and Development. Policy Implementation in Developing Countries* (Beverly Hills, Calif.: Sage).

Hart, D. K. (1972), 'Theories of government related to decentralization and citizen participation', *Public Administration Review*, vol. 32, no. 4. (October).

Hart, H. (1971), 'The village and development administration', in J. Heaphey (ed.), *Spatial Dimensions of Development Administration* (Durham, NC: Duke University Press).

Hartle, D. G., and Bird, R. M., 'The demand for local political autonomy: an individualistic theory', *Journal of Conflict Resolution*, vol. 15, no. 4.

Hatch, S., Fox, E., and Legg, C. (1977), *Research and Reform. The Case of the Southwark Community Development Project 1969–72* (London: Home Office Urban Deprivation Unit).

Haywood, S. C., and Elcock, H. J. (1982), 'Regional health authorities: regional government or central agencies?', in B. W. Hogwood and M. Keating (eds), *Regional Government in England* (Oxford: Clarendon Press).

Heald, D. (1983), *Public Expenditure: Its Defence and Reform* (Oxford: Martin Robertson).

Heaphey, J. J. (1971), *Spatial Dimensions of Development Administration* (Durham, NC: Duke University Press).

Heiberg, M. (1982), 'Urban politics and rural culture: Basque nationalism', in S. Rokkan and D. Urwin (eds), *The Politics of Territorial Identity* (Beverly Hills, Calif.: Sage).

Henderson, K. M. (1967), 'Towards an understanding of the local component of development administration', *International Review of Administrative Sciences*, vol. 33, no. 3.

Hepworth, N. P. (1976), 'Public expenditure controls and local government', *Local Government Studies*, vol. 2, no. 1.

Higgins, J. (1978), *The Poverty Business: Britain and America* (Oxford: Blackwell).

Hill, D. M. (1974), *Democratic Theory and Local Government* (London: Allen & Unwin).

Hill, R. C. (1978), 'Fiscal collapse and political struggle in decaying central cities in the United States', in W. K. Tabb and L. Sawers (eds), *Marxism and the Metropolis. New Perspectives in Urban Political Economy* (New York: Oxford University Press).

Hirsch, W. Z. (1970), *The Economics of State and Local Government* (New York: McGraw-Hill).

Hogwood, B. W. (1982a), Introduction to B. W. Hogwood and M. Keating (eds), *Regional Government in England* (Oxford: Clarendon Press).

Hogwood, B. W. (1982b), 'The regional dimension of industrial policy administration', in B. W. Hogwood and M. Keating (eds), *Regional Government in England* (Oxford: Clarendon Press).

Hogwood, B. W., and Lindley, P. D. (1982), 'Variations in regional boundaries', in B. W. Hogwood and M. Keating (eds), *Regional Government in England* (Oxford: Clarendon Press).

Home, R. K. (1976), 'Urban growth and urban government: contradictions in the colonial political economy', in G. Williams (ed.), *Nigeria: Economy and Society* (London: Rex Collings).

Hough, J. (1969), *The Soviet Prefects* (Cambridge, Mass.: Harvard University Press).

Hough, J. F. (1971), 'The prerequisites of areal deconcentration: the Soviet experience', in J. J. Heaphey (ed.), *Spatial Dimensions of Development Administration* (Durham, NC: Duke University Press).

Hough, J. F. (1980), 'USSR: The urban units', in D. C. Rowat (ed.), *International Handbook on Local Government Reorganisation. Contemporary Developments* (London: Aldwych Press).

Howell, J. (1977), 'Administration and rural development planning: a Sudanese case', *Agricultural Administration*, vol. 4, no. 2.

Humble, S. (1979), 'The parish review', *Local Government Studies*, vol. 5, no. 2.

Humes, S. (1973), 'The role of local government in economic development in Africa', *Journal of Administration Overseas*, vol. 12, no. 1.

Jackman, R. (1982), 'Does central government need to control the total of local government spending?', *Local Government Studies*, vol. 8, no. 3.

Jackson, J. E. (1975), 'Public needs, private behaviour and metropolitan governance: a summary essay', in J. E. Jackson (ed.), *Public Needs and Private Behaviour in Metropolitan Areas* (Cambridge, Mass.: Ballinger).

Jackson, P. M., Meadows, J., and Taylor, A. P. (1982), 'Urban fiscal decay in U. K. cities', *Local Government Studies*, vol. 8, no. 5.

Jackson, W., and Bergman, E. (1973), *A Geography of Politics* (Dubuque, Iowa: Brown).

Jacob, H. (1963), *German Administration since Bismarck* (New Haven, Conn.: Yale University Press).

Jones, G. W. (1974), 'Intergovernmental relations in Britain', *Annals of the Americal Academy for Political and Social Science*, vol. 416.

Jones, G. W. (1978), 'Central–local government relations: grants, local responsibility and minimum standards', in D. Butler and A. H. Halsey (eds), *Policy and Politics* (London: Macmillan).

Jones, G. W. (1980), Introduction in G. W. Jones (ed.), *New Approaches to the Study of Central–Local Government Relationships* (Aldershot, Hants: Gower and SSRC).

Katznelson, I. (1972), 'Antagonistic ambiguity: notes on reformism and decentralization', *Politics and Society*, vol. 2, no. 3 (Spring).

Kaufman, H. (1960), *The Forest Ranger* (Baltimore, Md: Johns Hopkins University Press).

Kaufman, H. (1963), *Politics and Policies in State and Local Governments* (Englewood Cliffs, NJ: Prentice-Hall).

Kaufman, H. (1969), 'Administrative decentralization and political power', *Public Administration Review*, vol. 29, no. 1 (January–February).

Kelsen, H. (1961), *General Theory of Law and the State*, 2nd edn (Cambridge, Mass.: Harvard University Press).

Khanna, B. S., and Bhatnagar, S. (1980), 'India', in D. C. Rowat (ed.), *International Handbook on Local Government Reorganisation. Contemporary Developments* (London: Aldwych Press).

King, D. N. (1973), *Financial and Economic Aspects of Regionalism and Separatism*, Research Paper no. 10, Commission on the Constitution (London: HMSO).

King, P. (1982), *Federalism and Federation* (London: Croom Helm).

Kjellberg, F. (1979), 'A comparative view of municipal decentralization: neighbourhood democracy in Oslo and Bologna', in L. J. Sharpe (ed.), *Decentralist Trends in Western Democracies* (Beverly Hills, Calif: Sage).

Kolinsky, M. (1981), 'The nation-state in Western Europe: erosion from above and below', in L. Tivey (ed.), *The Nation-State* (Oxford: Martin Robertson).

Kulski, W. W. (1959), *The Soviet Regime* (Syracuse, NY: Syracuse University Press).

Kuroda, Y. (1975), 'Levels of government in comparative perspective', *Comparative Political Studies*, vol. 7. no. 4.

Lang, N. R. (1975), 'The dialects of decentralisation: economic reform and regional inequality in Yugoslavia', *World Politics*, vol. 27.

Langrod, G. (1953), 'Local government and democracy', *Public Administration*, vol. 31 (Spring).

Laski, H. (1931), *A Grammar of Politics* (London: Allen & Unwin).

Lawless, P. (1979), *Urban Deprivation and Government Initiatives* (London: Faber).

Lawrence, R. J. (1956), 'Devolution reconsidered', *Political Studies*, vol. 4, no. 2.

Leemans, A. F. (1970), *Changing Patterns of Local Government* (The Hague: International Union of Local Authorities).

Lees, R., and Smith, G. (eds) (1975), *Action Research in Community Development* (London: Routledge & Kegan Paul).

Lindley, P. D. (1982), 'The framework of regional planning 1964–1980', in B. W. Hogwood and M. Keating (eds), *Regional Government in England* (Oxford: Clarendon Press).

Lipman, V. D. (1949), *Local Government Areas, 1834–1945* (Oxford: Blackwell).

Lipman, V. D. (1952), 'Town and country. The study of service centres and their areas of influence', *Public Administration*, vol. 30.

Livingstone, I. (1975), 'Experimentation in rural development. Kenya's special rural development programme', *Agricultural Administration*, vol. 2, no. 4.

Livingstone, W. (1956), *Federalism and Constitutional Change* (London: Oxford University Press).

Livingstone, W. (1968), 'Canada, Australia and the United States: variations on a theme', in V. Earle (ed.), *Federalism. Infinite Variety in Theory and Practice* (Itasca, Ill.: Peacock Publishers).

Lukes, S. (1974), *Power. A Radical View* (London: Macmillan).

Maas, A. (1959), *Area and Power* (New York: The Free Press).

Machin, H. (1977), *The Prefect in French Public Administration* (London: Croom Helm).

Mackenzie, W. J. M. (1961), *Theories of Local Government*, Greater London Papers, no. 2 (London: Greater London Group).

Mackintosh, J. P. (1964), 'Regional administration: has it worked in Scotland?', *Public Administration*, vol. 42 (Autumn).

Maddick, H. (1963), *Democracy, Decentralisation and Development* (Bombay: Asia Publishing House).

Maddick, H. (1981), 'Major approaches and strategies in decentralisation for development', paper to UN Interregional Seminar on Decentralization for Development, Khartoum, September.

Magnusson, W. (1979), 'The new neighbourhood democracy: Anglo-American experience in historical perspective', in L. J. Sharpe (ed.), *Decentralist Trends in Western Democracies* (Beverly Hills, Calif.: Sage).

Magnusson, W. (1981), 'Metropolitan reform in the capitalist city', *Canadian Journal of Political Science*, vol. 14, no. 3 (September).

Markusen, A. R. (1978), 'Class and urban social expenditure: a Marxist theory of metropolitan government', in W. K. Tabb and L. Sawers (eds), *Marxism and the Metropolis. New Perspectives in Urban Political Economy* (New York: Oxford University Press).

Mason, T. (1978), 'Area management – the progress of an idea in local government', *Local Government Studies*, vol. 4, no. 1.

Masterson, M. (1978), 'Forming community councils – East Kilbride', *Local Government Studies*, vol. 4, no. 4.

Masterson, M., and Masterman, E. (1980), 'Elections to the second generation of community councils – The Orkney and Shetland Islands, Lochaber, West Lothian and Berwickshire', *Local Government Studies*, vol. 6, no. 1.

Mathur, K. (1983), 'Administrative decentralization in Asia', in G. S. Cheema and D. A. Rondinelli (eds), *Decentralization and Development. Policy Implementation in Developing Countries* (Beverly Hills, Calif.: Sage).

Mawhood, P. M., and Davey, K. (1980), 'Anglophone Africa', in D. C. Rowat (ed.), *International Handbook on Local Government Reorganisation. Contemporary Developments* (London: Aldwych Press).

Mayntz, R. (1978), 'Intergovernmental implementation of environmental policy', in K. Hanf and F. W. Scharpf (eds), *Interorganizational Policy-Making. Limits to Co-ordination and Central Control* (Beverly Hills, Calif.: Sage).

Mayo, M. (1975), 'The history and early development of CDP', in R. Lees and G. Smith (eds), *Action Research in Community Development* (London: Routledge & Kegan Paul).

McAuley, M. (1977), *Politics and the Soviet Union* (Harmondsworth, Middx.: Penguin).

McKay, D. H. (1980), 'The rise of the topocratic state: U.S. intergovernmental relations in the 1970's', in D. E. Ashford (ed.), *Financing Urban Government in the Welfare State* (London: Croom Helm).

McKay, D. H. (1982), 'Fiscal federalism, professionalism and the transformation of American state government', *Public Administration*, vol. 60 (Spring).

Meadows, W. J. (1981), 'Local Government', in P. M. Jackson (ed.), *Government Policy Initiatives 1979–80: Some Case Studies in Public Administration* (London: Royal Institute of Public Administration).

Mill, J. S. (1859), *On Liberty*, Everyman edn (London: Dent, 1931).

Mill, J. S. (1861), *Representative Government*, Everyman edn (London: Dent, 1931).

Miller, C. (1981), 'Area management: Newcastle's priority areas programme', in L. Smith and D. Jones (eds), *Deprivation, Participation and Community Action* (London: Routledge & Kegan Paul).

Money, W. J. (1973), 'The need to sustain a viable system of local democracy', *Urban Studies*, vol. 10, no. 3.

Moulin, L. (1954), 'Local self-government as a basis for democracy: a further comment', *Public Administration*, vol. 32 (Winter).

Mukerji, B. (1961), 'Administrative problems of democratic decentralisation', *Indian Journal of Public Administration*, vol. 7, no. 3.

Nellis, J. R. (1983), 'Decentralization in North Africa. Problems of policy implementation', in G. S. Cheema and D. A. Rondinelli (eds), *Decentralization and Development. Policy Implementation in Developing Countries* (Beverly Hills, Calif.: Sage).

Newton, K. (1974), 'Community decision-makers and community decision-making in England and the United States', in T. N. Clark (ed.), *Comparative Community Politics* (Beverly Hills, Calif.: Sage).

Newton, K. (1975), 'Community politics and decision-making: the American experience and its lessons', in K. Young (ed.), *Essays on the Study of Urban Politics* (London: Macmillan).

Newton, K. (1976), 'Community performance in Britain', *Current Sociology*, vol. 26, no. 1, pp. 49–86.

Newton, K. (1980a), *Balancing the Books, Financial Problems of Local Government in West Europe* (Beverly Hills, Calif.: Sage).

Newton, K. (1980b), 'Central government grants, territorial justice and local democracy in post-war Britain', in D. E. Ashford (ed.), *Financing Urban Government in the Welfare State* (London: Croom Helm).

Newton, K. (1982), 'Is small really so beautiful? Is big so ugly? Size, effectiveness and democracy in local government', *Political Studies*, vol. 30, no. 2.

Norton, A. (1980), 'Britain: England and Wales', in D. C. Rowat (ed.), *International Handbook on Local Government Reorganisation* (London: Aldwych Press).

Oates, W. E. (1972), *The Political Economy of Fiscal Federalism* (Lexington, Mass.: Lexington Books).

O'Connor, J. R. (1973), *The Fiscal Crisis of the State* (New York: St Martin's Press).

Offe, C. (1975), 'The theory of the capitalist state and the problem of policy-formation', in L. Lindberg, R. Alford, C. Crouch, and C. Offe (eds), *Stress and Contradiction in Modern Capitalism* (Lexington, Mass.: Lexington Books).

Ostrom, E., Tiebout, C. M., and Warren, R. (1961), 'The organisation of governments in metropolitan areas: a theoretical inquiry', *American Political Science Review*, vol. 55, no. 4 (December).

Paddison, R. (1983), *The Fragmented State. The Political Geography of Power* (Oxford: Blackwell).

Padover, S. K. (1954), *Thomas Jefferson on Democracy* (New York: Mentor Books).

Page, E. (1981), 'The new gift relationship: are central government grants only good for the soul?', *Public Administration Bulletin*, no. 36 (August).

Panter-Brick, K. (1953), 'Local government and democracy – a rejoinder', *Public Administration*, vol. 31 (Winter).

Paris, C., and Blackaby, B. (1979), *Not Much Improvement. Urban Renewal Policy in Birmingham* (London: Heinemann).

Parry, G. (ed.) (1972), *Participation in Politics* (Manchester: Manchester University Press).

Pavic, Z. (1980), 'Yugoslavia', in D. C. Rowat (ed.), *International Handbook on Local Government Reorganisation. Contemporary Developments* (London: Aldwych Press).

Phillips, H. S. (1963), 'Development administration and the alliance for progress', *International Review of Administrative Sciences*, vol. 29, no. 1.

Phillips, T. J. (1979), 'Area planning committees in Walsall', *Local Government Studies*, vol. 5, no. 1.

Picard, L. (1980), 'Socialism and the field administrator: decentralization in Tanzania', *Comparative Politics*, vol. 12, no. 4 (July).

Plunkett, T. J. (1980), 'Canada: Ontario', in D. C. Rowat (ed.), *International Handbook on Local Government Reorganisation. Contemporary Developments* (London: Aldwych Press).

Porter, D. and Olsen, E. A. (1976), 'Some critical issues in government centralization and decentralization', *Public Administration Review*, vol. 36, no. 1 (January).

Premdas, R. R. (1982), 'The Solomon Islands: the experiment in decentralization', *Public Administration and Development*, vol. 2, no. 3.

Prest, A. R. (1982), 'Greener still and greener', *Local Government Studies*, vol. 8, no. 3.

Pusic, E. (1975), 'Intentions and realities: local government in Yugoslavia', *Public Administration*, vol. 53 (Summer).

Rai, H. (1967), 'The district officer in India to-day', *Journal of Administration Overseas*, vol. 6, no. 1.

Ramusson, R. (1975), 'Social emphasis of people's priorities in Kenya on results of decentralised planning', *Agricultural Administration*, vol. 21, no. 4.

Randall, P. J. (1972), 'Wales in the structure of central government', *Public Administration*, vol. 50 (Autumn).

Reagan, H. D., and Sanzone, J. G. (1981), *The New Federalism*, 2nd edn (New York: Oxford University Press).

Reddy, G. Ram (1967), 'The role of the BDO – promise and performance', *Journal of Adminstration Overseas*, vol. 6, no. 2.

Reddy, G. Ram (ed.) (1978), *The Patterns of Panchayati Raj in India* (New Delhi: Macmillan).

Reddy, G. Ram (1981), 'Institutional and organisational arrangements for decentralisation: the rural development experience', paper to UN Interregional Seminar on Decentralization for Development, Khartoum, September.

Rees, I. B. (1971), *Government by Community* (Croydon, Surrey: Charles Knight, 1971).

Regan, D. (1977), *Local Government and Education* (London: Allen & Unwin).

Reilly, W. (1981), 'District development planning in Botswana', in *Studies in Decentralisation*, Manchester Papers on Development, no. 3 (Manchester: Department of Administrative Studies, University of Manchester).

Rhodes, R. A. W. (1976), 'Centre – local relations', in app. 6 to Layfield Committee of Inquiry into Local Government Finance, *Report*, Cmnd 6453 (London: HMSO).

Rhodes, R. A. W. (1977), 'The future research into centre-local relations', Report to the Social Science Research Council Panel on Research into Local Government', April, mimeo.

Rhodes, R. A. W. (1979), 'Research into central-local relations in Britain: a framework for analysis', in Social Science Research Council, *Centre-Local Government Relationships*, app. 1 (London: SSRC).

Rhodes, R. A. W. (1981), *Control and Power in Central-Local Relations* (Aldershot, Hants.: Gower).

Richards, P. G. (1975), *The Reformed Local Government System*, 2nd edn (London: Allen & Unwin).

Richardson, N. (1966), *The French Prefectoral Corps, 1814–1830* (Cambridge: Cambridge University Press).

Ridley, F. F. (1973), 'Integrated decentralization: models of the prefectoral system', *Political Studies*, vol. 21, no. 1.

Ridley, F. F., and Blondel, J. (1964), *Public Administration in France* (London: Routledge & Kegan Paul).

Riker, W. H. (1964), *Federalism. Origin, Operation, Significance* (Boston, Mass.: Little Brown).

Riker, W. H. (1975), 'Federalism', in F. I. Greenstein and N. W. Polsby (eds), *Handbook of Political Science*, vol. 5 (Reading, Mass.: Addison-Wesley).

Rokkan, S., and Urwin, D. (eds) (1982), *The Politics of Territorial Identity* (Beverly Hills, Calif.: Sage).

Rondinelli, D. A. (1981a), 'Administrative decentralisation and economic development: the Sudan's experiment with devolution', *Journal of Modern African Studies*, vol. 19, no. 4.

Rondinelli, D. A. (1981b), 'Government decentralization in comparative perspective: theory and practice in developing countries', *International Review of Administrative Sciences*, vol. 47, no. 2.

Rondinelli, D. A. (1983), 'Decentralization of development administration in East Africa' in Cheema and Rondinelli (eds), op. cit. below.

Rondinelli, D. A., and Cheema, G. S. (1983), 'Implementing decentralization policies. An introduction', in G. S. Cheema and D. A. Rondinelli (eds), *Decentralization and Development. Policy Implementation in Developing Countries* (Beverly Hills, Calif.: Sage).

Rondinelli, D. A., and Mandell, M. B. (1981), 'Meeting basic needs in Asia. Part II: improving the performance of government and local communities', *Public Administration and Development*, vol. 1, no. 3.

Room, G. (1979), *The Sociology of Welfare* (Oxford: Martin Roberton).

Rose, R. (1977), 'The Constitution: are we studying devolution or breakup?', in D. Kavanagh and R. Rose (eds), *New Trends in British Politics* (Beverly Hills, Calif.: Sage).

Rossetti, F. (1978), 'Politics and participation: a case study', in P. Curno (ed.), *Political Issues and Community Work* (London: Routledge & Kegan Paul).

Roth, D. F. (1975), 'Dimensions of policy changes: towards an explanation of rural change policy in Thailand', *Asian Survey*, vol. 15, no. 10.

Rothenberg, J. (1972), 'Local decentralization and the theory of optional government', in M. Edel and J. Rothenberg (eds), *Readings in Urban Economics* (New York: Macmillan).

Rowe, A. (1975), *Democracy Renewed: The Community Council in Practice* (London: Sheldon Press).

Royal Commission on Local Government in England (1969) (Redcliffe-Maud Report), *Report*, Cmnd 4040 (London: HMSO).

Samoff, J. (1979), 'The bureaucracy and the bourgeoisie: decentralization and class structure in Tanzania', *Comparative Studies in Society and History*, vol. 21, no. 1.

Saunders, P. (1980), *Urban Politics. A Sociological Interpretation* (Harmondsworth, Middx.: Penguin).

Saunders, P. (1982), 'Why study central-local relations', *Local Government Studies*, vol. 8, no. 2.

Saxena, A. P. (ed.) (1980), *Administrative Reform for Decentralised Development* (Kuala Lumpur, Malaysia: Asian and Pacific Development Administration Centre).

Scharpf, F. W. *et al.* (1978), 'Policy effectiveness and conflict avoidance in intergovernmental policy formation', in K. Hanf and F. W. Scharpf (eds), *Interorganisational Policy-Making. Limits to Co-ordination and Central Control* (Beverly Hills, Calif.: Sage).

Schmandt, H. J. (1972), 'Municipal decentralization: an overview', *Public Administration Review*, vol. 32, no. 3 (October).

Schnur, R. (1969) 'Area and administration', *International Social Science Journal*, vol. 21, no. 1.

Schulz, A. (1979), *Local Politics and National-States. Case Studies in Politics and Policy* (London: Clio Books).

Scottish Office (1971), *Reform of Local Government in Scotland*, Cmnd 4583 (London: HMSO).

Selznick, P. (1949), *TVA and the Grassroots* (Berkeley, Calif.: University of California Press).

Senior, D. (1969), 'Memorandum of Dissent', Vol. 2 of Royal Commission on Local Government in England, *Report*, Cmnd 4040 (London: HMSO).

Sharpe, L. J. (1965), *Why Local Democracy?* Fabian Tract no. 361, June.

Sharpe, L. J. (1976), 'Instrumental participation and urban government', in J. A. G. Griffith (ed.), *From Policy to Administration* (London: Allen & Unwin).

Sharpe, L. J. (1978), ' "Reforming" the grass roots: an alternative analysis', in D. Butler (ed.), *Politics, Administration and Policy* (London: Macmillan).

Sharpe, L. J. (1979), 'Decentralist trends in Western democracies: a first appraisal,' in L. J. Sharpe (ed.), *Decentralist Trends in Western Democracies* (Beverly Hills, Calif.: Sage).

Sharpe, L. J. (1981a), 'Does politics matter? An interim summary with findings', in K. Newton (ed.), *Urban Political Economy* (New York: St Martins Press).

Sharpe, L. J. (1981b), 'Is there a fiscal crisis in Western European local government? A first appraisal' in L. J. Sharpe, (ed.), *The Local Fiscal Crisis in Western Europe* (Beverly Hills, Calif.: Sage).

Sharpe, L. J. (1981c), 'The failure of local government modernization in Britain: a critique of functionalism', *Canadian Public Administration,* vol. 24, no. 1.

Sharpe, L. J. (1981d), 'Theories of local government', in L. D. Feldman (ed.), *Politics and Government of Urban Canada* (London: Methuen).

Sharpe, L. J. (1984), 'Functional allocation in the welfare state', *Local Government Studies*, vol. 10, no. 1.

Shepard, W. B. (1975), 'Metropolitan political decentralization: a test of the life-style values model', *Urban Affairs Quarterly*, vol. 10, no. 3.

Sherwood, F. (1969), 'Devolution as a problem of organizational strategy', in R. T. Daland (ed.), *Comparative Urban Research* (Beverly Hills, Calif.: Sage).

Smailes, A. E. (1947), 'The analysis and delimitation of urban fields', *Geography*, vol. 32, no. 2.

Smith, B. C. (1967), *Field Administration. An Aspect of Decentralisation* (London: Routledge & Kegan Paul).

Smith, B. C. (1969), *Advising Ministers. A Case-Study of the South-West Economic Planning Council* (London: Routledge & Kegan Paul).

Smith, B. C. (1972a), 'Field administration and political change: the case of

Northern Nigeria', *Administrative Science Quarterly*, vol. 17, no. 1 (March).

Smith, B. C. (1972b), 'The justification of local government', in L. D. Feldman and M. D. Goldrick (eds), *Politics and Government of Urban Canada*, 2nd edn (London: Methuen).

Smith, B. C. (1976), *Policy-Making in British Government, An Analysis of Power and Rationality* (Oxford: Martin Robertson).

Smith, B. C. (1980), 'Measuring decentralisation', in G. W. Jones (ed.), *New Approaches to the Study of Central-Local Government Relationships* (Aldershot, Hants: Gower and SSRC).

Smith, B. C. (1981a), 'Federal-state relations in Nigeria', *African Affairs*, vol. 80, no. 320 (July).

Smith, B. C. (1981b), 'The powers and functions of local government in Nigeria, 1966–1980', *International Review of Administrative Sciences*, vol. 47, no. 4.

Smith, B. C. (1982), 'The revenue position of local government in Nigeria', *Public Administration and Development*, vol, 2, no. 1.

Smith, B. C., and Owojaiye, G. S. (1981), 'Constitutional, legal and political problems of local government in Nigeria', *Public Administration and Development*, vol. 1, no. 3.

Smith, B. C. and Stanyer, J. (1976), *Administering Britain* (Oxford: Martin Robertson).

Smith, C. S., and Anderson, B. (1972), 'Political participation through community action', in G. Parry (ed.), *Participation in Politics* (Manchester: Manchester University Press).

Smith, G., Lees, R., and Topping, P. (1977), 'Participation and the Home Office Community Development Project', in C. Crouch (ed.), *Participation in Politics* (London: Croom Helm).

Smith, L. (1981), 'A model for the development of public participation in local authority decision-making', in L. Smith and D. Jones (eds), *Deprivation, Participation and Community Action* (London: Routledge & Kegan Paul).

Sommer, R. (1969), *Personal Space: The Behavioural Basis of Design* (Englewood Cliffs, NJ: Prentice-Hall).

Stanyer, J. (1976), *Understanding Local Government* (Oxford: Martin Robertson).

Stanyer, J. (1979), 'Have the world's big cities become ungovernable?' *Municipal Review*, no. 596 (September-October).

Stanyer, J. (1980), 'The logic of metropolitan local government structure', paper to SSRC Urban Political Geography Seminar, Exeter University, April.

Stephens, G. R. (1974), 'State centralization and the erosion of local autonomy', *Journal of Politics*, vol. 36, no. 1.

Stewart, J. D. (1980a), 'Grant characteristics and central-local relations', in G. W. Jones (ed.), *New Approaches to the Study of Central-Local Government Relationships* (Aldershot, Hants.: Gower and SSRC).

Stewart, J. D. (1980b), 'The governance of the conurbation', in G. C. Cameron (ed.), *The Future of The British Conurbations* (London: Longman).

Stubbings, B. J. (1975), 'Integrated rural development in Pakistan', *Journal of Administration Overseas*, vol. 14, no. 2.

Subramanian, V. (1980), 'Developing countries', in D. C. Rowat (ed.), *International Handbook on Local Government Reorganisation. Contemporary Developments* (London: Aldwych Press).

Tarrow, S. *et al.* (eds) (1978), *Territorial Politics in Industrial Nations* (New York: Praeger).

Taylor, E. G. R. (1950), 'The definition of regions for planning purposes', in *Town and Country Planning Textbook* (London: Association for Planning and Regional Reconstruction).

Tennant, P. (1973), 'The decline of effective local government in Malaysia', *Asian Survey*, vol. 13, no. 4.

Thoenig, J. C. (1978), 'State bureaucracies and local government in France', in K. Hanf and F. W. Scharpf (eds), *Interorganizational Policy-Making. Limits to Co-ordination and Central Control* (Beverly Hills, Calif.: Sage).

Tiebout, C. M. (1972), 'A pure theory of local expenditures' in M. Edel and J. Rothenberg (eds), *Readings in Urban Economics* (New York: Macmillan).

Tordoff, W. (1967), 'Provincial and district government in Zambia', *Journal of Administration Overseas*, vol. 6, no. 3.

Tordoff, W. (1981), 'Decentralisation in Papua New Guinea', in *Studies in Decentralisation*, Manchester Papers on Development, no. 3 (Manchester: Department of Administrative Studies, University of Manchester).

United Nations (1962), *Decentralisation for National and Local Development*, UN Technical Assistance Programme (New York: UN).

United Nations (1979), *Rural Development Administration in India: Some emerging policy issues*, Economic and Social Committee for Asia and the Pacific (New York: UN).

Urwin, D. (1982a), 'Conclusion: perspectives on conditions of regional protest and accommodation', in S. Rokkan and D. Urwin (eds), *The Politics of Territorial Identity* (Beverly Hills, Calif.: Sage).

Urwin, D. (1982b), 'Germany: from geographical expression to regional accommodation', in S. Rokkan and D. Urwin (eds), *The Politics of Territorial Identity* (Beverly Hills, Calif.: Sage).

van Putten, J. G. (1971), 'Local government in the seventies', *International Review of Administrative Sciences*, vol. 37, no. 3.

Vielba, C. A. (1979), 'Public participation', *Local Government Studies*, vol. 5, no. 2.

Vile, M. J. C. (1973), *Federalism in the United States, Canada and Australia*, Research Paper no. 2, Commission on the Constitution (London: HMSO).

Vile, M. J. C. (1977), 'Federal theory and the "new federalism" ', *Politics* (November) (Journal of the Australian Political Studies Association).

Walker, B. (1981), *Welfare Economics and Urban Problems* (London: Hutchinson).

Webster, B. A. (1979), 'Area management', *Local Government Studies*, vol. 5, no. 2.

Webster, B. A. (1982), 'Area management and responsive policy making', in S. Leach and S. Stewart (eds), *Approaches in Public Policy* (London: Allen & Unwin).

Wells, M. (1981), *Poverty and Educational Action*, Occasional Paper (Sheffield: Department of Political Studies, Sheffield Polytechnic).

Whalen, H. (1960), 'Ideology, democracy, and the foundations of local self-government', *Canadian Journal of Economics and Political Science*, vol. 26, no. 3 (August).

Wheare, K. G. (1963), *Federal Government*, 4th edn (London: Oxford University Press).

Wickwar, W. Hardy (1970), *The Political Theory of Local Government* (Columbia, SC: University of South Carolina Press).

Wilson, C. H. (1948), *Essays on Local Government* (Oxford: Blackwell).

Wilson, V. Seymour (1979), 'Federal – provincial relations and federal policy processes', in G. B. Doern and P. Aucoin (eds), *Public Policy in Canada* (Toronto: Macmillan of Canada).

Wiswawarnapala, D. W. A. (1972), 'District agencies of government departments in Ceylon', *International Review of Administrative Sciences*, vol. 38, no. 2.

Wood, B. (1974), *The Process of Local Government Reform 1966–74* (London: Allen & Unwin).

Wood, G. D. (1977), 'Rural development and the post-colonial state', *Development and Change*, vol. 8, no. 3 (July).

Wood, R. C. (1959), *Metropolis against Itself* (New York: Doubleday).

Wright, D. S. (1974), 'Intergovernmental relations: an analytical overview', *Annals of the American Academy of Political and Social Science*, vol. 416.

Wright, V. (1979), 'Regionalism under the French Fifth Republic: the triumph of the functional approach', in L. J. Sharpe (ed.), *Decentralist Trends in Western Democracies* (Beverly Hills, Calif.: Sage).

Yates, D. (1973), *Neighbourhood Democracy: The Politics and Impacts of Decentralisation* (Lexington, Mass.: D. C. Heath).

Yates, D. (1974), 'Making decentralisation work: the view from city hall', *Policy Sciences*, vol. 5, no. 3 (September).

Yin, R. K., and Lucas, W. A. (1973), 'Decentralisation and alienation', *Policy Sciences*, vol. 4, no. 3 (September).

Yin, R. K., and Yates, D. (1974), 'Street-level governments: assessing decentralisation and urban services', *Nation's Cities*, vol. 12 (November).

Ylvisaker, P. (1959), 'Some criteria for a "proper" areal division of governmental powers', in A. Maas (ed.), *Area and Power: A Theory of Local Government* (New York: The Free Press).

Young, S. (1982), 'Regional offices of the Department of the Environment: their roles and influence in the 1970s', in B. W. Hogwood and M. Keating (eds), *Regional Government in England* (Oxford: Clarendon Press).

Zawadzka, B., and Zawadzki, S. (1980), 'Socialist countries of central and southeastern Europe', in D. C. Rowat (ed.), *International Handbook on Local Government Reorganisation. Contemporary Developments* (London: Aldwych Press).

Zimmerman, J. F. (1980), 'United States', in D. C. Rowat (ed.), op. cit. above.

Index